EurographicSeminars

Tutorials and Perspectives in Computer Graphics

Edited by W. T. Hewitt, R. Gnatz, and D. A. Duce

Frontispiece: An image produced with a Doré dynamic renderer. Doré, the design of which is presented in Chapter 10, is an object-oriented graphics system. The portability and extensibility essential in graphical systems, where the hardware is developing very rapidly, was provided by the underlying object-oriented design of the system. For example, the dynamic renderer used runs on a new graphics supercomputer system and the picture was produced in a few seconds. The image is stillframe from an interactive sequence featuring real-time texture mapping, true transparency, environment mapping, shadows and in-scene light sources (spotlights and point light sources). Previously, a picture containing these effects could only have been produced using one of Doré's production renderers. Now, however, these effects are available in interactive time, through exactly the same interface as before.

Created using Doré on a Stardent 3000VS computer. Image by Daniel R. McLachlan with contributions from Helga Thorvaldsdóttir and Michael A. Toelle. The resolution of the image is 1280x1024. For antialiasing, images are computed at 2x2 subpixel resolution, and filtered using a 3x3 filter kernel. Each update takes 137 seconds. Without the antialiasing the image takes 14 seconds. At a resolution of 640x512 it takes 72 seconds with the antialiasing and 7 seconds without.

E. H. Blake P. Wisskirchen (Eds.)

Advances in Object-Oriented Graphics I

With 74 Figures, Including 7 in Color

Springer-Verlag
Berlin Heidelberg New York
London Paris Tokyo
Hong Kong Barcelona
Budapest

EurographicSeminars

Edited by W. T. Hewitt, R. Gnatz, and D. A. Duce
for EUROGRAPHICS -
The European Association for Computer Graphics
P. O. Box 16, CH-1288 Aire-la-Ville, Switzerland

Volume Editors

Edwin H. Blake

Centrum voor Wiskunde en Informatica
P. O. Box 4079, NL-1009 AB Amsterdam, The Netherlands

Peter Wisskirchen

Institute for Applied Information Technology, National Research Center
for Computer Science (GMD), Postfach 1240
W-5205 Sankt Augustin 1, FRG

Library of Congress Cataloging-in-Publication Data. Advances in object-oriented graphics I / E. H. Blake, P. Wisskirchen (eds.). p. cm. - (EurographicSeminars) Papers presented at the First Eurographics Workshop on Object-Oriented Graphics, held Oct. 1990 in Königswinter, Germany, and sponsored by the German National Research Center for Computer Science et al. Includes bibliographical references.

ISBN-13: 978-3-642-76305-2 e-ISBN-13: 978-3-642-76303-8
DOI: 10.1007/ 978-3-642-76303-8

1. Computer graphics - Congresses. 2. Object-oriented programming (Computer science) - Congresses. I. Blake, E. H. (Edwin H.), 1952-. II. Wisskirchen, P. (Peter) III. Gesellschaft für Mathematik und Datenverarbeitung. IV. Eurographics Workshop on Object-Oriented Graphics (1st: 1990: Königswinter, Germany) V. Title: Advances in object-oriented graphics one. VI. Title: Advances in object-oriented graphics 1. VII. Series: Eurographic seminars. T385.A37 1991 006.6-dc20 90-26971

Softcover reprint of the hardcover 1st edition 1991

45/3140-5 4 3 2 1 0 - Printed on acid-free paper

Preface

This book contains extensively revised versions of some of the papers presented at the first EUROGRAPHICS workshop on Object-Oriented Graphics. This workshop took place during June 1990, in Königswinter, near Bonn in the Federal Republic of Germany. It was held in an atmosphere of lively discussion and the results of these discussions were incorporated into the various chapters of this book.

The aim of the workshop was to investigate the applicability of object-oriented methods to computer graphics—computer graphics in a very broad sense, including human computer interaction, image synthesis, dynamic graphics and computer-aided design. Another aim of the workshop was to develop a constructive critique of the object-oriented methods themselves from the point of view of computer graphics. These aims were realized not only in the papers, but also in the discussions. In fact a number of research areas were uncovered by the participants and we hope to see results in the near future.

The diversity of contributions did not lend themselves to easy classification, but in the end we decided to split the book into three parts. These three parts reflect the main areas in which object-oriented methods were applied.

The first part of this book deals with *Interaction Theory and Practice.* It is a characteristic of object-oriented user interfaces that they are Direct Manipulation interfaces. This fact is illustrated not only by the contents of this first part of the book, but also by the chapters in other parts. The first contribution is on an extension of the Smalltalk Model-View-Controller framework. The influence of Smalltalk is of course pervasive in object-oriented computer graphics. The next contribution introduces the topic of constraints in the context of a mathematical modelling system. The use of constraints is an important recurring theme in object-oriented graphics. Many discussions centred around this topic during the workshop. It is clear that the integration of constraints into object-oriented user interfaces and graphics systems remains an important research area. The next chapter deals with user interfaces for object-oriented databases. The one following is a presentation of a complete object-oriented model for interaction. This model leads to a much higher-level interface for programmers developing user interfaces. The last chapter also presents a programmer's tool for developing user interfaces. It concentrates particularly on the demands placed by multi-user interfaces and the object-oriented solutions to them. Once again constraints play a major role.

The second part is on *Modelling and Design.* One important issue here is how one deals with complex objects which are built up out of components. Such objects arise in any situation where the geometrical properties of physical objects are important, but of course this is not the only source of such complex structures. At issue is both the creation and persistence of these kinds of objects without violating object-oriented principles that have proved their worth in other contexts. Persistent objects is the term used for objects which are stored beyond the lifetime of the process which created them.

Here we find a contribution on persistent graphical objects followed by one on generating different views of complex objects on-the-fly — this is an important problem in CAD systems. Geometric problems are combined with constraints in the next chapter, whose point of departure is the importance of coordinate systems and coordinate transformations. The last chapter in this part of the book presents a complete environment for the design of three-dimensional objects. It actually spans all three parts of the book since it deals with direct manipulation user interfaces, design and modelling issues, and looks ahead to the graphics systems issues of the last part.

The third and last part of this book addresses *Graphics Systems.* The first chapter deals with the design of the influential Doré application interface. It presents a synthesis of many of the design principles of object-oriented graphics in one practical system. The second chapter aims to introduce the benefits of these object-oriented principles to the wider graphics community via the development of a new graphics standard. The advantages of object oriented methods are reviewed and the expected difficulties analysed.

The workshop was made possible by the efforts of the authors who prepared and revised the papers which established the scientific content of the workshop and of this book. The editors gratefully thank the members of the Programme Committee for the efforts they invested in the preparation of the workshop. Their reviews of the papers contributed to the overall scientific standard of the workshop.

The success of the workshop also depended on the organizational support of the German National Research Center for Computer Science (GMD), Mrs. C. Harms for the local organization of the workshop, and the Dutch Centre for Mathematics and Computer Science (CWI), and in particular Ms. Marja Hegt. Financial and promotional support was provided by Eurographics, the German Society for Informatics (GI 4.1.1 Special Interest Group for Graphics Systems, GI 4.1.5 German Chapter of Eurographics). We also thank the CWI for the use of their typesetting facilities.

Amsterdam, September 1990

Edwin Blake
Peter Wisskirchen

First Eurographics Workshop on Object-Oriented Graphics

Co-Chairmen

Dr. P. Wisskirchen, German National Research Center for Computer Science.

Dr. E.H. Blake, Centre for Mathematics and Computer Science, Netherlands.

Programme Committee

Alan Borning	Rank Xerox EuroPARC, U.K.
Jan van den Bos	University of Leiden, Netherlands.
Michael R. Kaplan	Apple Computer Inc., USA.
Brad A. Myers	Carnegie Mellon University, USA.
Xavier Pintado	Université de Genève, Switzerland.
Mel Slater	University of London, U.K.
Tapio Takala	Helsinki University of Technology, Finland.
Tetsuo Tomiyama	The University of Tokyo, Japan.

Table of Contents

Part I

Interaction Theory and Practice

1

An Object-Oriented Framework for Direct-Manipulation User Interfaces

Yen-Ping Shan

This chapter describes an object-oriented framework for building direct-manipulation user interfaces. Based on the concept of "mode", the framework extends the Model-View-Controller (MVC) paradigm to accommodate an orthogonal design. It provides a clean structure for the user interface components and increases their reusability.

A Mode Development Environment (MoDE) has been built to demonstrate the framework. Users of MoDE can easily create a wide variety of interfaces (mostly by direct manipulation).

1. Introduction

Many user interface systems are based on, or influenced by, the Smalltalk Model-View-Controller (MVC) paradigm [Alexander, 1987; Binding, 1988; Krasner and Pope, 1988; Hartson, 1989; McAffer and Thomas, 1988; Stepstone, 1988; Meulen, 1989]. Although the MVC concept provides an attractive object-oriented division at the abstract level, this division is rather hard to implement. Most implementations of the MVC concept have view and controller pairs associated with models. When this is done, the use of a controller, for instance, is limited to the view and model with which it is associated. Assigning a different controller to a view does not change the interaction but often breaks the code. From the implementer's point of view, it makes little sense to separate the view and controller into two modules. Because of that, some implementations lump the two parts together. As explained in Section 4, this often hinders the reuse of software components and produces awkward inheritance structures.

Although the MVC concept has its problems, its principle of dividing user interface components into three parts can still be used to guide the design of orthogonal interface components. While object-oriented inheritance alone does not guarantee good reuse of user interface components, an orthogonal design of those components, along with inheritance, can make for good reusability. In addition, orthogonality results in a more general and versatile system for building user interfaces.

This chapter presents an object-oriented framework for building direct-manipulation user interfaces. In so doing, it shows how the MVC concept can be extended to provide for orthogonal user interface components. After a brief introduction to the Smalltalk MVC paradigm in the next section, Section 3 defines the concept of "mode". Section 4 illustrates why the orthogonality introduced in Section 3 supports generality and good reusability of user interface components. To demonstrate these ideas, a Mode Development Environment (MoDE) has been built. Section 5 introduces the kernel classes of MoDE. The Mode Composer, MoDE's direct-manipulation user interface, is described in Section 7. Section 8 then closes with some final remarks.

2. MVC

The MVC paradigm divides the responsibility for a user interface into three types of objects:

Model: The model represents the data structure of the application. It contains or has access to information to be displayed in its views.

View: The view handles all graphical tasks; it requests data from the model and displays the data. A view can contain subviews and be contained within superviews. The superview/subview hierarchy provides windowing behaviour such as clipping and transformations.

Controller: The controller provides the interface between its associated model/view and the user input. The controller also schedules interactions with other controllers.

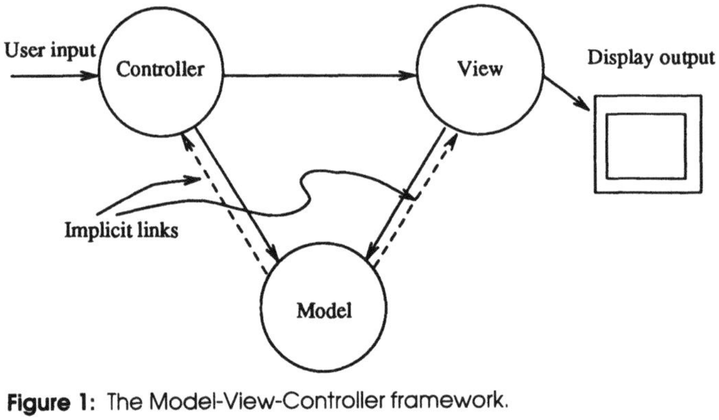

Figure 1: The Model-View-Controller framework.

The three parts of a user interface are interconnected as shown in Figure 1. The standard interaction cycle is that the user takes some input action and the active controller responds by invoking the appropriate action on the model. The model carries out the prescribed operation, possibly changing its state, and broadcasts to all its dependent views (through the implicit links) that it has changed. Each view can then query the model for its new state and update its display if necessary.

3. A Design for a Mode Framework

"Modal" user interfaces interpret the same user input differently depending on the state of the system. They are generally considered inferior because they make it hard for the user to find out:

- which mode it is in,
- how the mode is reached,
- what operations are allowed in the mode,
- and how to get out of the mode.

Direct-manipulation user interfaces, on the other hand, are modal systems that are not characterized by the shortcomings listed above. These interfaces actually divide the screen into little modes—areas on the screen that interact with the user differently from surrounding areas. Because these modes are always clearly visible and are entered and exited simply by moving the cursor, direct-manipulation user interfaces appear to be modeless [Jacob, 1986]. Further, the operations allowed in each mode are unambiguously presented by menus and dialogue boxes that can be invoked by simple, generic actions (for example, a button click).

By extending these ideas, a "Mode framework" can be defined to describe and build user interfaces. The basic building block of the Mode framework is called a *mode*. A mode is a composite defined by its three attributes: *appearance, interaction,* and *semantics*. It is distinguished by an area on the screen in which it is likely that at least one of its attributes is different from those of other modes in surrounding areas. The *Mode framework* includes the definition of modes and provides rules of composition. Thus, a user interface might be composed of a group of hierarchically structured modes. A mode in such a structured interface could contain other modes as submodes. Any given mode, however, would be a submode of only one mode—its "supermode". The set of modes in a structured interface forms a hierarchy.

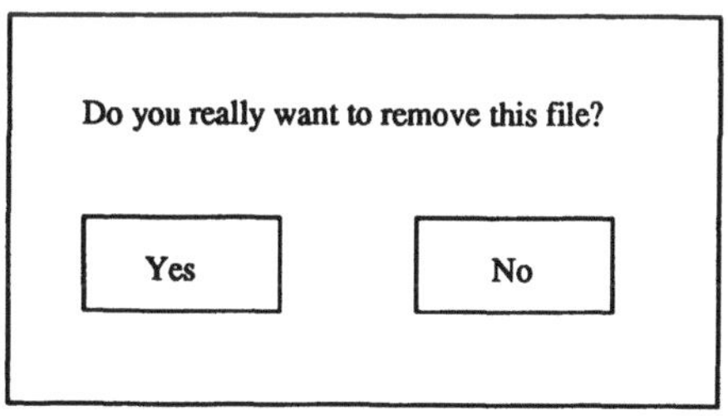

Figure 2: A dialogue box can be viewed as a mode with two submodes.

To illustrate, the dialogue box shown in Figure 2 can be thought of as a mode with two submodes: a "yes" submode and a "no" submode. The yes and no buttons highlight themselves when the left mouse button is pressed within them, and they dehighlight themselves when the cursor moves away or the left mouse button is released. Their behaviour is different from that of their supermode which does not respond to a left mouse button press. Notice that the text in the dialogue box is not a mode. It affects the appearance of the dialogue box, but it does not form an area that provides a different interpretation of the user's input.

Each individual mode is defined by its appearance, its semantics, and the way it interacts. For example, the "yes" submode has the following definition:

Appearance: White background with black border of width one and a piece of text (yes) centred. The highlighted appearance is the inverse of the normal appearance.

Semantics: Confirm to remove the file.

Interaction: Highlight when the left mouse button is pressed inside; dehighlight when the cursor leaves or the button is released.

Notice that the "no" submode shares exactly the same interaction part with the "yes" submode. The differences between them comes from the appearance and semantic parts.

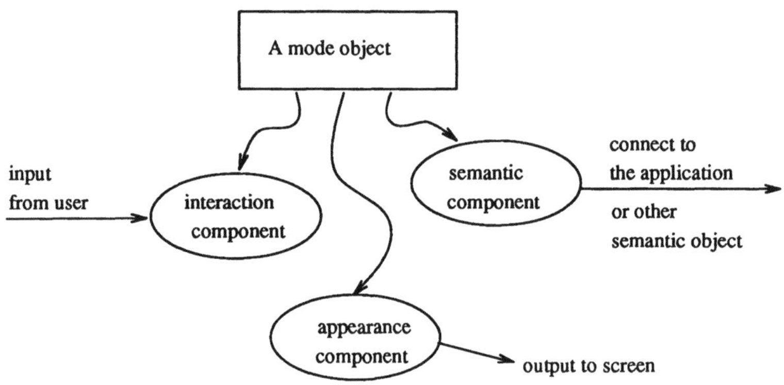

Figure 3: The structure of a mode.

In an object-oriented design, a mode is an object. The appearance, semantic, and interaction components are three different objects possessed by a mode object, as shown in Figure 3. The mode object provides a structure in which the three objects can be plugged. An internal protocol is defined so that the component objects have a standard way of communicating with each other. The appearance of a mode is changed by replacing its appearance object with a different one. This is the same as the way for changing the semantics and interaction of a mode. For example, a mode that highlights has two different appearance objects: one for normal state, the other for highlighted state. When the mode highlights, it replaces the normal display object with the highlight display object. When it dehighlights, the normal display object is switched back.

The standard interaction cycle of a mode is similar to that of the MVC paradigm. The interaction object detects the user's input and tries to process it locally (for example, to highlight the mode). When the user's action indicates a semantic command, the semantic object is activated to process the command. The semantic object may pass control to the application or to other semantic objects that it is connected to, change the appearance and interaction of the mode, or simply update its own state. Notice that while a view in the MVC paradigm queries the model and updates the display, a mode in the Mode framework only provides the structure within which its three components collaborate to perform the interaction.

4. A User Interface Component Space and Its Axes

Each simple mode is the composition of three parts. Assigning an axis to each part, we get the three-dimensional space shown in Figure 4. The three axes define a type-space for modes. Each point in the space represents a new mode type. The "yes" and "no" submodes of the dialogue box example occupy two points in the space. They have the same interactive behaviour but different appearance and semantics. This is reflected in their sharing the same value on the "Interaction" axis.

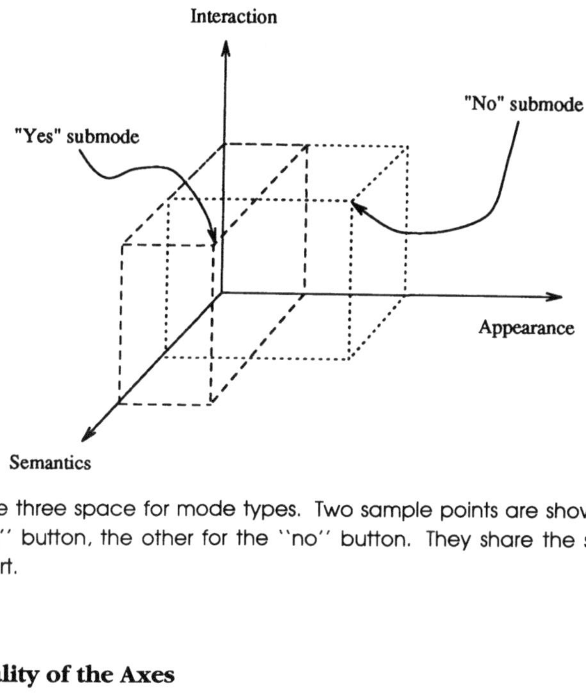

Figure 4: The three space for mode types. Two sample points are shown. One for the ''yes'' button, the other for the ''no'' button. They share the same interaction part.

4.1. Orthogonality of the Axes

Axes that span a space are orthogonal if changing the value on one axis does not affect the values on the other axes. That is to say that the axes are independent of each other.

In defining a type-space for modes, one would like to have as many axes as possible and to have them as orthogonal as possible. Though it is possible to use just one axis to describe the whole type-space with each type occupying a value on this single axis, this is an inferior approach since creating a new point on the axis defines only one new type. In the case of a three-space, creating a new point on one of the axes defines a plane of new types. In user interface construction, the one-dimensional approach represents lumping all three parts of a mode together in a single object. (Keeping them in three separate but closely coupled objects is essentially the same). The parts can only be reused when the whole object can be reused. In the three-dimensional case, three parts of a mode are put into three independent objects. The chances for reuse are increased.

For example, suppose there are two buttons. One is square shaped and responds to a left mouse button click to perform operation A. The other one has a round shape and responds to middle mouse button click to perform operation B. In a single-dimensional design, to create a square button that responds to a middle button click to perform operation A, one needs to create a new subclass of the first button to accommodate the changes. In a three-dimensional orthogonal type-space for design, such a button can simply be obtained by replacing the interaction part of the first button with the interaction part of the second. No new class is needed. Actually, by permuting the parts, one can have eight different buttons without creating any new classes.

Notice that the three-dimensional orthogonal design is different from parameterizing the appearance and interaction of a single object. When a new appearance is invented (say a triangular display object), the three-dimensional approach immediately gives four additional new buttons. This is in contrast to the parameterized single dimension approach where editing the code and recompilation is necessary to incorporate the new shape.

Assuming the total number of types in the type-space is N, a single axis must have N distinctive values to represent all the types. With three orthogonal axes, each axis would only need $\sqrt[3]{N}$ distinctive values in general. The sum of the number of distinctive values for all three axes is $3 \times \sqrt[3]{N}$, as opposed to N for the single-axis case. In the above example, N is equal to 12, and the three-dimensional approach requires 7 values (three appearances, two interactions, and two semantics). The single-dimensional approach will need 12 values on its axis. Since N is usually much larger than 12, the three-space representation is more efficient.

4.2. Generality

The generality of the user interface framework depends heavily on the choice of the axes. The more orthogonal axes a framework has, the more mode-types it can span and the more general it is. In reality, it is difficult to find fully orthogonal axes. One can only strive for axes that are as orthogonal as possible. The Mode framework is an attempt to find those orthogonal axes. An implementation of this framework is described in the next section. New axes will evolve as new interaction techniques (for instance, sound) emerge.

5. Realization

The MoDE (Mode Development Environment) is the realization of the Mode framework. It is implemented on top of Smalltalk-80 and an event-driven mechanism [Shan, 1989]. Four classes make up the Mode framework. They are *Mode, MController, MDisplayObject*, and *SemanticObject*. The *Mode* class is responsible for event dispatching and window management. The other three classes correspond to the three orthogonal axes discussed in Section 4.

5.1. Mode

The *Mode* class implements the basic structure of a mode discussed in Section 3. In the current implementation, each *Mode* has a *MController*, an *MDisplayObject* and a *SemanticObject*. *Mode* coordinates the activities of these three objects to perform the interaction.

5.1.1. Event Handling

A major responsibility of *Mode* is to handle event dispatching. Two methods provide this functionality. The **interestedIn:** method takes an event as an argument and returns true when the *Mode* is active (mapped) and the event happened in the area controlled by the *Mode*. The **processEvent:** method asks the controller to process the event when **interestedIn:** returns true.

5.1.2. Windowing

Mode provides window management functions. Each instance of *Mode* can be "mapped" or "unmapped". When a *Mode* is mapped, it can interact with the user by receiving the input events and responding to them. An unmapped *Mode* does not receive any events, and therefore can not interact with the user. Each *Mode* has its own local coordinate system and a transformation (both translation and scaling) that maps between the local coordinates and the screen coordinates.

A simple constraint system provides a convenient way to specify the position and size of a mode when its supermode changes its position and size. An example of this would be to specify a vertical scroll bar in a window. When the window is resized, the constraints can be used to stretch the scroll bar vertically so that the top and the bottom touch the border of the window while maintaining its width as a constant.

Several methods are provided to support operations that manage the sub/super mode hierarchy. These operations include adding and removing submodes and reordering the order of the submodes (like bring to top, send to bottom, etc.).

5.1.3. Displaying

A *Mode* displays itself by first asking its display object to display its background and then asking all contained submodes to display themselves. The built-in clipping algorithm draws only the portions of the mode that are unobscured.

5.2. MController

The *MController* class realizes the interaction component of a mode.

5.2.1. The eventResponses Table

The *MController* executes interactions by sending out messages according to the type of events it receives. The instance variable eventResponses of this class holds a table that stores the mapping between interesting event types and messages. Table 1 shows a simple eventResponses table. The keys of the table (enterMode, leaveMode, and leftButtonDown) are the event types and the values (**highlight**, **deHighlight**, and **action:**) are message selectors. When a *MController* is asked by its mode to process an event, it checks whether the event type matches any of the keys in the eventResponses table. If there is no match, a false is returned immediately and the event is sent to the next mode for processing. If there is a match, the value (a message selector) of that key is examined. If the selector ends with a colon (for example **action:**), a message is sent to the semantic object using the selector with that event as the argument. Otherwise, the message is sent to the controller itself and is handled by the shared-behaviour mechanism described below. Since the controller has access to the event, it does not need the event as a message argument. This is why the message selectors (for example, **highlight** and **deHighlight**) intended for the controller do not end with a colon.

Event Type	Message
enterMode	**highlight**
leaveMode	**deHighlight**
leftButtonDown	**action:**

Table 1: A simple 'eventResponses' table.

In Smalltalk syntax, a message selector ending with a colon requires an argument. A *MController* can query a message selector at run-time to decide whether it ends with a colon or not. In a more conventional language that does not support this querying capability, such as C++, one can associate tags to function pointers to implement this feature.

5.2.2. Shared Behaviours

The *MController* class and its subclasses implement a set of shared behaviours as instance methods. They include common behaviours like menu invocation, rubber-band lines and boxes, mode dragging, mode highlighting, and mode resizing. These behaviours are shared since any instance of the class or the subclass can invoke them. A shared behaviour is invoked by placing the name of its corresponding method into the controller's eventResponses table as a value.

New behaviours are included if they are used frequently and do not require semantic information. That is, they can be handled by the controller and the mode.

5.2.3. Inheritance of Controllers

A single inheritance class hierarchy is not adequate for supporting the sharing of interaction behaviours among controllers. For example, suppose controller A highlights the mode when the cursor moves into its area, and controller B allows the user to drag the mode with the mouse. If one would like to have a controller C which behaves like a combination of A and B (both highlight and drag), what would the inheritance structure be? If C were made a subclass of A, the behaviour of B (dragging) would not be inherited and would have to be duplicated in class C. Making C a subclass of B requires the behaviour of A (highlighting) to be duplicated. Neither solution is satisfactory.

This kind of problem is not unique to user interface construction—many object-oriented applications have the same problem—but the situation here is particularly severe. In other application areas, one may be able to treat the problem as a special case and work around it with *ad hoc* solutions. Here, it is very common to have controllers that would like to inherit from two, three, or even more controllers. Instead of maintaining a multiple inheritance mechanism just for this need, MoDE provides the eventResponses table to solve the problem. Instead of having a lot of controller classes, all controllers are instances of the *MController* class. Inheriting from a controller is achieved by copying the contents of its eventResponses table. Multiple inheritance is simulated by copying the contents from multiple eventResponses table. Using a table instead of an actual multiple inheritance mechanism also provides the extra run-time flexibility essential for interactive construction and editing of user interfaces.

Under this scheme, the creation of a class for a controller is used mainly for grouping the code of the shared behaviours and limiting assess to them. In some cases, a frequently used controller can be made a class for ease of reference.

5.3. SemanticObject

The semantic object supplies the semantics of a mode. The term "supply" is used instead of "generate" because in MoDE the semantic objects usually serve as the connection points to the underlying application which generates the semantics. Semantic objects reside in a domain maintained by the MoDE connection model [Shan, 1990]. Objects in the domain have knowledge of both the user interface and the application. They form a layer that insulates both sides from the effects of changes.

The connection model is de-centralized so that interface objects no longer deal with a single large application interface. Instead, an interface object sees, through its semantic object, a small piece of the application that implements its semantics. A complicated internal interface between the user interface and the application can be divided into small, independent, and manageable pieces maintained by the system. With object-oriented message sending occurring through the pieces, a wide communication bandwidth between the interface and the application is maintained.

Semantic objects are programmable. If an interaction technique is created by coding (instead of using the Mode Composer introduced in Section 7), it will have its own class, which is a subclass of the *SemanticObject* class. Instances of this interaction technique are created by sending creation messages to its class. The *SemanticObject* class defines a set of initialization methods to set up the parts in the Mode framework. They are **setUpMode**, **setUpController**, and **setUpAppearance**. Whenever a subclass of *SemanticObject* is sent a creation message, these three methods are invoked automatically to create and initialize the parts of a mode and to connect them to one another.

Subclasses of *SemanticObject* implement a "controller-msg" protocol to support the messages sent from the controller. Recall that, in the eventResponses table, message selectors that end with a colon are sent to the semantic object. The "controller-msg" protocol implements those messages.

The subclasses of *SemanticObject* that use menus to interact with the end user follow the convention described below. Each class implements two protocols. The "Menu Access" protocol contains methods that return menus. The "Menu Support" protocol contains methods that perform the menu options.

SemanticObject defines a default instance variable to store the connection to other objects. New instance variables are defined in the subclasses of *SemanticObject* as more connections are needed.

5.4. MDisplayObject

Instances of the *MDisplayObject* class control the "background" of modes. The "background" includes the inside colour, the border, and zero or more displayable objects. The instance variable contents holds a table that keeps these displayable objects. All objects that know how to display themselves can be put into this collection. They can be text, drawings, forms, and animated pictures.

The display method accepts two arguments from the mode: a display box and a collection of visible rectangles. The display box defines the size and position of the mode. The visible rectangles define the visible portion of the mode computed by the clipping algorithm.

The *MDisplayObject* has the capability to buffer its output as a bitmap. This speeds up the display of complex objects.

5.5. Interactions Amongst the Four Kernel Classes

This section discusses how the four classes described above relate to one another. Figure 5 illustrates the message-sending relationships among the four kernel classes. Each class is represented by a box with its important instance variables listed in the box. An arrow at the end of a line indicates the direction of messages. Message arguments are omitted; only the message names are shown. The number of colons in a message name corresponds to the number of arguments. Descriptions of message groups are indicated by a serif fount.

The *Mode* class is responsible for event dispatching. When the user performs an action that generates an event, the modes on the screen cooperate to find the receiving mode and send the event to it. The receiving mode then asks its controller to process the

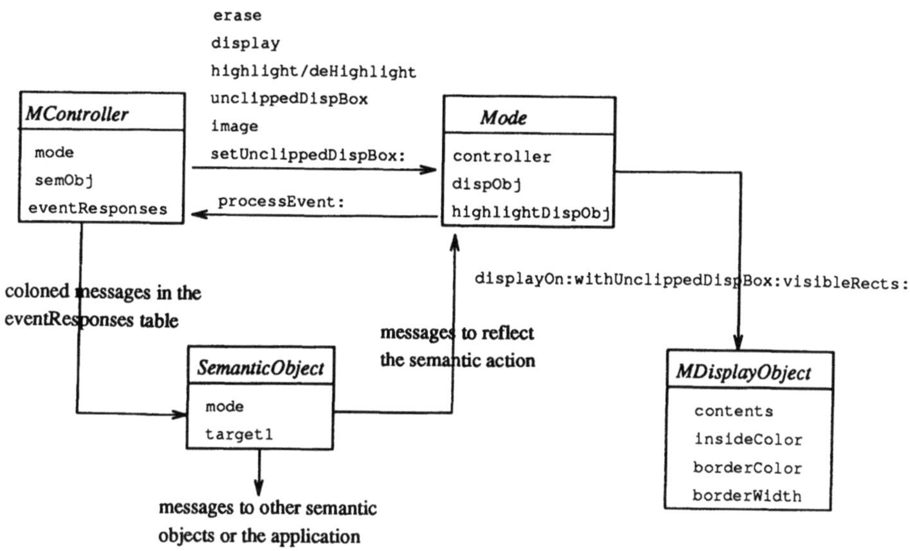

Figure 5: The relationships among the four kernel classes.

event by sending the **processEvent:** message with the event as an argument.

Upon receiving the message, an *MController* checks the event type against the keys in its eventResponses table. If the value of the key that matches the event type is a message selector that does not end with a colon, the event is processed by local methods defined in the controller. These methods, in turn, use methods defined in the *Mode* class to perform the interactions. The **erase** method erases the mode before it is moved, and the **display** method displays it after it is moved. The **highlight** method switches the mode's-dispObj and highlightDispObj and redisplays it. The **deHighlight** method does the reverse. The **unclippedDispBox** method returns the display box of the mode without being clipped by the the display box of the supermode. The unclipped display box is used to draw the indication box when a mode is moved with its frame. The **image** method returns the image of the mode that can be used to move the mode with its actual image. All operations that change the mode's position use the **setUnclippedDispBox:** method to set it to its final position.

If the message selector ends with a colon, the event is processed by the semantic object. A subclass of the *SemanticObject* class should be created to implement the method corresponding to the message. This method, in turn, may send messages to the mode to reflect the semantic action.

No specific messages are used by the *SemanticObject* class, but the subclasses of the *SemanticObject* class may use all the public messages of the *Mode* class. An instance of the subclass of the *SemanticObject* may use those messages to alter the appearance of the mode, switch the mode's controller, or activate/inactivate the mode. The semantic object may also send messages to other semantic objects or the underlying application to further propagate the semantic action.

The *MDisplayObject* does not send messages to other objects. It merely maintains the appearance of the mode (inside colour, border colour, border width, and the displayable objects in its contents collection) and displays itself upon request. The full message sent from the mode is **displayOn:** aMedium **withUnclippedDispBox:** aBox **visibleRects:** aRectCltn. aMedium can be the screen or a bitmap. The latter is for buffering the output to speed up the displaying. The aBox and aRectCltn are necessary for the display object to follow the clipping algorithm and to display itself efficiently.

The following is a simple example to illustrate how the four classes described above interact with one another.

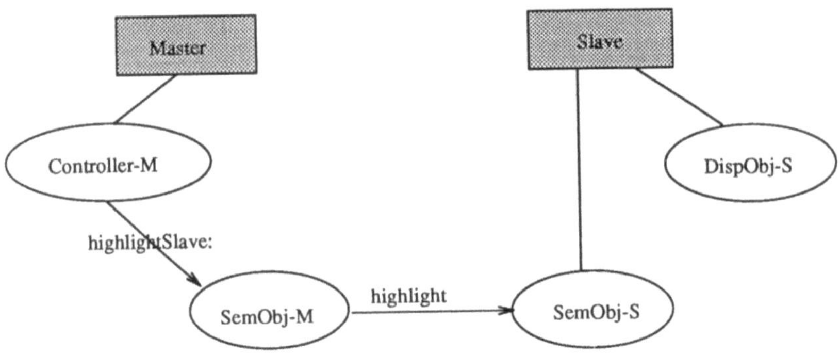

Figure 6: A simple example interface with two modes: 'Master' and 'Slave' (represented by the gray boxes).

Figure 6 shows the example interface. It has two modes: Master and Slave. When the user pushes the left mouse button in the Master mode, the Slave mode is highlighted. To accomplish this interaction, the following sequence of actions takes place:

- After the user pushes the button, the event generation mechanism that underlies MoDE generates a leftButtonDown event.
- The event dispatching mechanism, implemented in the *Mode* class, delivers the event to the Master mode.
- The Master mode asks its controller (Controller-M) to process the event.
- Controller-M matches the event type against the keys in its eventResponses table (not shown in the figure) and finds that there is a match. The value of the matched key (a message selector **highlightSlave:**) ends with a colon. This indicates that the message should be sent to the semantic object (SemObj-M) with the event as an argument.
- SemObj-M in turn, sends an **highlight** message to SemObj-S (the semantic object of the Slave mode).
- The **highlight** method defined in SemObj-S highlights the Slave mode by asking the mode's display object (DispObj-S) to display the inverse of itself. This completes the interaction.

This example shows the basic internal interactions among the kernel objects. The next section discusses how these objects are used in designing and constructing an interface.

5.6. Designing an Interface with MoDE

The mode concept provides a unified architecture for interfaces. An interface is composed of nothing but modes. Given a specification of a user interface, a developer using MoDE first identifies the areas on the screen that should have different appearance, interaction, and semantics relative to the surrounding contexts. Each of these areas becomes a mode in the Mode framework. This approach decomposes the interface into modes that can be refined individually. For each mode, the developer reuses or creates display objects to define the mode's appearance. Often, an existing controller can be used to define the interactions of a mode. If no controller provides exactly the interaction wanted, a new controller can be created by editing a copy of the eventResponses table from an existing controller. The semantic object of a mode is then programmed to handle the messages from both the controller and the underlying application. The Mode Composer, described in Section 7, supports the above activities as well as the creation and management of the connections among the semantic objects and between the semantic objects and the underlying application.

6. Decoupling the User Interface Parts

The *MController*, *MDisplayObject*, and *SemanticObject* classes define user interface components that are largely orthogonal to one another. As a consequence, these parts are more likely to be reused.

Many systems, such as the X Toolkit [McCormack and Asente, 1988], come with a set of interaction techniques (widgets); however they do not separate the interaction, appearance, and semantics components into objects. Consequently, it is impossible to reuse individual component objects since they do not exist. ICpak 201 [Stepstone, 1988] does incorporate the concept of a separate interaction component, but the appearance of an interaction technique is hard-wired. The NeXT Application Kit [NeXT, 1988] allows parameterized appearance (subject to the limitations discussed in Section 4) but does not have a separate interaction object[1].

The Smalltalk MVC framework comes close to the ideal of orthogonality since it separates the model, view, and controller into three different objects. Unfortunately, these three objects are closely coupled, resulting in what is, essentially, a one-dimensional type-space, as discussed in Section 4. The Mode framework solves this coupling problem by re-partitioning the responsibilities of the interface components and abstracting the dependency among them into the semantic object. This frees the *MDisplayObject*, *MController*, *Mode*, and the underlying application from the need to be coupled with one another. Figure 7 shows the partition of responsibilities in the Mode

1 Graphical user interface specifications, such as OpenLook and Motif, are not discussed since they are independent to the internal architecture of the user interfaces that conform to the specified styles.

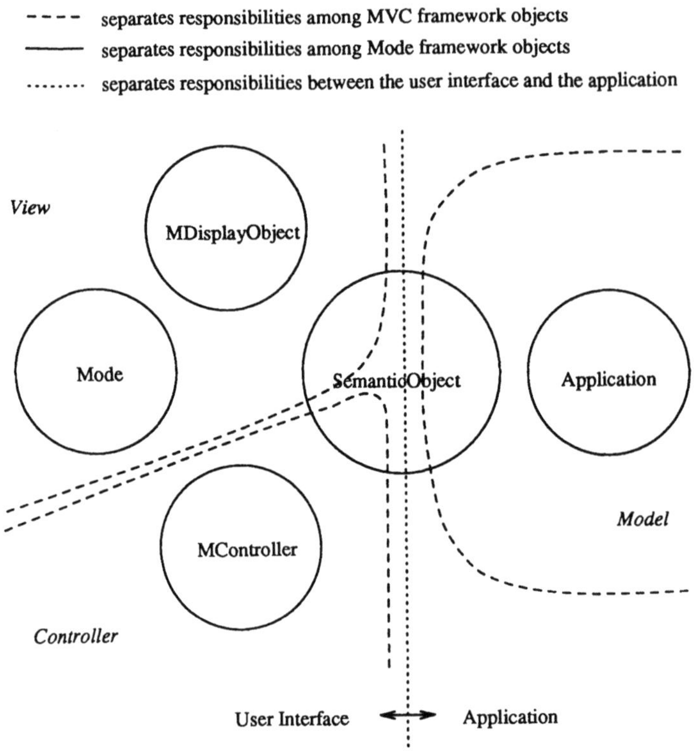

Figure 7: The responsibilities in the Mode framework are partitioned differently from those in the MVC framework.

framework and in the MVC framework. The circles indicate the objects in the Mode framework. The dashed lines show the corresponding MVC objects (their names are in italics).

7. Mode Composer

The Mode Composer is the direct-manipulation user interface of MoDE. It allows the user to create an interface, edit it, and connect the interface to the application through direct manipulation.

The user creates interfaces by dragging modes out of the interactive technique library (the right-hand window in Figure 8) and pasting them together. Visual representatives of semantic objects and application objects can be created and manipulated directly.

All interfaces created with the Mode Composer are immediately testable at any stage of the development. There is no need to switch to a test state. After the interface is created and tested, it can be promoted into the library for future use. In Figure 9, the upside-down window has been promoted into the interactive technique library and is represented by an icon. The user can also store it in a file and share it with other user interface developers.

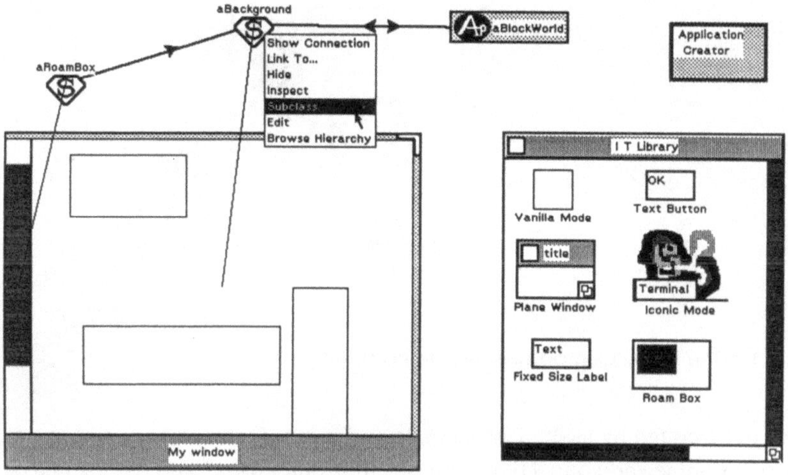

Figure 8: Using MoDE. The user has finished the layout and connection of the interface (an upside-down window) and is asking the system to create a subclass of the "aBackground" semantic object.

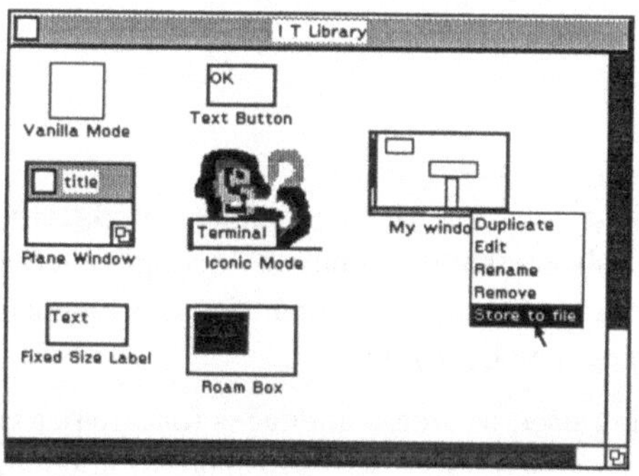

Figure 9: The interactive technique library.

The interaction technique library of the Mode Composer stores prototypes of the interaction techniques. As a consequence, each library object represents a prototype instead of a class. Once an interaction technique is promoted into the library, it can be reused immediately by making copies of its prototype.

Besides the orthogonal design of the Mode framework, the ability to easily introduce new objects to the library is also essential to the generality of the system. If an interface builder were to have a fixed set of library objects, the kinds of interfaces that it could create would be limited. Since the user of MoDE can freely promote new objects into the interaction technique library, MoDE is not limited in this respect.

Not only is the Mode Composer an important component of MoDE, it is also an important application of MoDE. To demonstrate the generality of MoDE, the user interface of the Mode Composer is created using itself. Because of this self-creative ability, the Mode

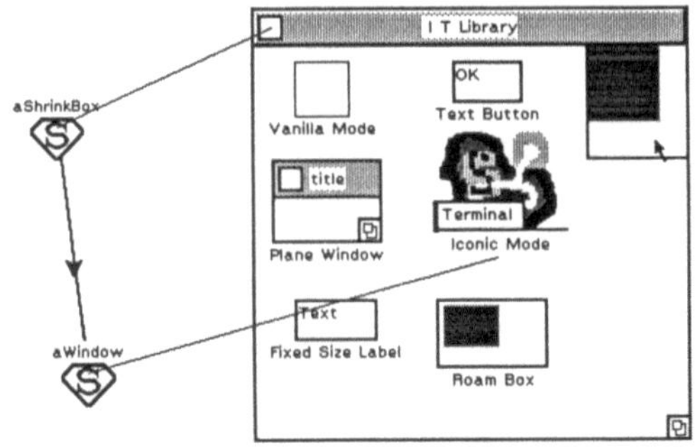

Figure 10: The Mode Composer is used to edit itself.

Composer can be edited by itself. For example, in Figure 10, the user is using the Mode Composer to examine the connection between the "ShrinkBox" and the "Window" of the interaction technique library. The user has also made some changes to the Mode Composer. The two scroll bars of the interaction technique library have been removed, and a "Roam Box" (a two-dimensional scrolling device) has been attached.

Since it is easy for users to customize the user interface of the Mode Composer, the interface images shown in this document represent only a sampling used by the author.

8. Conclusion

The Mode framework provides a clean structure for direct-manipulation interfaces. Experience with MoDE shows that the ability to uncouple the constituent parts of modes not only increases reusability, but also results in a more general system with which a wide variety of interfaces can be created.

MoDE is currently being used to create interfaces for a hypertext software engineering system. The author is also exploring the possibility of augmenting MoDE to generate code automatically for the X Window System. (A similar project has been done by hand.)

Acknowledgements

This work was performed while studying at the University of North Carolina at Chapel Hill. A number of organizations and people have contributed to the work reported here. The author is grateful to the National Science Foundation (Grant # IRI-85-19517) and the Army Research Institute (Contract #MDA903-86-C-0345) for their support of this research. John B. Smith, Richard Hawkes, John Maloney, Barry Elledge, and Gordon Ferguson provided valuable comments and suggestions for this chapter. The Textlab Research Group within the Department of Computer Science at the University of North Carolina at Chapel Hill has provided a provocative and supportive intellectual environment for this work.

References

Alexander, J.H. (1987) "Painless panes for Smalltalk windows," In: *OOPSLA'87: Object Oriented Programming, Systems and Applications*, pp. 287-294.

Binding, C. (1988) "The architecture of a user interface toolkit," In: *UIST '88: ACM SIGGRAPH Symposium on User Interface Software*, pp. 56-65. October 1988

Hartson, R. (January 1989) "User-interface management control and communication," *IEEE Software*, 62-70.

Jacob, R.J.K. (1986) "A specification language for direct manipulation user interfaces," *ACM Transactions on Graphics*, vol. 5, no. 4, 283-317.

Krasner, G.E. and Pope, S.T. (1988) "A cookbook for using the Model-View-Controller user interface paradigm in Smalltalk-80," *Journal of Object-Oriented Programming*, vol 1, no. 3, 26-49.

McAffer, J. and Thomas, D. (1988) "Eva: An event driven framework for building user interfaces in Smalltalk," In. *Graphics Interface '88*, pp. 168-175.

McCormack, J. and Asente, P. (October, 1988) "An overview of the X toolkit," *UIST '88 ACM SIGGRAPH Symposium on User Interface Software*, 46-55.

Meulen, P.S. van der (1989) "Development of an interactive simulator in Smalltalk," *JOOP*, 28-51. January/February 1989

NeXT Inc. (1988) *NeXT System Reference Manual*, Palo Alto, Calif.

Shan, Yen-Ping (1989) "An event-driven Model-View-Controller framework for Smalltalk," In: *OOPSLA'89: Object Oriented Programming, Systems and Applications*, pp. 347-352.

Shan, Yen-Ping (1990) "Mode offers direct manipulation for Smalltalk," *IEEE Software*, vol. 7, no. 3, 36

Stepstone corp. (1988) *ICpak 201 Reference Manual*, Sandy Hook, Ct.

2

Snap Together Mathematics

Michael Gleicher and Andrew Witkin

Large numbers of applications involve building complicated mathematical models out of predefined functions and repeatedly evaluating the combined function and its derivatives. For interactive applications it is important that the evaluations be efficient and that the model can be altered dynamically. Snap Together Mathematics is a facility that provides this functionality. Primitive functions are defined at compile time and can be composed dynamically to create larger models. Evaluation of both the composed function and its derivatives is accomplished by traversal of the expression graph. The sparse derivative matrix of a subset of a model's outputs with respect to any set of its inputs can be computed efficiently. Snap Together Mathematics is implemented as a set of class definitions that provide a base for application specific objects. Among the applications we have developed are interactive systems for geometric modelling, constrained optimization, and constrained dynamics.

1. Introduction

The increasing availability of high performance computers has for the first time made it feasible to perform non-trivial numerical computations at interactive speeds. There are two central issues in making applications like iterative simulations, constrained optimization, or physics based animation, interactive. First, achieving the 20+hz frame rates of such systems requires very high-performance evaluation of the models. Second, the user must be able to alter the structure of the model without "breaking stride." Without the ability to define and modify the objects being simulated dynamically, such systems are not truly interactive.

All of these applications, and many others, involve mixing alterations of a mathematical model with repeated evaluations of the model and the derivatives of its input/output relationships. We have isolated this functionality in a general purpose facility which we call "snap-together mathematics." The package allows an application to build complicated models dynamically by snapping together smaller pre-defined mathematical functions, the set of which is fixed at compile time. Expression graphs built out of these primitives can then be manipulated and evaluated at run time. The derivatives of the expressions can be computed in addition to the values.

As an example, consider a modeller which lets the user experiment with parametric surfaces. The user can interactively edit the defining function which must be evaluated for each sample point when the object is rendered. Surface normals can be computed from the derivatives of the function with respect to the parameters. Snap Together Mathematics provides support for applications like this. It allows applications to compose mathematical functions dynamically, and then to evaluate them and their derivatives rapidly.

Evaluating mathematical expressions is a standard practice. Repeatedly and rapidly evaluating a dynamically defined expression and its derivatives is much less so. The two primary contributions of this work are the encapsulation of this functionality into a general purpose facility which can be mixed into applications, and the efficient evaluation of the derivatives of these dynamically constructed functions.

2. Evaluating Expressions

Mathematical expressions can be represented by directed acyclic graphs. An expression graph or network consists of one type of vertex, one type of arc, and two types of leaves. The leaves are either constants or variables, the only distinction being that we may differentiate with respect to the variables. Leaf nodes can be thought of as functions of 0-arity that return the value of their constant or variable. The non-terminal nodes represent primitive functions, referred to as function blocks. The edges of the graph represent function composition.

Any interpreter, compiler or calculator must be able to evaluate expressions, so the techniques required are well known[1]. Providing for rapid repeated evaluation of dynamically defined expressions creates challenges not addressed in the literature.

One way to evaluate an expression graph is first to compile it to machine code, then execute the code as needed. This technique offers the fastest evaluations, but each time an expression changes it needs to be compiled and re-linked—which is expensive.

The other approach to implementing expression evaluation is interpretive: traverse the graph for each evaluation. A set of pre-defined primitive operations are compiled ahead of time and composed by the traversals. We can build complicated functions by "snapping together" these basic building blocks.

The most straightforward process for expression evaluation is recursive descent. When a non-leaf node is asked for its value it recursively asks its children for their values, and then applies its local function to those intermediate results. The recursion bottoms out at the leaf nodes, which return their values. This approach is fully lazy: a value is not computed until it is needed.

Performance can be enhanced by using caching to exploit two types of redundancy: (1) within an evaluation common subexpressions need only be evaluated once, and (2)

1 See [Aho and Ullman, 1977] for example.

between evaluations certain old values might still be correct if some of the inputs did not change.

Recomputation can be avoided by storing the results of a calculation and, for a later request, deciding whether this stored value is still correct. We have implemented this decision using a global time clock which is updated whenever any one of the expression's inputs change. Each block contains a time-stamp containing the value of the clock when it was last computed. A block must recompute if its time-stamp is older than the current clock. This method has the advantage that it is simple and fast. It has the problem that inter-evaluation coherence is not exploited because all blocks are invalidated whether or not they depended on the inputs that have changed.

The time-stamp cache-coherence scheme is a variant of flag based schemes in which each block has a valid flag which is reset when its cache becomes invalid. The time-stamp scheme resets all flags by changing the time on the clock. Instead of the constant time time-stamp invalidation process, most flag implementations involve resetting a list of flags when an input changes. In order to exploit inter-evaluation coherence, flags must be reset selectively. Schemes such as this have two problems: first, dependency information must be maintained; second, changing an input might be expensive because many flags may need to be reset.

A recursive descent of the tree can also be used to validate caches. A node checks its children to see if any of them have recomputed since it last did so. A coherency check causes a complete descent of the tree which is expensive. This recursive descent scheme minimizes recomputation at the expense of coherency checking.

Eager systems offer an alternative to cache checking. An eager system is one which evaluates all blocks in a graph at its first opportunity. Time at network configuration is traded for time during evaluations. When the network is reconfigured a total ordering for the expression graph is found by topological sorting. Evaluating the blocks in this order insures that no block is evaluated before its children. Eager systems do not exploit inter-evaluation coherence and evaluate all blocks in the graph at each evaluation whether their values will be needed or not.

3. Evaluating Derivatives

We would like to be able to differentiate a set of the outputs of an expression graph with respect to a set of the inputs, $\mathbf{w}$. In the case of first derivatives, which will be our concern in this paper, this result is a matrix called the Jacobian, which is typically sparse. The techniques discussed do extend to higher derivatives. The two general approaches for computing derivatives are to build the expression symbolically, or to approximate it numerically.

Numeric approximation of the derivative can be done by using finite differences. Instead of taking the limit, we look at the change of the function over a small range, using multiple evaluations of the function

$$\frac{df(x)}{dx} \approx \frac{f(x+\Delta x)-f(x)}{\Delta x}.$$

The finite difference approach's primary advantage is that it only requires us to be able to evaluate the function. A disadvantage is that it is only an approximation to the derivative[2]. It is also difficult to exploit sparsity in the derivatives. In order to take the derivative with respect to n variables, the function must be evaluated at least $n+1$ times. To avoid redundant computation we must be extremely clever about exploiting inter-evaluation coherence.

Instead of estimating the derivative numerically, we can use the basic properties of derivatives to build expressions for them, and then evaluate these new expressions. The chain rule allows us to decompose complicated functions into smaller pieces. For example,

$$\frac{\partial f(a,b,\ldots)}{\partial \mathbf{w}} = \frac{\partial f(a,b,\ldots)}{\partial a}\frac{\partial a}{\partial \mathbf{w}} + \frac{\partial f(a,b,\ldots)}{\partial b}\frac{\partial b}{\partial \mathbf{w}} + \cdots. \tag{1}$$

Symbolic differentiation involves recursive applications of the chain rule. If we are able to evaluate the derivative of each of the primitive functions with respect to their inputs then we can apply Equation 1 recursively to build the compound expressions. The recursion bottoms out at the constants, whose derivatives are 0, and at the variables, whose derivatives are 1 with respect to themselves and 0 with respect to others variables.

Symbolic differentiation is ordinarily applied to an expression graph to transform it into a new expression for evaluating the derivative. The resulting expression must then be simplified to take advantage of the sparsity of the derivatives. Even then, the symbolic differentiation of a vector with respect to a vector yields a matrix of *expressions* which is unwieldy to manage.

Instead, we perform symbolic differentiation "in place." The existing expression graph is augmented with the ability to pass derivatives as well as values along arcs. In addition to being able to compute its output values, each node of the expression graph must also be able to compute the value of its internal derivative, also a function of its inputs.

We implement the evaluation of the derivative by a recursive descent of the expression graph. Each block asks its children for their derivatives with respect to $\mathbf{w}$, computes its local derivative as a function of its inputs, and multiplies these two matrices together to yield its derivative with respect to $\mathbf{w}$. The base cases of the recursion are the leaf nodes of the tree whose derivatives are constants.

It is important to recognize the generality of the derivative composition process. Each node of the expression graph need only to be able to compute its local, internal derivative matrix: the derivative of its outputs with respect to its inputs. This matrix is a function only of the input values, not their derivatives. Given the internal Jacobians, the composition process merely multiplies the matrices together to build the global derivatives.

---

2 For a discussion see [Mitchell and Griffiths, 1980]

3.1. Building Sparse Matrices

Derivative matrices are composed by multiplying the local derivatives of function blocks by the intermediate result fed into the function block. By passing the entire intermediate result matrix along the arcs of the graph, the derivative matrix can be built in one traversal of the expression graph (Figure 1).

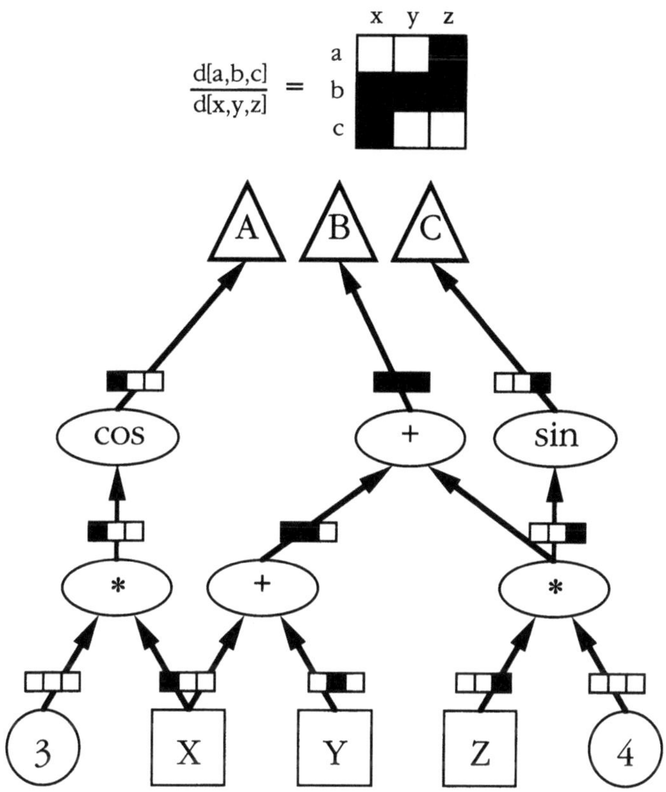

Figure 1: Passing Matrices
By passing entire intermediate results along the arcs of an expression graph, the Jacobian matrix can be composed in one traversal. The result matrices here are depicted as sparsity patterns, with non-zero entries shaded. Leaf nodes have constant derivatives. Other nodes compute their output derivatives by multiplying their internal Jacobians by the Jacobians of their inputs.

Alternatively, the complication of managing the intermediate results can be reduced by passing scalars, making each derivative in the network be with respect to an extra variable $u \notin \mathbf{w}$. Successively setting u equal to each member of $\mathbf{w}$ builds the Jacobian a column at a time, requiring a tree traversal for each variable. The internal Jacobians need only be computed once as they do not depend on derivatives of inputs.

The critical performance issue in building the matrix is exploiting sparsity. Matrix passing schemes exploit sparsity by using sparse representations for the intermediate matrices. Usually, the internal derivatives of primitives are too small to warrant the overhead of sparse matrices.

There are many possible ways to represent a sparse matrix, with many tradeoffs to consider in selecting a representation [Duff et al., 1986]. This decision is central to the design of a Snap Together Mathematics implementation. One particular representation with which we have had success is the half sparse matrix: a full vector of sparse vectors. We call a Snap Together Mathematics system based on these data structures a *sparse vector* scheme, since this is the most important data structure.

In the sparse vector scheme we consider every output in the expression as an independent scalar, even if higher levels will interpret them as pieces of larger structures. A function block can have multiple scalar outputs. The gradient of each scalar is a sparse vector ($\frac{\partial x}{\partial \mathbf{w}}$).

Sparse vectors can be represented as a list of pairs *(index, value)*, taking space linear with the number of non-zero elements. If this list is sorted by index, we can perform the essential vector operations in time linear to the number of non-zero elements. For single vector operations, such as 'multiply by scalar' or 'find magnitude', the algorithms simply run through the list. For multi-vector operations, such as addition, linear combination, or dot product, we exploit the sortedness of the lists and step through both in parallel, advancing which ever has the least index. These algorithms maintain the representation invariant, so $O(n \log n)$ sorting is not needed.

Each derivative in the expression graph is represented as a sparse gradient vector, a derivative of a scalar with respect to a set of variables. For each graph, one set of variables is denoted as current: all derivatives are with respect to this set. Each set of variables also must contain a mapping to the corresponding column of the Jacobian. A working set is a collection of inputs and a mapping.

We implement the sparse vector scheme as a lazy recursive descent of the tree. Each node in the graph is able to respond to requests for the derivative of its output with respect to the current working set. Constants and variables not in the working set return zero in response to this query. A state variable in the current working set returns a vector with a single 1 in the position corresponding to the variable, and zeros elsewhere. After determining that its cached value is not valid, a non-terminal node recursively asks its children for their derivatives, computes its internal Jacobian, and multiplies these together to produce its derivative with respect to the current working set.

Storage management is potentially an issue in a sparse matrix passing scheme since our intermediate results are dynamically sized objects. In adding sparse vectors, there is a simple way to determine an upper bound on the space needed for a result: the number of entries in a result cannot be more than the sum of the numbers of entries in the inputs. By being generous with initial space allocations, we rarely need to resize them. The vectors can grow in their pre-allocated space. In the rare event that new space is needed, pools of various standard sizes can be kept.

4. Implementing Snap Together Mathematics

4.1. A Function Blocks Library

The most straightforward approach to implementing Snap Together Mathematics would be to a build a library. Classes are created for major abstractions, such as function blocks, inputs and outputs, and wires. To make such a library more usable, facilities such as graph management are added.

Although we desire a large variety of primitive functions, there is a very high degree of regularity in these different types of function blocks. Since they differ only in the function and internal derivative they compute, given a facility for symbolic differentiation it is easy to build tools for automatically building new function block subclasses from algebraic expressions.

Although such a library is very easy to build and extend, a design such as this has the problem that it is too restrictive to support some applications. It creates a tendency to have separate mathematical and conceptual models. For example, in an earlier mechanical simulator, we kept a separate description of the mechanical object in addition to a function block network which computed the equations required for the simulation. The user operated on the mechanical model which in turn "stuck its fingers" into the mathematical model. The complications of maintaining the dual representations made building and maintaining the system more difficult than it should have been.

4.2. Definition by Protocol

The lazy recursive descent sparse vector scheme outlined in the preceding sections can be defined in terms of a simple protocol. In order to "speak mathematics" an object must support two methods: return the value of your ith scalar output; and return the sparse vector which is the derivative of your ith scalar output with respect to the current working set. At any given time, one subset of variables are defined as current: meaning that all derivatives in the graph are to be taken with respect to it.

This minimal protocol places few restrictions on what objects can have mathematics connected to them, making the system very simple and allowing a large variety of possible types of objects in the graph. We can have objects in the graph which are not primitive functions, such as subgraphs, or which choose to implement the required functionality differently.

The minimal protocol pushes the issues of network wiring into the objects themselves, but insulates them from what they are connecting to. A function block, which is one class of object which can have mathematics snapped to it, must take care of managing its own network connection.

Other classes can have the mathematics protocol mixed in with their application specific duties. For example, in an electrical circuit simulator's electrical components, in addition to being able to depict themselves graphically and maintain their connectivity information, could have mathematical outputs that computed the current flowing through them. Our constrained dynamic simulation library, described later, also takes advantage of adding snap-together functionality to objects.

The major classes of Snap Together Mathematics, such as function blocks and variables, still exist, but are rarely used "raw." Typically their capabilities are mixed into application specific objects.

Our implementation employs sparse vectors and lazy recursive descent. In addition to being simple and clean, this approach to derivative evaluation performs extremely well. It makes the maximum possible exploitation of inherent and randomly occurring sparsity. The inner loop of the computation is the linear combination of sparse vectors, a linear time routine which is small enough that an optimizing compiler can create efficient code for it. The lazy nature of the evaluation ensures that no unneeded blocks are traversed.

5. Supporting Interactive Dynamics

Interactive physical simulation was the application which primarily motivated the development of Snap Together Mathematics. The goal is to build systems which allow the user to build mechanical gadgets and manipulate them. Doing this requires the ability to dynamically construct the equations defining the model and to be able to evaluate these equations rapidly. The facilities of Snap Together Mathematics are designed to meet these challenges.

Interactive Dynamics is presented here as a case study not only because it is a natural use of Snap Together Mathematics, but also because the techniques of constraint based simulation are useful in a broad class of applications. A more detailed discussion of constrained dynamics can be found in [Witkin et al., 1990].

5.1. Constrained Dynamics

Consider a system whose state is described by a vector $\mathbf{q}$. The behaviour of this system in response to a force vector $\mathbf{f}$ can be found by integrating the differential equation of motion, typically some form of Newton's second law $\mathbf{f} = \mathbf{M}\ddot{\mathbf{q}}$. We often write this in terms of the inverse of the mass matrix, $\mathbf{W}$, so $\ddot{\mathbf{q}} = \mathbf{WF}$.

When the machinery of constrained dynamics is to be used as a tool for manipulating purely geometric or otherwise non-physical objects, it is often desirable to replace the second order equations of motion with a first order system of the form

$$\dot{\mathbf{q}} = \mathbf{W}\mathbf{F}, \tag{2}$$

in effect replacing $f = ma$ by $f = mv$, approximately modelling the behaviour of a highly damped system with negligible mass. The effect of this change is that things stop moving the instant forces are withdrawn, which facilitates accurate positioning in geometric modelling applications. We present the derivations for the first order case, noting that the second order case is similar and presented elsewhere [Witkin et al., 1990].

A constraint is a relationship on the system which must hold true. The class of constraints we are concerned with are holonomic equality constraints, which can be written as $c(\mathbf{q}) = 0$. The problem is to simulate the behaviour of the system in response to an applied force, $\mathbf{f}_a$. Simulating requires ensuring that the system does not violate the constraints. Integrating an arbitrary applied force might lead to violations of the constraints, so the total force $\mathbf{f}$ must be the sum of $\mathbf{f}_a$ and a force generated by the constraints, $\mathbf{f}_c$.

Assume that, at the present instant, all of the constraints are met ($\mathbf{c} = 0$). In order for the constraints to be maintained, $\mathbf{c}$ must be unchanging, so $\dot{\mathbf{c}}$ (and higher derivatives) must equal zero. From the chain rule,

$$\dot{\mathbf{c}} = \frac{\partial}{\partial t}\mathbf{c}(\mathbf{q}) = \frac{\partial \mathbf{c}}{\partial \mathbf{q}}\dot{\mathbf{q}}.$$

Denoting the constraint Jacobian by $\mathbf{J} = \frac{\partial \mathbf{c}}{\partial \mathbf{q}}$, we obtain $\mathbf{JWf} = 0$ by substituting in the equation of motion (2). Recalling that $\mathbf{f} = \mathbf{f}_a + \mathbf{f}_c$, a little manipulation yields

$$\mathbf{JWf}_c = -\mathbf{JWf}_a, \tag{3}$$

which is a system of *linear* equations with only the constraint force vector $\mathbf{f}_c$ unknown.

In words, Equation 3 just says that the constraint force, added into the applied force, must cause the first time derivative of the constraints to be zero. This condition is generally too weak: if the system is under constrained, as is usually the case (otherwise nothing can move at all!) we have fewer equations than unknowns, and there exist many values for $\mathbf{f}_c$ that satisfy Equation 3. In order to remove this ambiguity, we require that the system obey the principle of virtual work, which requires that the constraints do not change the energy in the system. For this to occur, the constraint forces must lie in the null space compliment of the Jacobian, so that $\mathbf{f}_c = \boldsymbol{\lambda}\mathbf{J}$ for some vector $\boldsymbol{\lambda}$. We write the equation as

$$\mathbf{JWJ}^T\boldsymbol{\lambda} = -\mathbf{JWf}_a, \tag{4}$$

and solve for $\boldsymbol{\lambda}$, the vector of *Lagrange Multipliers*.

The constraint formulation assumed that the constraints are met. In order to allow for drift due to numerical problems and initial conditions where the constraints are not met, we use feedback to pull the system back into a legal state. This is implemented by adding a force in the direction of the constraint Jacobian proportional to the deviation of the constraint.

5.2. Implementing Interactive Dynamics

Equation 4 provides a method for simulating the behaviour of a physical system. Given the constraint Jacobians, mass matrix, and the applied forces, we can compute the actual derivatives by solving a sparse linear system, then integrating the result.

Although Equation 4 is a global relationship, the problem of setting up the linear system can be decomposed into smaller pieces. This allows us to build interactive simulation systems despite the fact that the constraint equations grow complex quickly. All of the global quantities can be built by composing a small set of local ones.

Gadgets are built by connecting predefined parts together with constraints. Treating each part as a separate entity with its own state and mass matrix, the global state and mass can be created by concatenating these smaller elements into the required global quantities.

Mechanical constraints typically involve particular points on the objects they relate. A connector is a place on an object where constraints and forces can be attached. Mathematically, connectors may be viewed as "outputs" of the objects, pieces of geometry that "move with" the object in the sense that their values depend on state. In addition to representing points on surfaces, connectors can also represent surface normals, areas and volumes, or anything that might be subjected to a constraint, or to which a force might be applied.

The benefit of introducing connectors is that they allow us to formulate generic constraints—e.g. attaching two points together—without the need to know anything in advance about the objects being constrained. Consider an arbitrary equality constraint c on a pair of points a and b, which could be written

$$c(q) = f(a(q), b(q))$$

where f is whatever function defines the constraints (which is simply subtraction in the case of an attachment constraint) using whatever formulae determine a and b as functions of their respective objects' state. From the standpoint of decomposition and encapsulation, it is significant that the function $f(a, b)$ is only a property of the constraint and not of the constrained objects, while the position functions $a(q)$ and $b(q)$ are properties only of the two constrained objects and not of the constraint.

Connectors and constraints provide the mapping from mechanical systems to Snap Together Mathematics. By mixing in the ability to speak mathematics to connectors, snapping together mechanical objects with constraints also snaps together the required constraint functions. There is only one graph representing the mechanical system. Figure 2 shows the decomposition of a simple system, a double pendulum in the plane built from two rods, a nail, and two attachment constraints.

For dynamic simulation, we require not only the constraint equation but its time derivative. We achieve this by adding time derivatives to each part of the mechanical hierarchy. The configuration of the object is given in phase space, the combination of configuration and velocity spaces. Since they are provided with time derivative information as input, connectors can provide not only their outputs but the time derivatives of these outputs as well. Constraints have the same property. Since these time derivatives are just like any other Snap Together Mathematics outputs, they can be differentiated against the state variables.

We have built prototype mechanical construction sets in two and three dimensions. These interactive systems allow the user to build complicated gadgets by connecting simple pieces and then "playing" with these objects. The systems are completely without modes: construction and experimentation can be intermixed.

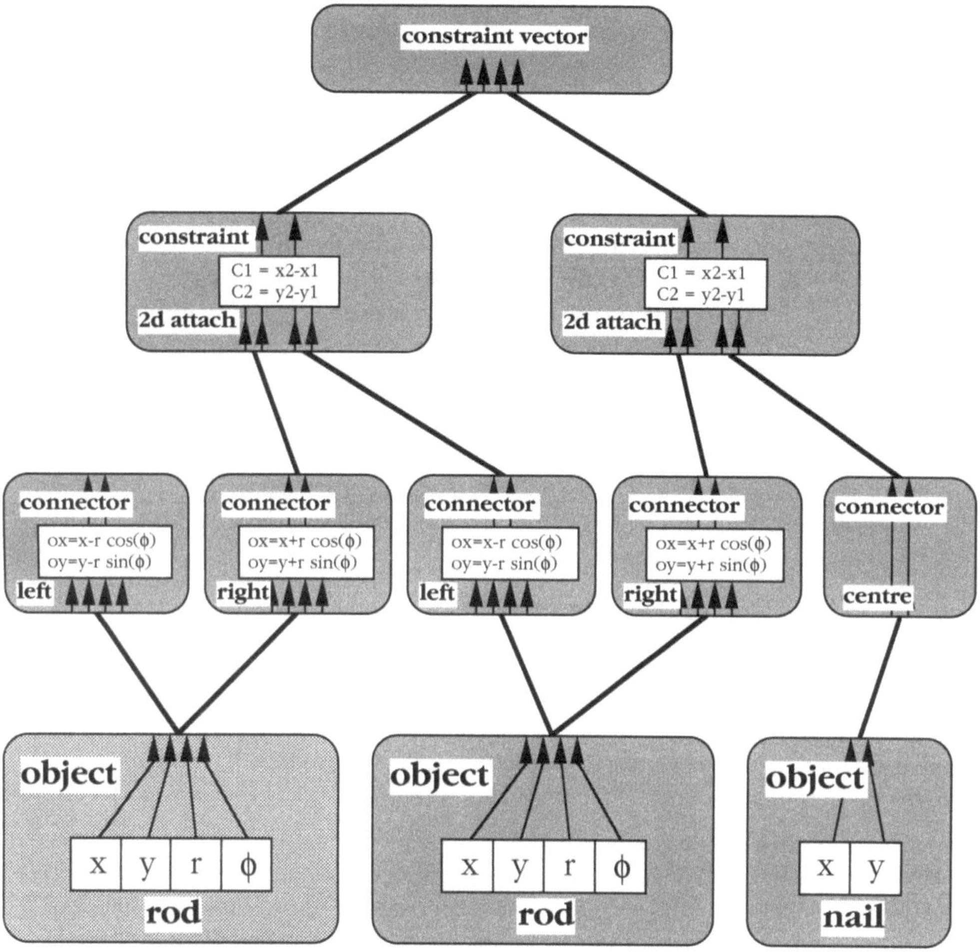

Figure 2: Interactive Dynamics Implemented
This single tree represents both the mechanical and mathematical structure of a double pendulum in the plane.

By building on top of Snap Together Mathematics, we have made it easier to define new classes of basic objects and constraints. Without the ability to do general dynamic composition of derivatives, a system must either make composition easier by restricting the objects or constraints possible ([Witkin and Welch, 1990] restricts both) or else precompose all possible permutations of objects and constraints (as in the drawing program by [Spreen, 1989]).

6. Other Applications

6.1. A Graphical Calculator

The *Slideroo* application allows the user to type symbolic expressions which are then parsed into Snap Together Mathematics networks. The inputs and outputs of the functions are connected to sliders.

The user can not only set inputs and view the outputs, but can also move the outputs and have the required change in the inputs computed from the derivative. Unlike [Vander Zanden, 1988], we do not actually create the inverse function by manipulating our tree, but rather use the ability to evaluate the derivatives. Unlike [Borning, 1981], we achieve bi-directionality without use of our constraint mechanism.

Since derivatives of functions are available, we can use our constraint simulation techniques. Relations on the inputs and outputs can be enforced as either equality or inequality (one sided) constraints. The user can then explore the solution space by pulling the inputs or outputs around in it. With this, the graphical calculator can be used to solve constrained optimization problems.

6.2. Geometric Modelling

We have been experimenting with the use of physical simulation as an interface for geometric modelling. A parametric curve can be interpreted as a physical object with uniform mass and drag. Under this model, a curve responds to forces applied to it in accordance with the functions that define it. The parameterization of the object is completely hidden from the user.

By having derivative information available, a more direct form of direct manipulation is possible. The user can point to a place on an object and manipulate that point directly, since motion of the point can be translated into motion of the representation. Traditional manipulation schemes require the user to manipulate the parameters for an object, which may be unintuitive or difficult to control.

For example, consider manipulating an ellipse in a traditional drawing program such as [Claris, 1988]. The user alters the ellipse by changing its parameters directly. Fortunately, the programmer chose a parameterization which is convenient for the user: an axis aligned bounding box. In our two-dimensional drawing program, the user can grab any point on the ellipse and pull it. Since the user is isolated from the parameterization, we could choose a more complicated one that does not limit ellipses to be aligned with the axes.

Derivative information also makes it possible to use dynamic simulation techniques, such as constraints, in geometric modelling. The addition of constraints and direct manipulation to a drawing program allows it to be used for experimenting with the drawings as mechanisms.

7. Status and Directions

We have been using facilities for dynamic composition of expressions and evaluations of them their derivatives for two years. Our first realization, built in C, implemented an eager scalar passing scheme in a very complete library. Our experiences in building applications on top of this substrate led to the design of a simpler system.

Our present implementation is built in C++ [Lippman, 1989] and is based on sparse vectors, lazy recursive descent, and a minimal protocol as described previously. Multiple inheritance is used to give objects the ability to "speak mathematics."

Our present set of tools for building interactive mathematical applications includes classes to support function composition and evaluation, support for basic mathematical entities (vectors, matrices, etc.), and a variety of numerical tools. We have built automatic code generation tools, built into a symbolic mathematics package [Wolfram, 1988], to define function blocks from algebraic expressions.

By encapsulating the often needed functionality of dynamic expression composition and evaluation into a general purpose library, we have created a substrate on which to build a wide variety of interactive applications. We are already building two and three dimensional geometric modellers and physical simulators. We have plans to create systems for interactive optimization, computer vision, analog circuit design, and diagram layout.

Acknowledgements

This research was sponsored in part by Apple Computer. The first author is supported in part by a fellowship from the Schlumberger Foundation, Inc. The views and conclusions contained in this document are those of the authors and should not be interpreted as representing the official policies, either expressed or implied, of Schlumberger or Apple.

References

Aho, A and Ullman, J. (1977) *Principles of Compiler Design,* Addison Wesley.

Borning, A. (1981) "The programming language aspects of ThingLab, a constraint-oriented simulation laboratory",," *ACM Transactions on Programming Languages and Systems,* vol. 3, no 4, 353–387.

Claris Corp. (1988) *MacDraw II.* computer program

Duff, J.S., Erisman, A.M., and Reid, J.K. (1986) *Direct Methods for Sparse Matrices,* Oxford University Press, Oxford, UK.

Lippman, S. (1989) *C++ Primer,* Addison Wesley.

Mitchell, A.R. and Griffiths, D.F (1980) *The Finite Difference Method in Partial Differential Equations,* John Wiley and Sons.

Spreen, R. (Summer 1989) *Personal Communication.*

Vander Zanden, B.T. (1988) "Constraint grammars in user interface management systems," In: *Proc. Graphics Interface,* pp. 176–184.

Witkin, A. and Welch, W. (August 1990) "Fast animation and control of non-rigid structures," *Computer Graphics,* vol. 24. Proceedings Siggraph '90

Witkin, A., Gleicher, M., and Welch, W. (March 1990) "Interactive dynamics," *Computer Graphics,* vol. 24, no. 2, 11-21. Proceedings 1990 Symposium on Interactive 3d Graphics

Wolfram, S (1988) *Mathematica,* Addison Wesley

3

Building User Interfaces with the LOOKS Hyper-Object System

Didier Plateau, Patrick Borras, Didier Lévêque, Jean-Claude Mamou and Didier Tallot

In this chapter, we present the *LOOKS* system which is designed to support the construction of user interfaces for object-oriented database applications. The *LOOKS* system provides high level capabilities to display and manipulate database objects interactively and to build end-user ↔ application dialogue based on object manipulation.

1. Introduction

End-user dialogue management represents a large part of the application code. Designing and implementing a powerful direct-manipulation graphic user interface requires time and expertise from the programmer. Such user interfaces are often out of reach, unless appropriate user interface tools are provided.

In this chapter, we focus on the user interface tools needed by a programmer writing object-oriented database applications. Object-oriented database applications cover various domains such as business, office automation, CAD, hypertext and hypermedia systems.

Object-oriented database (OODBMS in the following) applications have specific problems for two reasons:

- The information manipulated by the applications (and therefore the end-users) is a graph connecting large composite objects.

  Think, for instance, of a travel agency organizing tours. The database stores information about cities, hotels, monuments, restaurants, customers, flights, etc. Cities and hotels are objects linked together: a hotel is located in a city and a city contains a set of hotels. A travel agency application needs basic tools to display, browse, and update this graph to allow the end-user to perform functions such as "What about Rome ?" or "Make a room reservation in the Ritter Hotel".

- Database programmers have to compromise between application usability and software productivity.

  What they need are "easy to learn", "easy to use" tools which relieve them from most of the user interface design and implementation workload. These tools also guarantee the usability and consistency of the resulting user interfaces.

Thus, object-oriented database programmers need a set of built-in facilities to display, browse and manipulate a graph of *hyper-objects* interactively. Let us now discuss how these needs relate to facilities of the existing user interface tools.

User interface toolkits ([OSF, 1989], [Devin and Duquesnoy, 1988], [Schmucker, 1986], etc.) constitute a mature technology moving towards standards. However, they only provide a library of basic dialogue components (widgets) such as buttons and menus. The gap to meet OODBMS applications requirements is huge. To display a piece of data, one needs to compose widgets as well as implement editing operations.

User interface editors ([Cardelli, 1988], [Karsenty, 1987], [Smith, 1988], [Devin and Duquesnoy, 1989], and [Hullot, 1986]) allow one to create and to combine widgets interactively and to store their description in resource files for use by a program. This relieves the programmer from writing the corresponding code and provide a nice framework to tune the user interface (colour, layouts, fonts, etc.). However, *user interface editors* rarely capture the dynamic dimension of widgets: dynamic creation of widgets, reaction to user command, etc.

While *toolkits* and *user interface editors* focus on widgets creation, *User Interface Management Systems* (UIMS) as defined in [Betts et al., 1987] and [Rhyne et al., 1987] address the complete construction of the dialogue: not only the description of the different screen components but also how these components relate to one another, to the application and to the user, in order to capture user↔application dialogue completely. Many UIMS have been prototyped ([Sibert et al., 1986], [Olsen, 1986], [Myers and Buxton, 1986], [Hermann and Hill, 1988], etc) but UIMS technology is still not mature. The UIMS research community is quite active, but few products are available and none is widely spread.

Last, *application generators* are dedicated to a specific application domain. A domain is characterized by a data model describing the information manipulated by the application. Within this framework, *application generators* provide facilities to control data layout, editing and interactive behaviour. Application semantics is represented by scripts.

Application generators include Fourth Generation Languages (4GLs) [Martin, 1985] and Hypercard-like systems [Goodman, 1987]. 4GLs are parts of relational database systems programming environments. In relational systems, data is modelled by tables and tuples. 4GLs provide display, editing and scripting (usually SQL queries) facilities.

Information handled by Hypercard is represented by stacks and cards instead of tables and tuples (this is not very different). Hypercard provides a nice environment to specify the graphic appearance and the interactive behaviour of cards and stacks.

Application generators meet our initial requirements. The *LOOKS* system we present in this chapter belongs to this category. It is built on top of a data model and it provides facilities to display and manipulate interactively objects.

However, various features make *LOOKS* significantly different from other *application generators*. *LOOKS* is based on an object-oriented data model which is much more powerful than relational or "card and stack" model. To control data layout, interactive manipulation and dialogue construction, *LOOKS* provides various original features like masks, links and modes which are described in this chapter.

The rest of this chapter is organized as follows. The O_2 object-oriented data model is described in Section 2. The various features of the system are described from Section 3 to 10. Section 11 illustrates these features with a short programming example. As a conclusion, Section 12 presents the current state of the *LOOKS* system and discusses the future of the project: evaluation, tuning and improvements, additional functions, etc.

We assume the reader familiar with the basic object-oriented and programming concepts. The few required to understand the content of this chapter are: typing, message passing, encapsulation, object identity, methods and classes.

2. The LOOKS Data Model

This section is an informal description of the data model underlying the *LOOKS* system. This data model is part of an object-oriented database system named O_2 [Deux, 1989]. Extensive presentation and theoretical justifications of the model can be found in [Lécluse and Richard, 1989].

An object is either atomic (integer, float, string, bits, boolean, etc) or composite. A composite object is built from atoms combined with list, set or tuple constructors. These constructors can be arbitrarily nested.

In order to illustrate our discussion on object display, we use the following example:

```
class Hotel
 type tuple(name:string,
          address: Address,
          facilities: set(string),
          rate: integer);

class Address
 type tuple(number: integer,
          street:string,
          city: City);

class City
 type tuple(name:string,
          map: bitmap,
          hotels:set(Hotel));
```

Hotel type is a composite type built with a tuple, the attributes of which are a name (an atom of type string), an address (a reference to the Address class), a set of facilities (set of string) and a room rate (integer).

It should be noticed that these three classes form a cycle: Hotel has an Address field which in turn has a City field while finally, City contains a set of Hotels.

The next example shows a Hotel object:

```
ritter: tuple(name: ''Ritter Hotel'',
              address: addr_ritter,
              facilities: set(''swimming-pool'',
                              ''bar''),
              rate: 100,000)
```

3. Generic Presentations

LOOKS provides a generic algorithm to display objects. It can be applied to any object to build an interactive presentation. A generic presentation is an interactive component which can be edited and saved in the database. Application/end-user dialogue can be organized by means of menus that are hooked to the presentations. There is one menu per object. Menu items correspond to object methods.

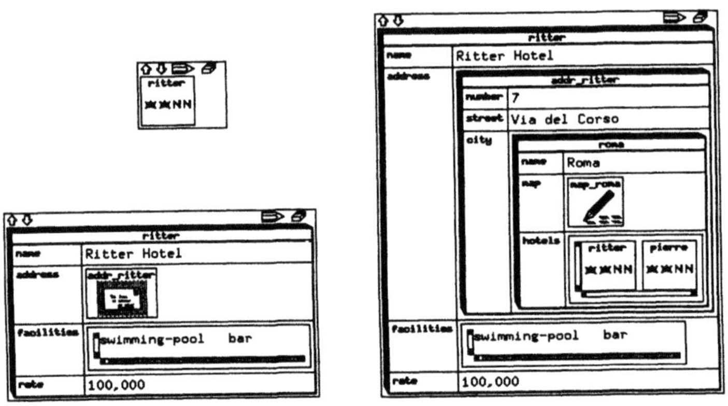

Figure 1: Generic presentations with depth 0, 1 and 3.

Figure 1 shows three generic presentations of the same ritter object as defined above.

Several generic presentations can be created from the same ritter object. The difference is the amount of information visible. To control this, a depth parameter is used. Let us illustrate how the algorithm works on the ritter example.

Displaying an object with depth 0 creates an icon (see the upper left window of Figure 1. A menu is hooked to the icon: the menu items correspond to ritter methods.

Displayed with depth 1, the content of ritter is shown (see the lower left window of Figure 1). In this case, the display algorithm shows each ritter sub-objects as icons (addr_ritter in this example). Menus are hooked to ritter and addr_ritter.

Recursively, a depth 2 presentation is obtained applying depth 1 to ritter and again to addr_ritter. Depth *i* is the expansion obtained applying depth 1 to ritter and depth *i*-1 to addr_ritter. For instance, the right window of Figure 1 shows depth 3 applied to ritter.

The next section describes how generic presentations can be edited, while Section 9 explains how the object menus are created and used.

4. Editing Presentations

Generic presentations show atoms (integers, strings, ...), structures (list, set, tuple) and objects. Each of these components can be edited.

Atoms (integer, string, etc.) are edited in a textual manner. Boolean (viewed as a two state button) and bits, which cannot be edited as text, are exceptions. Atoms can be copied and pasted within a presentation and between different presentations. *LOOKS* type-checks dynamically. For instance, one cannot type something other than a digit in an integer field.

Structures can be copied and pasted. The end-user can copy a tuple and paste it on a tuple having the same type. Within lists and sets, it is also possible to cut and create elements.

Again, *LOOKS* performs synchronous type-checking. Any type inconsistent manipulation is forbidden. Consistency is based only on internal (O_2) type consistency. Thus, even if two views of the same O_2 structure do not show the same information (hidden attributes in a tuple for instance) the copy/paste will still be allowed by *LOOKS.*

Objects can be copied, pasted and cut when they are in a list or a set. They can also be shared: this is different from the copy because the copy operation performs an object copy (a new object is created) while the share operation manipulates the object identity.

5. Masks

With generic presentations, the control of the programmer on the amount of visible information is limited to control of the depth. Besides, generic presentations are completely editable. Masks provide the capability to control how much information is displayed and which part(s) of this information can be edited.

Let us show some masks which can be used to control the presentation of the ritter object.

```
O2 type mask1
  read object
      read tuple(name: write string,
                 address: read object,
                 facilities: read set( read string),
                 rate: private integer);
```

Basically a mask is a structure similar to the corresponding object. The various components of the mask are labeled by private/read/write properties: private means hidden, read means visible but not editable, and write means visible and editable.

For instance, attribute rate is hidden because it is declared private in mask1. The complete object and the tuple structure cannot be pasted because they are declared read.

To see the content of the address, the following mask can be used:

```
O2 type Mask_Hotel
      read object
         tuple(name: string,
               address: read object
                             tuple(number: integer,
                                   street: string,
                                   city: City)
               facilities: write set(read string));
```

In this second example, the mask forces the address to be visible. private/read/write properties are inherited through the mask structure but can be overridden. Notice also that the rate attribute has disappeared which is equivalent to declaring it private.

6. Placements

Whether a generic presentation or a mask is used, once a presentation is created, it has to be displayed on the screen. The *placement* capability provide high level control on screen layout.

LOOKS provides eight layout strategies (MANUAL, MOUSE, STACK, TOP, DOWN, RIGHT, LEFT and COORDINATE).

The first two (MANUAL, MOUSE) let end-users control the layout. The last six layouts (STACK, TOP, DOWN, RIGHT, LEFT, COORDINATE) position a presentation P1 relative to another presentation P0, provided P0 is already on the screen. In the following, we assume that a presentation P0 is already on the screen and that the program has to map another presentation P1.

MANUAL simply consists in asking the end-user to perform the placement of P1 interactively at run time. This is done by moving a ghosted P1 on the screen.

MOUSE requires that the upper left corner of P1 matches the current position of the mouse.

STACK placement consists in placing P1 over P0, slightly translated down and right (see Figure 2).

TOP, DOWN, RIGHT and LEFT tiles P1 and P0. DOWN makes P1's upper left corner match P0's lower left corner. RIGHT makes P1's upper left corner match P0's upper right corner. LEFT makes P1's upper right corner match P0's upper left corner.

In the COORDINATE strategy, (x,y) coordinates are explicitly defined in the program.

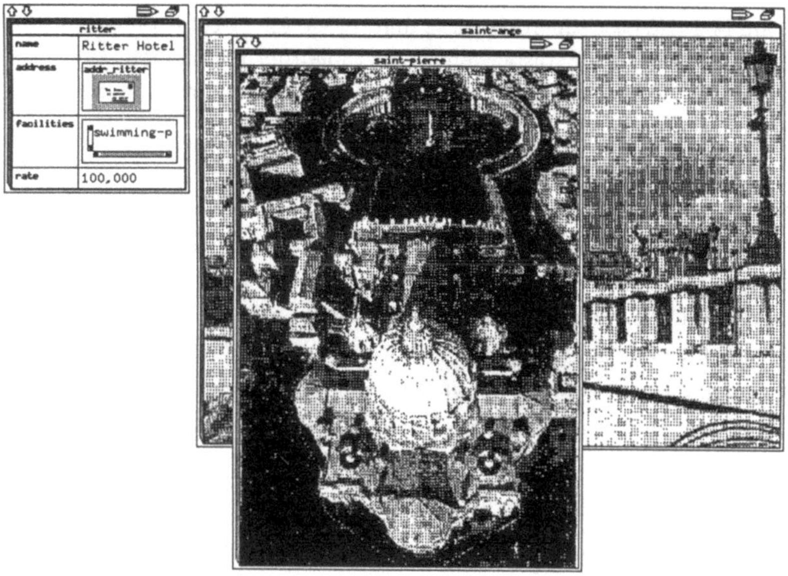

Figure 2: *Tile* and *stack* placements.

On Figure 2, the saint-ange presentation is at the RIGHT of ritter while saint-pierre is STACKed on saint-ange.

7. Modes

Modes address the problem of dialogue control. When an application is running, it is either waiting for an end-user operation (user control) or executing a method (application control). Control transfer from the application to the user and back is a complex problem.

A method can be interrupted to get some information from the user. Later on, this method will be restarted or maybe canceled. Meanwhile, the end-user is either constrained to input the required information or free to perform any other operation before.

LOOKS modes implement each of these alternatives. Assume a presentation P was created with the mode mode. At the time P is displayed, mode will affect the execution of the application as follows:

> If mode is WAIT, the application is interrupted. Control is transferred to the end-user who is free to manipulate P as well as any other presentation.
>
> If mode is GRAB, the application is interrupted but the end-user is constrained to manipulate exclusively P.

In both cases (WAIT and GRAB), the end-user restarts the method either by a "continue" or a "cancel" command. The method can then get the contents of P, remove P from the screen and give any meaning to the "continue" or "cancel" commands.

Because we are in a database environment, a third mode (BROWSE) is provided. If P is created with the BROWSE mode, displaying P won't interrupt the method. However, if later on, the end user gets control, it will be possible to edit P and save it in the database without any application control.

8. Links

When a presentation P0 is laid out on the screen relative to another presentation P1 using TOP, DOWN, RIGHT, LEFT, STACK or COORDINATE, a link (or a constraint) from P0 to P1 can be created by *LOOKS*. These links group presentations in trees and affect operations such as resizing, moving, removing from the screen and saving in the database.

To do so, four kinds of link are supported: FREE, GEOMETRIC, CONTENT and SLAVE. We illustrate each of them by a P1 and P0 example and then generalize to a tree.

FREE expresses the fact that P1 and P0 are not linked. The end user is free to move, resize, erase, edit and save P1 and P0 independently in the database.

GEOMETRIC links P0 to P1 geometrically. Each time P1 or P0 are pushed, popped, moved or resized, the other is pushed, popped or moved so that the primary layout (RIGHT, STACK, etc) is preserved. More generally, if P1 is part of a presentation tree, each time P1 is moved or resized, all the tree nodes are moved in order to preserve the layout.

CONTENT links P0 to P1 from the application point view. Assume for instance that P0 and P1 were created with a WAIT mode. Each time a "continue" or a "cancel" operation (see section 7) is applied to P1, the same operation is applied automatically on P0 beforehand. More generally, when a "continue" or a "cancel" operation is performed on a presentation linked to a presentation tree, the same operation is performed in suffix order on the subtree issued from the presentation

Lastly, SLAVE cumulates the properties of GEOMETRIC and CONTENT links.

9. Interactive Method Activation

As mentioned in Section 3, menus are hooked to object presentations. Each item of an object menu corresponds to a method of this object. *LOOKS* allows one to control which methods can be activated through this menu (i.e., a subset of the object methods). The menu item's name can be different from the method's name.

When an item (or a method) is selected in a menu, *LOOKS* automatically displays a presentation to collect the arguments if there are some. Once the arguments are collected, the method is executed. At any time during argument collection, the end-user may also cancel the method activation.

10. Specific Presentations

Generic presentations and masks allow the specification of which parts of an object are visible and editable. But they do not help to control the graphical aspect of the object.

Furthermore, the application cannot trap user operations. For instance, one might wish to display a list of integers as a pie or a chart (see Figure 3).

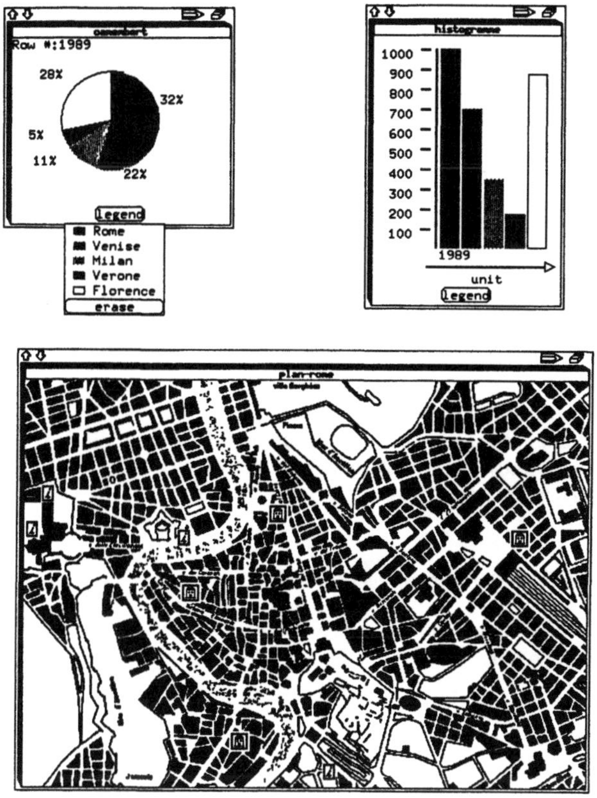

Figure 3: Presentations customized by program

A specific presentation is a programming extension of *LOOKS*. When displaying an object, the application can require the use of a specific presentation. Programming a specific presentation is similar to adding a new widget in a toolkit. The precise description of this programming process is beyond the scope of this chapter.

11. A Programming Example

The following example illustrates how to use the capabilities of *LOOKS* from the programming perspective. Our example is simply the creation of a new Hotel.

```
/* Creation of a new database Hotel
 */

  hotel = new(Hotel);

/* This new hotel is displayed with a depth 2 generic
```

```
* presentation. Mode is WAIT so that the application
* will be interrupted and control transferred to the
* user when the presentation is mapped on the screen.
*/

  presentation2 = present(hotel,GENERIC,2,WAIT);

/* presentation2 is mapped at the RIGHT of a presentation1
 * we assume to be already on the screen. This RIGHT
 * constraint will be maintained against GEOMETRIC
 * operations (moving presentation1 or presentation2).
 * The result will be either CONTINUE or CANCEL.
 */

  result = map(presentation2,RIGHT,presentation1,GEOMETRIC);

/* ''map'' has interrupted the execution until the user
 * has either canceled the creation or filled this new
 * hotel with the required information.
 * In both cases, presentation2 is erased from the screen
 * and removed. It the result is CONTINUE, then the content
 * of presentation2 is transferred in hotel.
 */

  if (result = CONTINUE) consult(presentation2,hotel);

/* Here, the code should check the consistency of the
 * data returned by the user.
 */

  unmap(presentation2);
  destroy(presentation2);
```

12. Conclusion

In this chapter, we have described the main features of the *LOOKS* system: generic presentations, masks, placements, links, modes. The current prototype is written in Le_Lisp [Chailloux, 1986] on top of the Aïda toolkit [Devin and Duquesnoy, 1988]. *LOOKS* has been tested against the development of significant applications: a travel agency application (from which the examples and figures of this chapter are extracted) and a complete programming environment for the O_2 OODBMS system.

We believe the strong point of *LOOKS* is the possibility given to the programmer to write a reasonable user interface very quickly and without dealing directly with widgets, event queue and other typical graphic toolkit notions.

As compared to Hypercard and existing 4GLs, *LOOKS* provides additional power. The data model is richer and extensible (one can define new classes). For each object, *LOOKS* proposes several predefined display algorithms.

Unlike most 4GLs, but like Hypercard, object presentations are graphical components which can be directly manipulated.

Like most 4GLs but unlike Hypercard, *LOOKS* is a programmer tool. The programming methodology is *(1)* to define the internal structures of the data manipulated by the application and use the generic presentations to test it. Then, *(2)*, use the various tools available in *LOOKS* (masks, programming extensions) to refine the aspect and interactive behaviour of the presentations.

Let us now discuss the current and future improvements and evolutions.

Firstly, we are currently redesigning the external aspect and behaviour of generic presentations. To do so, we are collaborating with graphic designers.

Secondly, we plan to add an interactive presentation editor. In the current prototype, building a specific presentation (that is changing the graphical aspect or interactive behaviour of objects presentations) requires programming. What we plan is an interactive tool to "redraw" presentations. It can be viewed as a user interface editor specialized to the problem of displaying and manipulating structures and objects.

Lastly, we are porting *LOOKS* on top of Motif.

Acknowledgements

The authors are employed by Altaïr, a consortium funded by IN2 (a Siemens subsidiary), INRIA (Institut National de Recherche en Informatique et Automatique) and LRI (Laboratoire de Recherche en Informatique, University of Paris XI).

References

Betts, B., Burlingane, D., Fisher, G., Foley, J., Green, M., Kasik, D., Kerr, S., Olsen, D., and Thomas, J. (1987) "Goals and objectives for User Interface Software," *Computer Graphics*, vol. 21, no 2 (April), 73.

Cardelli, L. (1988) "Building user interface by direct manipulation," In: *Symposium on User Interface Software*, ACM SIGGRAPH, pp 152-166. (October) Banff, Alberta, Canada

Chailloux, J (1986) *Le-Lisp Version 15 2 Manuel de Reference*, INRIA, Domaine de Voluceau BP 105, Rocquencourt 78153 Le Chesnay Cedex, France.

Deux, O. (1989) *The Story of O2*, GIP Altair.

Devin, M. and Duquesnoy, P. (1988) *Manuel de reference Aida version 1 2*, ILOG, 2, Avenue Gallieni - 94250 Gentilly, France.

Devin, M. and Duquesnoy, P (1989) *Manuel de reference Masai version 1*, ILOG, 2, Avenue Gallieni - 94250 Gentilly, France.

Goodman, D. (1987) *The complete Hypercard handbook*, Bantam Books.

Hermann, M. and Hill, R. D. (1988) *Abstration and declarativeness in user interface development— The methological basis of the composite object architecture*, ECIRC.

Hullot, J.M. (1986) "SOS Interface," *Journées AFCET*.

Karsenty, S (1987) *Graffiti un outil interactif et graphique pour la construction d'interfaces homme-machine adaptables*, Université de Paris XI

Lécluse, C. and Richard, P. (1989) "The O_2 Database Programming Language," In. *VLDB*

Martin, J (1985) *Fourth-Generation Languages*, Prentice-Hall

Myers, B A and Buxton, W (1986) "Creating highly-Interactive and Graphical User Interface by Demonstration," *Computer Graphics*, vol. 20, no. 3, 249-258

Olsen, D.R. (1986) "MIKE : The Menu Interaction Kontrol Environment," *ACM Trans. on Graphics*, vol. 5, no. 4, 318.

OSF (1989) "Motif 1.0 Programmer's Guide," *OSF*.

Rhyne, J., Ehrich, R., Bennett, J., Hewet, T., Sibert, J., and Bleser, T. (1987) "Tools and Methodology for User Interface Development," *Computer Graphics*, vol. 21, no. 2 (April), 78.

Schmucker, K. (1986) "MacApp . An Application Framework," *Byte*, vol. 11, no 8, 189-193.

Sibert, J.L., Hurley, W.B., and Bleser, T.W (1986) "An object-oriented user interface management system," *Computer Graphics*, vol. 20, no. 4, 259-168.

Smith, D N. (1988) "Building user interface interactively," In: *Symposium on User Interface Software*, ACM SIGGRAPH, pp. 144-151. (October) Banff, Alberta, Canada

4

A Layered Object-Oriented Model for Interaction

Chris Laffra and Jan van den Bos

We present a layered model of human computer interaction based on an object-oriented programming language. The model gains increasing abstraction with each layer that is added to the model. At the lowest layer parsing of physical events generated by a window system is dealt with. At the highest level we find interaction panels that no longer refer to events as such. Instead, interaction panels are solely described as aggregations of messages from High level interaction tools such as buttons, slider, menus, etc. The interaction tools are separated into three components: the interaction methods, the presentation, and the interaction style. The model can be used as a toolbox for programmers, or as a basis for automatic generation of user interfaces by interactive development tools.

1. Introduction

Good language facilities are indispensable for the design of good human-computer interfaces. There is a clear need for languages that are specifically deigned for human-computer interface definition. Conventional programming languages do not offer sufficient facilities for dealing with input. For example, it is not in general possible to specify a choice from more than one input source like a keyboard and a mouse. One should also be able to activate and de-activate input tools at will. In some cases we want to be able to start receiving input, while the program is doing something else (asynchrony). In other cases we want to allow parallel processing of two or more input sources. Often we only have these abilities in low-level (assembler/interrupt driven) languages. In practice one notices that a large part of a (graphical) application is concerned with event identification and processing.

Because of this concern with details, it is hard to concentrate on designing a good human-computer interface. The programmer should be able to specify an interface in terms of input patterns [van den Bos et al., 1981; van den Bos, 1988], including prompt, acknowledgement and feedback.

Interaction modules present a first good approach [van den Bos et al., 1981; van den Bos, 1988]. Following the rules of structured design and structured programming, an interactive system is considered to consist of a hierarchical set of dialogues, or interaction modules. only on the lowest level do we specify the physical input. This approach can be realized by defining modules that are activated (triggered) when a certain internally defined input pattern becomes available. The processing of the input, results in output that can in turn be used as input for higher level modules. Facilities for *Prompt* and *Echo* are part of the approach.

In this chapter the focus is moved to *object-oriented* interaction techniques. The model proposed consists of layers of objects that provide increasing levels of abstraction for each layer added (see Figure 1). At the lowest layer we are concerned with the (complicated) details of physical input. The second layer consists of objects forming abstract representations of physical input events. The third layer consists of interaction tools (ITs), such as *buttons, sliders* and *menus.* The ITs at this level are activated by one or more abstract events, the input pattern, from layer 2. ITs describe their input in terms of input patterns consisting of messages being sent by the abstract event objects from the second layer. Input patterns are specified in a high-level regular expression, so the model can easily be extended with new input tools. This is in contrast with existing (and popular) toolkits, whose contents is fixed. ITs can be considered to be compositions of abstract events extended with semantics and a physical representation on the screen. At the highest layer of our model we can combine interaction tools from the third layer into interaction Panels.

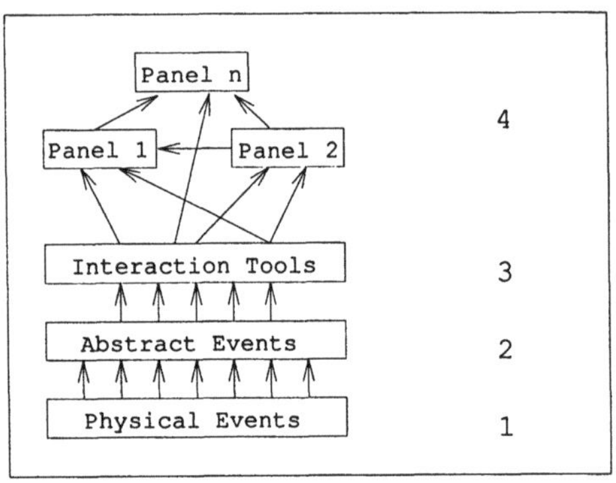

Figure 1: The Interaction Layers

We will relate our work to other (object-oriented) models for human computer interaction (HCI) in Section 2. We will describe the individual layers of the model in more detail in Sections 3 to 6. In Section 7, we will give a short introduction to *Procol,* the general-purpose object-oriented language used to develop our layered model. Following this introduction, two example applications are given developed according to our layered model of interaction.

2. Related Work

Object oriented models for HCI have been investigated many times before [McCormack et al., 1988; Swick and Weissman, 1988; Digital, 1988; OSF, 1989; Sun, 1989; Weinand et al., 1988; Linton et al., 1989; Webster, 1989; Goldberg, 1983; Shan, 1989; Aitken, 1990].

What most of these models have in common is their lack of extendibility. As indicated in [Myers, 1990], the familiar class-inheritance paradigm, adopted by most object oriented models, is too static and inflexible. What is more appropriate, and also applied in garnet [Myers, 1990], is a prototype-instance model. Instances are not created from a class description, but from a (possibly initialized) prototype. Garnet also provides a special tool for extending the current set of ITs.

The X Toolkit [McCormack et al., 1988; Swick and Weissman, 1988], and its derivates [Digital, 1988; OSF, 1989; Sun, 1989], tend to hide the implementation of individual ITs as much as possible Most of them do not provide a frame work to create new ITs if the currently available set is insufficient. Too many details need to be provided, and too much study is needed to be able to implement a new IT successfully.

We believe that the implementation model should be open and clear to understand. Abstraction of concept (layers) and clear communication protocols between these layers of abstraction is mandatory. When the protocols are simple and well understood, programmers are encouraged to create new ITs. Specialized interactive tools like Peridot [Myers and Buxton, 1986], can produce new ITs, simply be adhering to these clear descriptions.

A problem found in many toolkits is the problem of *control*. Who is in control, the user interface, or the application? Who is the active party? Who has the initiative? In all known toolkits the user sets up the environment and determines the context for its user interface and application. After this initialization, a special routine (or method) has to be called. This special routine never returns, and the initiative is never returned to the application. From time to time some user-specified action will be activated, and the appropriate "callback" routine is executed. This kind of model leaves little room for applications performing some complicated task, and wishing to inform the end-user of the percentage of the work that has been done already. Also, infinite loops in the application can cause problems. Of course, the problem of control is closely related to single thread *vs.* multiple thread programming, but little work has been done on "mixed-control" interfaces.

Another problem that emerges from the available toolkits, is that almost all toolkits are specifically directed towards *dialogue programming*. Buttons are merely extensions of function keys, as function keys are accelerators for typing a command. Menus allow for retrieval of commands and attributes in a more user friendly way. Scrollbars are replacements for commands such as "scroll up 1 page". These are all examples of tools supporting the (textual) *dialogue* between the user and the program.

Few toolkits pay attention to the graphical aspects of user interface programming. Entering lines and circles, indicating regions of interest in a work area, and direct manipulation of graphical objects (and resulting semantic feedback) are examples of graphical interactions that are badly supported by existing toolkits. Generally speaking, toolkits do not interfere with anything happening inside an "application window". All interaction inside such a window has to be programmed using the low level window system libraries for input and output. The programmer has to provide many confusing details or write a program using hazardous nested loops [Liebeskind and O'Neal, 1990]. See the NeXT book [Webster, 1989] for an illustrative example (page 330).

Graphics support in toolkits tends to be minimal and graphics tends to be slow [Liebeskind and O'Neal, 1990] when toolkits are applied. Another problem is introduced in many toolkits when text with multiple founts or sizes are to be used in one single area.

In general existing toolkits or interaction models tend to lack extendibility and support for both interaction based on direct manipulation, and for interaction concerning more graphically oriented aspects, such as specifying coordinates in a drawing area. Too often low level programming is needed to compensate the shortcomings of these existing toolkits.

3. Physical Event Layer

The lowest level of abstraction in our layered object-oriented model is layer 1. Input from the window system, handled here, is referred to as physical events. The objects at this level are of the type WINDOW. Both input and output have to go through a WINDOW. The WINDOW objects are the *only* link to the underlying window system. An advantage of this approach is that the model is highly independent of a window system. Because of this reduction in dependency, applications that have been developed on a layered interaction model are very portable. Our current implementation is based on X [Scheifler and Gettys, 1987] as the underlying window system.

4. Abstract Event Layer

At the second layer of abstraction, physical events from the first level are represented by their abstract counterparts (see Table 1 for a list of abstract events). There are two reasons for creating this second level. First, it is possible to *compose* events from layer 1 into abstract events at layer 2. Depressing and releasing a mouse button, two distinct physical events, can be composed to form an abstract event, that may perhaps not be supported by the current window system at all (e.g. a click or a double click from the mouse). The second reason for the existence of layer 2 is that each abstract event is represented by a Procol language object acting as a resource manager for this particular type of abstract event. The object has a dynamic list of currently active clients and notifies the appropriate clients when an event arrives. This dynamic and flexible nature is one of the most important features of the layered model.

type	*corresponding physical event*
down	a mouse button press
up	a mouse button release
click	a mouse button click
motion	a motion of the mouse
enter	entering an area
leave	leaving an area
key	pressing a keyboard key
resize	resizing a window

Table 1: Abstract Events

5. Interaction Tool Layer

The third level of abstraction, layer 3, is composed of the set of basic interaction tools (ITs) from which a graphic user interface is built. Examples are MENUS, SLIDERS, BUTTONS, etc. An IT has a client-server relation with a number of these abstract event objects. The IT may register itself with one or more of the second layer objects. An IT is free to register and unregister at will during its existence. This provides for an easy way to create a dormant IT: an IT visible on the screen, but temporarily not reacting to events from outside.

In our model, events can be delivered at a much higher abstraction level, so less detail needs to be provided by a programmer and more efficient programming can be the result. This strategy is in sharp contrast with the strategy used for instance in NeXT [Webster, 1989] and OpenLook, where input is typically handled at the physical event level.

5.1. Interaction Tools

An interaction tool consists of three independent parts (see Figure 2), an interaction method part IT_M, a presentation (graphics) part IT_P, and an interaction style part IT_S, or more formally:

$$IT = (IT_M, IT_P, IT_S)$$

The method part IT_M is independent of the user interface constructed. The method part has at least the components *init, enable, disable, handler(1..n).* The *init* component takes care of initialization of the IT after creation, *enable* prepares the IT for handling input tokens, *disable* disallows the handling of input, and one or more *handlers* process the actual input. The method part may contain other components, such as *SetBox* and *SetPos* to adjust the size and position, respectively.

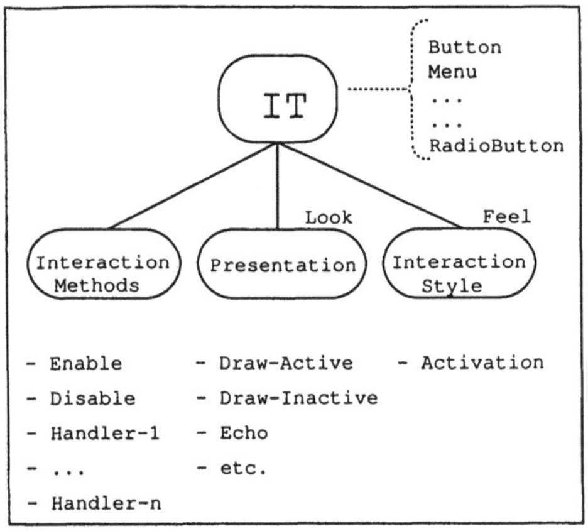

Figure 2: The three Parts that form an Interaction Tool (IT)

The presentation (graphics) part IT_P may and usually does differ from one target user interface to the next one. It is in general defined as:

$$IT_P = (dormant,\ \ active\text{--}on,\ \ active\text{--}off,\ \ echo)$$

Together *active-on* and *active-off* are called the *active* presentation. The difference between the two is most relevant for switchable ITs (with return tokens *on..off*). Normally, following *init* or *disable*, the IT is graphically presented in the *dormant* (ghostified) form; *enable* presents the *active* form; *handler* starts with presenting the *echo*, and ends with the *active* form of presentation; but depending on the IT differences may occur.

The interaction style part IT_S is an adjustable part of the IT. It is dependent on the physical interaction devices used for the IT. It can be used to vary interaction style from one IT to the next, but it seems more advisable to enforce a uniform style for (each part of) the target user interface constructed, by having the IT call on a global interaction style *object*. This object can be passed as an attribute of the IT. The style object is in fact an event manager. In some cases it may therefore influence the functionality of the IT. For example, if STROKE is registered with the CLICK event manager (interaction style), it may act as an input method for connected line segments, but if it registers with the MOTION event manager, it may act as a sampler or tracker.

By convention, ITs are those tools that can be manipulated by the end-user. It is however quite useful to allow the application to influence the interface indirectly, either by displaying information, or sometimes even by modifying its state. This is called semantic feedback. Examples are a slider used as a thermometer, or a scrollbar as indicator of "percentage of work done".

The layered interaction model provides a set of *basic* interaction tools. The basic set consists of the necessary and sufficient ITs to construct any composite IT in a user interface. In addition some composite ITs have been provided because they are either frequently used in practice, or because they facilitate the task of constructing a user interface.

The contents of this basic toolkit is given in Table 2. After the right arrow the type of value produced by the IT is given, as well as an indication whether the IT possesses a local state (*yes*) or not (*no*). For example, RADIOBUTTON produces an integer (the item selected) and whether this item is toggled on or off. A RADIOBUTTON has a local state (memory), which it remembers.

Interaction Tool	*Type of Value*	*Local State*
Button	⇒ *()*	*no*
Menu	⇒ *int*	*yes*
Locator		
- InPoint	⇒ *point*	*yes*
- InLine	⇒ *point(2)*	*yes*
- InTriangle	⇒ *point(3)*	*yes*
- InBox	⇒ *point(2)*	*yes*
- InCircle	⇒ *point,real*	*yes*
- InPolygon	⇒ *point(n)*	*yes*
- Stroke	⇒ *point(n+1)*	*yes*
Switch	⇒ *(on..off)*	*yes*
Radiobutton 1-of-n	⇒ *int,(on..off)*	*yes*
Key	⇒ *char*	*yes*
String	⇒ *string*	*yes*
Valuator (Slider):		
- 1D discrete	⇒ *int*	*yes*
- 1D continuous	⇒ *real*	*yes*
- Interval discrete	⇒ *int(2)*	*yes*
- Interval continuous	⇒ *real(2)*	*yes*

Table 2: Basic Toolkit

IT BUTTON is in fact a one element MENU. The state of MENU is the most recent element selected. This is displayed in the *active-on* form, the other elements are displayed in the *active-off* form. IT SWITCH is similarly a special case of RADIOBUTTON.

Note that variants of the same IT may exist, e.g. INBOX may produce the coordinates of half the diagonal, or the whole diagonal of the box echoed. Or a rubber circle may be echoed for INCIRCLE by giving the center and the radius, or by giving two points on the circumference of the circle. Although the function of these ITs are the same, the user of the ITs experiences them as different interaction methods. At the same time different ITs, such as INLINE and INBOX may produce the same result. In fact nothing prevents the application to use INBOX to produce the coordinates for a line segment or for a circle.

The interaction tools in the tool kit consist of prototypes of all the ITs in the table above. These prototypes have defaults for the interaction style, the presentations, as well as standard method components. Prototypes may be used as such, or instances of the prototype may be constructed graphically. If a prototype is changed, the change propagates through the target UI wherever the prototype is employed. Instances may be affected as well, unless they have overridden all of the components of the prototype. The standard handlers can easily be used for 'dry-runs', while linking to stubs provides an efficient vehicle for simulation.

Most ITs will be situated in an interaction window. The application is supposed to render its own output in one or more application windows. The designer defines the screen real estate for the application, but the interface is not involved in the possibly complex (graphics) output of the application. However, the layered model does provide for ITs in the application window: the generalized Locator tools appear to be of particular use. The GKS input class PICK is not provided by the model, because this would run counter to the idea of separating interface and application, since PICK is heavily dependent on the knowledge of application structure. The IT INPOINT would be an appropriate front end to an application supported PICK.

6. Interaction Panel Layer

The fourth layer in our model is formed by the highest level of interaction objects: Panels. Panels play an important role as composite ITs; they are also used to order interactions in sequences, alternatives and repetitions, the so-called interaction patterns [van den Bos, 1988]. This ordering is specified in Panel protocols.

Panels only receive events (messages) from objects in layer 3 (ITs) or in layer 4 itself (abstract Panels). Panels can be composed to form a hierarchy of interaction Panels constituting the target user interface. Panels can also be added to the interaction toolkit for reuse.

The application produced by the designer using the layered interaction model is a hierarchy of a Panels, (Sub-)Panels, and ITs. The hierarchy can be represented as a tree, with a Panel as root. Panels may contain (Sub-)Panels. The leaves of the tree are basic ITs, that is, the ITs in the IT set presented in Section 5.1. The root Panel is mapped on the entire window or viewport of a workstation. Panels are mapped as rectangles parallel to the x and y-axis of the workstation. As indicated before, each Panel has been implemented as an object in Procol. Each Panel contains the actions listed in Table 3.

In general, a Panel contains a set of ITs. The first thing a Panel does when it is created, is to create this set of ITs. This is done in the Init Section of the Panel. The Init section is a special section in a Procol object that is executed (once) when the object is created.

To understand the design of the layered interaction model and the protocols, the next section gives a brief expose on Procol; this is followed by two example applications using the layered interaction model.

action name	*measures undertaken*
Init	new IT_1; ... ; new IT_n
Enable	send Enable to $IT_{(1 .n)}$
	Draw(Active)
Disable	send Disable to $IT_{(1\ n)}$
	Draw(InActive)
IT_1	*perform action for* IT_1
	send message to parent panel
IT	..
IT	
IT_n	*perform action for* IT_n
	send message to parent

Table 3: Panel Actions. IT_i and $IT_{(1\ n)}$ are arbitrary names referring to ITs constituting the panel.

7. Procol

This section gives a short summary of Procol; further details can be found in [van den Bos and Laffra, 1989; van den Bos, 1989]. Procol is a parallel object-oriented language supporting a distributed, incremental and dynamic object environment. It also supports parallel delegation.

A Procol object definition consists of the sections listed in Table 4.

OBJ	*Name Attributes*
Description	natural language description
Protocol	(sender-message-action)-expression
Declare	local data, procs, type definitions
Init	section executed once at creation
Cleanup	section executed once at deletion
Actions	definition of public methods
IntActions	definition of interrupt methods
EndOBJ	*Name*

Table 4: The Sections constituting a Procol Object Definition.

An object offers a number of services to other objects. In Procol the services are specified as *Actions*. The name of an action is known externally. The body of an action may include, besides standard C-code, send and request primitives with the following syntax, respectively:

sendTargetObject.ActionName(msg)

requestTargetObject.ActionName(msg) → *(result)*

ActionName is the name of the action in *TargetObject* to which a message *msg* is sent for processing. The message *msg* is comparable to a set of parameters. The values returned by the request are deposited in the variables indicated in the list *result*. The advantage of send over request is that the objects are only bound during actual message transfer and not during the processing of the message.

The body of an Action may further contain the Procol primitives new, which creates a new instance of an object and executes its Init section, and del which deletes an existing instance of an object after executing its Cleanup section. Deletion is only allowed by the creator of the object, the identity of which is acquired by the Procol primitive *Creator*. The bodies of the Init and Cleanup sections have the same form as the bodies of the Actions.

Procol constrains possible communications by controlling access to the object's actions, specified by a *Protocol* in each object. Protocols also define a sequential order on input (messages from other objects to this object), thus acting as a major aid towards structuring input patterns. The protocol has the form of an expression over *interaction* terms, the counterparts of send statements and request statements. During the life of an object this expression is matched against actual communications. The protocol is repeated. The form of an interaction term is:

SourceObject(ms) → *ActionName*

The semantics is that upon receipt of message *msg* from *SourceObject*, *ActionName* will be executed. *SourceObject* can be specified as: object instance, object type (class), and *ANY* object. In the receiving object, the Procol primitive *Sender* contains the identification of the communication partner. Expressions over interaction terms are constructed with the four operators listed in Table 5.

E	+	F	*selection:*	E or F is selected
E	;	F	*sequence:*	E is followed by F
E	*		*repetition:*	Zero of more times E
ϕ	:	E	*guard:*	E only if ϕ is true

Table 5: The four Operators for constructing Expressions over Interaction Terms. In this table E and F themselves stand for interaction terms or for expressions.

We will illustrate the expression operators with a few simple examples. Let us assume that we specify the protocol in a server object S with Actions actionA and actionB triggered by messages msg1 and msg2. There also exist clients A and B. Then the following protocol in S

ANY(msg1) → actionA + ANY(msg2) → actionB

is equivalent to no protocol as far as access control is concerned, because it specifies that any client may send msg1 to trigger actionA, or msg2 to trigger actionB. The protocol does however play a role as interface specification for the outside world.

The following protocol in S

A(msg1) → actionA + B(msg2) → actionB

specifies that only clients A and B have access to object S; A can send a message that triggers actionA and B can send a message that triggers actionB. This with the exclusion of any other access patterns.

The following protocol in S

A(msg1) → actionA ; A(msg2) → actionB

specifies that only client A is allowed access to object S; furthermore A first has to send a message S.actionA(msg1) to trigger actionA, before it can send a message S.actionB(msg2) to trigger actionB. Since the protocol repeats this doublet of messages repeats as well.

Although the protocol as a whole repeats, it is sometimes necessary to repeat a subexpression in it as well. The following protocol accomplishes that:

A(msg1) → actionA * ; B(msg2) → actionB

It specifies that client A may tiger actionA zero or more times, and that such a repetition always must be concluded by B triggering actionB once. Hence the interaction with object B serves as a terminator in this example.

8. Example 1: Hello World

The first example we present is the well-known "Hello World" example. The example implements a program that is able to print the string *Hello World* on the computer display. We use the layered interaction model for this purpose. Figure 3 shows how the program looks on the screen. The example program contains two buttons. One button is labeled with Hello World. When we click the mouse button on this screen button, the string in question is displayed. When we click on the Bye button, the program stops execution.

Figure 4 contains the definition of the Procol object HELLO. In our model, the HELLO object is a Panel. The object is divided into four sections. From top to bottom they are:

line 3-5, the Declare section

The Declare section contains the declarations of all variables local to the object. In this case the HELLO object contains three object variables: object variable window (which is of type WINDOW), and two LABEL_BUTTON objects, named hello_button and bye_button.

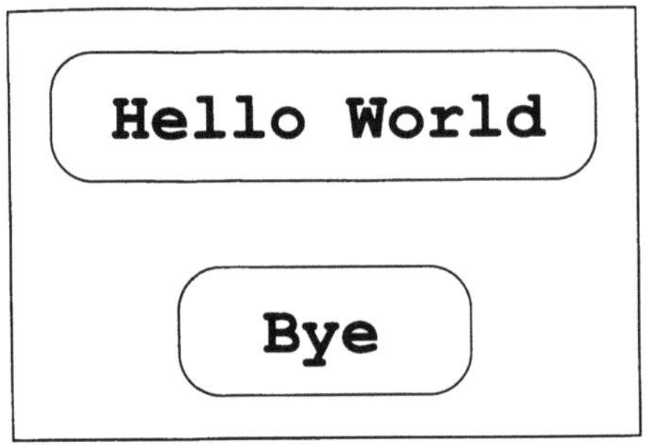

Figure 3: Example 1: Hello World

```
1.  Obj       HELLO
2.
3.  Declare   object WINDOW window;
4.            object LABEL_BUTTON hello_button;
5.            object LABEL_BUTTON bye_button;
6.
7.  Protocol  hello_button -> Handler1 +
8.            bye_button   -> Handler2
9.
10. Init new   window(100,100,300,200,300,200);
11.      send window.FillBox(10, 0, 0, 300, 200);
12.      new  hello_button(window,40,20,220,60,
13.                                "Hello World");
14.      new  bye_button(window,100,130,100,40,
15.                                        "Bye");
16.      send hello_button.Enable();
17.      send bye_button.Enable();
18.
19. Actions   Handler1 = { printf("Hello World0); }
20.           Handler2 = { exit(0); }
21.
22. Endobj    HELLO;
```

Figure 4: Definition of the Hello World Object

line 7-8, the Protocol section

The Protocol specifies the senders that are allowed to call the actions of the HELLO object. In this case the legal senders are hello_button and bye_button. After the → the name of the action is listed that can be called by the sender in question.

The way to read the Protocol is as follows:

- When object hello_button sends a message, action Handler1 is executed.
- When object bye_button sends a message, action Handler2 is executed.

line 10-17, the Init section

The Init section is called when a HELLO object is being created. In this section a window is allocated (line 10). The window is passed a number of attributes. The attributes 100,100 specify that the window is to be displayed at position [100,100] on the display. The attributes 300,200 specify that this window should cover an area on the display of 300 by 200 pixels. Furthermore, the second occurrence of the attributes 300,200 indicate to the window that it will have to accept coordinates in the range 0-299 and 0-199. If we had made the latter attribute pair larger than the first, we could *pan* over the corresponding window.

At line 11, the window is filled with a box of a gray scale of 10 percent (0 percent is white, 100 percent is black). The other four parameters indicate a rectangle with top-left coordinate 0,0, a width of 300, and a height of 200.

At line 12, the "Hello World" button is created with parameter window indicating the window in which the button should be drawn. The parameters 40,20,220,60 determine the position and size of the button, and the string "Hello World" (see line 13) will be the text on the face of the button. At line 14, the "Bye" button is created.

line 19-20, the Actions section

The Actions section contains the implementation of the actions that an object provides. The two actions that are provided by the HELLO object are Hello (used to print the appropriate string) and Bye (used to stop the program).

The HELLO object uses a window object and two LABEL_BUTTON objects. We will now show how the BUTTON is implemented. The LABEL_BUTTON object type is implemented using the BUTTON object.

```
 1. Obj         BUTTON(BOX box, ANY drawer)
 2. Protocol    creator -> Enable    ;
 3.             CLICK   -> Handler *;
 4.             creator -> Disable
 6. Actions
 7.   Enable    = { drawer.Active(box);
 8.                 CLICK.AddClient(box); }
 9.   Disable   = { drawer.InActive(box);
10.                 CLICK.RemoveClient(box); }
11.   Handler   = { drawer.Echo();
12.                 creator.();
13.                 drawer.Active(); }
14. EndObj      BUTTON;
```

Figure 5: Button Object Definition

The protocol (see lines 2 to 4 in Figure 5) indicates that button is able to perform the following actions: first Enable, then zero or more times Handler, followed by Disable, In action Enable at line 7, the button draws itself by sending a message to its drawer object. The drawer object is supplied by the creator of the button, and functions to parameterize the look of the button. The button registers itself at the CLICK device at line 8. The message AddClient is sent to the CLICK object with box as a parameter. With this statement the button announces its candidacy for selections inside box. Whenever such a selection takes place the Handler action is performed. The button then echoes by sending a message to its drawer (line 11) and tells its creator that it has been selected (line 12). The creator of the button will then receive a message via action Handler(i). The button merely sends an empty message; the Procol run-time system will bind the call to the correct routine, based on sender identification in the receiving object. Coming back to Figure 5, the button also removes the echo at line 13, again by sending a message to its drawer object.

9. Example 2: Draw

We will now give the second example of a Procol program that has been developed using our layered interaction model. Figure 6 shows the example program: draw. Draw is a simple drawing editor that allows the user to draw rectangles and lines on an imaginary sheet of paper. The sheet of paper is represented by a window that can be scrolled with two scrollbars. At the bottom we find a panel containing 4 buttons. Two buttons function to set the current drawing mode, that is, line-mode or box-mode. The other two buttons print the current drawing on disk, or quit the application.

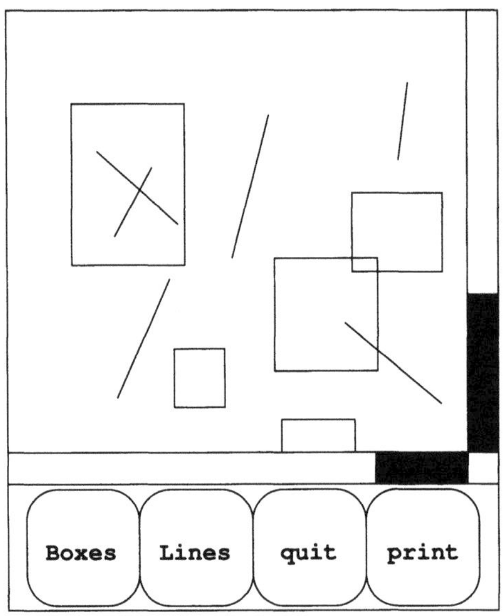

Figure 6: Example 2: the Draw Application

The first object we will examine, is the draw object (see Figure 7). The draw object creates a window, and in this window a canvas (which is a scrollable window), and a Panel. The draw object reacts to messages from the panel, thereby creating an IT to cover the canvas. This IT is either an in_box or an in_line object. Both are generalized locator devices. These devices send a message to the draw object when the user has produced a box or a line. With the coordinates in this message, the draw object interprets this input, and creates a box or a line object accordingly.

```
Obj      DRAW
Declare  object WINDOW window;
         object DRAW_PANEL panel;
         object SCROLL_WINDOW canvas;
         object ANY element;
         object LIST list;
         object PSFILE file;
         object IN_BOX in_box;
         object IN_LINE in_line;
         object ANY current_IT;
         int    x1, y1, x2, y2;

Protocol in_box(x1,y1,x2,y2) -> AddBox  +
         in_line(x1,y1,x2,y2)-> AddLine +
         panel -> BoxMode  +
         panel -> LineMode +
         panel -> Print    +
         panel -> Quit

Init
   new window(100,100,500,600,500,600);
   new panel(window,10,510,580,80);
   new canvas(window,0,0,500,500,612,792);
   new list;
   send canvas.Enable();
   send panel.Enable();
   new in_box(canvas, 0, 0, 612, 792);
   current_IT = in_box;
Actions
    AddLine = {
        new line(x1, y1, x2, y2);
        send list.AddElement(line);
    }
    AddBox = {
        new box(min(x1,x2), min(y1,y2),
                abs(x2-x1), abs(y2-y1));
        send list.AddElement(box);
    }
    LineMode = {
        del current_IT;
        new in_line(canvas,0,0,612,792);
        current_IT = in_line;
    }
    BoxMode = {
        del current_IT;
        new in_box(canvas,0,0,612,792);
        current_IT = in_box;
    }
    Print = {
        new  file("draw.ps");
        send list.Print(file);
        del  file;
    }
    Quit = {
        del canvas, panel, window;
    }
Endobj DRAW;.
```

Figure 7: Definition of the Draw Object

Also, the panel object will report to the draw object (its creator) when the user has activated the Print option or the Quit option.

Note that the draw object has not the faintest notion of how the panel object has been implemented. It could contain a set of buttons, a radiobutton, a menu, etc. Right now, we are not interested in how the panel achieves its task, as long as it informs us when the user has made a choice.

Now we will describe the individual statements in the draw object. Line 1 and line 57 contain the header and the trailer of the object definition. The declare section (line 2 to 11) contains the declaration of the private variables of the draw object.

The Protocol (lines 13 to 18) specifies the clients that are allowed to call the actions of the draw object. In this case these are in_box, in_line, and panel. After the → the name of the action is listed that can be called by the sender in question. The actions AddLine, and AddBox are called with the message (x1, y1, x2, y2). That is, the four integers that are being sent by in_box, and in_line are copied into (x1, y1, x2, y2).

The Init section (line 20 to 28) is called when the object draw is created. In this section a window is allocated (line 21), and a panel and a scrollable window are created inside this window (line 22 and 23). A list object is created at line 24 to contain the boxes and lines that make up the drawing. Then the canvas and the panel object are activated by sending them the *Enable* message (line 25 and 26). Finally at line 27 and 28, an IT is created to initialize the drawing process. Now, when the program starts, the user can add boxes to the drawing.

The Actions section (line 29 to 56) contains the implementation of the actions mentioned in the Protocol section at line 13 to 18. In order of appearance they are:

- AddLine receives four integers from the in_line object (see line 14). These four integers are interpreted as the two end-coordinates of a line: a line object is created at line 31. Then, at line 32, the newly created line object is added to the existing list of objects by sending the object identity to the list object.
- AddBox is similar to AddLine, yet here the four integers are interpreted as two vertices defining a rectangle (box).
- LineMode is an action that is called by the panel object (see line 16). What is done is the following: the interaction tool that is currently covering the canvas is deleted (line 40). Then a new in_line locator object is created. The attributes that are passed are exactly the dimensions of the canvas object. Now the user can only add lines to the drawing.
- BoxMode is identical to LineMode with the difference that calling this action results in being able to add boxes to the drawing, until the user switches mode again.
- Print is called when the drawing should be printed to a file. Therefore we create a file object with in this case a constant name *draw.ps*. Then we send the Print command to the list object, with the file object as the argument of the message. The list object will accordingly send the Print command to each item in the list (a box or a line). Each box and line has the knowledge to print itself to a file (in a Postscript

format). So, the Print action results in a file that is directly printable on a Postscript printer.

- Quit will delete all objects owned by the draw object. The Procol run-time system will now detect that there are no more *active* objects, and no more messages will be sent in the future. Therefore, the run-time system will stop the program.

10. Interaction Styles

For the sake of simplicity, in our examples the ITs react to a fixed set of abstract events (see line 3, 8 and 10 in Figure 5). Actually, interaction styles can be parameterized (see Section 5.1). For instance, two or more types of a button could be defined that need to be operated in quite different ways. We think that tools or environments for building user interfaces should provide methods to maintain global consistency in interaction style. It is not acceptable that one slider is operated using the left mouse button and another slider using the right mouse button. To prevent this from happening we would like to force a global *interaction style* to which all interaction objects in a user interface adhere. This global interaction style is not fixed, but should be adaptable from one target user interface to another. Interaction style objects provide for this purpose. Instead of registering with a fixed type of abstract event, an IT should first consult the interaction style object for the appropriate abstract events. For example, the BUTTON given in Figure 5 registers with the CLICK abstract event manager. In the situation where global interaction styles are to be used, the button would be passed the identity of the style object (line 1 in Figure 8). Next, the BUTTON would ask the style object for the applicable *Selector* abstract event type (line 7 in Figure 8). This type could be CLICK, DOWN, DOUBLE CLICK, or any other abstract event. After retrieving the abstract event for making selections corresponding with the current interaction style, the IT registers with this abstract event as before (compare line 8 in Figure 5 with line 10 in Figure 8). The object definition of the button object with variable interaction style is given in Figure 8. As compared with Figure 5, lines 6 and 7 are added to this object definition, Changes have been made to lines 1, 4, 10, and 12.

An interaction style could be chosen once for all or part of an interactive application and all interaction tools involved will use this style object.

The advantages are that a user interface will be consistent in interaction style, and interaction tools are parameterized with a style object, and are therefore generic for more than one interaction style. If interaction styles also contain output elements, the "look" of an application can also be made dependent on the interaction style that is adapted. In this way the "look and feel" of a user interface is made independent of the implementation strategy.

11. Conclusion

We presented a layered model for human-computer interaction. Because of the growing abstraction from physical events, increasing with each layer added to the model, we achieve a highly extendable and high-level user-interface toolkit. Interaction tools are described as a composition of high-level abstract events. Interaction tools can be combined into abstract interaction panels, and stored away for later use. The model is both usable by system programmers and by interactive user-interface development tools. The use of protocols allows us to specify input patterns and sequencing. Because all access to the underlying window system has to go through a window object, we created a highly portable framework for designing and developing interactive systems.

The model presented here makes a clear separation between three components that constitute an IT: the interaction methods, the presentation, and the interaction style. The model provides extendibility, adaptivity of interaction styles, and support for graphical interaction such as required in for instance CAD systems. This support is lacking in most existing toolkits or interaction models. To overcome these shortcoming, these toolkits require too low a level of programming, as opposed to the model presented.

References

Aitken, G. (1990) "OI: A Model Extensible C++ Toolkit for the X Window System," In: *Proceedings of the X Technical Conference*, Boston. January

Bos, J. van den (1988) "ABSTRACT INTERACTION TOOLS: A Language for User Interface Management Systems," *ACM-TOPLAS (Transactions on Programming Languages and Systems)*, vol. 10, no. 2 (April), 215-247.

Bos, J. van den (1989) "Procol — A Protocol-Constrained Concurrent Object-Oriented Language," *Information Processing Letters*, vol. 32, no. September, 221-227.

Bos, J. van den and Laffra, C. (1989) "Procol — A Parallel Object Language with Protocols," In: *ACM—OOPSLA '89 Conference Proceeding*, New Orleans, pp. 95-102

Bos, J. van den, Plasmeijer, M.J., and Stroet, J.W.M (1981) "Process communication based on input specifications," *ACM-TOPLAS (Transactions on Programming Languages and Systems)*, vol. 3, no. 3, 224-250.

Digital, Inc (1988) *XUI Style Guide, Digital XUI Manual Set.*

Goldberg, A. (1983) *Smalltalk-80, The Interactive Programming Environment*, Addison-Wesley, Reading.

Liebeskind, S. and O'Neal, M. (1990) "Pitfalls in Widget Writing and In Using Widgets in Applications," In: *Proceedings of the X Technical Conference*, Boston. January

Linton, M , Vlissides, J M., and Calder, P.R. (1989) "Composing User Interface with InterViews," *Computer*, vol. 22, no 2 (February), 8-22.

McCormack, J , Asente, P , and Swick, R.R. (1988) *X Toolkit Intrinsics — C Language X Interface, X Window System, X Version 11, Release 2.*

Myers, B. (1990) "An Object-Oriented, Constraint-Based, User Interface Development Environment for X in CommonLisp," In. *Proceedings of the X Technical Conference*, Boston. January

Myers, B.A. and Buxton, W.A (1986) "Creating highly interactive graphical user interfaces by demonstration," *Computer graphics*, vol 20, no. 4, 249-258

Open Software Foundation, Inc (1989) *OSF/Motif Programmer's Reference Manual.*

Scheifler, R.W. and Gettys, J. (1987) "The X window system," *ACM Transactions on Graphics*, vol 5, no. 2 (April), 79-109.

Shan, Yen-Ping (1989) "An Event-Driven Model-View-Controller Framework for Smalltalk," In: *ACM—OOPSLA '89 Conference Proceedings*, New Orleans, pp. 347-352.

Sun Microsystems (1989) *OPEN LOOK Graphical User Interface Functional Description, Sun Microsystems.*

Swick, R.R. and Weissman, T. (1988) *X Toolkit Widgets — C Language X Interface, X Window System, X Version 11, Release 2*

Webster, B.F. (1989) *The NeXT Book*, Addison-Wesley Publishing Company, Inc.

Weinand, A., Gamma, E., and Marty, R (1988) "ET++ — An Object Oriented Application Framework in C++," In: *ACM—OOPSLA '88 Conference Proceedings*, pp 46-57. San Diego

5

A 2-D Graphics System for Multi-User Interactive Graphics Based on Objects and Constraints

Ralph D. Hill

The MEL project is developing an object-based tool for the rapid development of graphical direct manipulation user interfaces. We emphasize interfaces to be used by multiple people from multiple workstations simultaneously. The specific requirements that multi-user interfaces place on the graphics system are discussed, as are the solutions that we have developed. In particular, the MEL graphics system is based on a hierarchical display structure of graphical objects and makes extensive use of constraints to maintain graphical consistency and link together various parts of a complete multi-user graphical program.

1. Introduction

The Human-Computer Systems Research District of Bellcore is developing tools and techniques for rapidly developing software systems that can be used by multiple users from multiple workstations, simultaneously. These multi-user systems can range from games for entertainment and education, to systems for collaboration in the work place (e.g., co-operative report writing, meetings), to adversarial negotiation (e.g., contract negotiation, stock and commodities trading). These applications are all characterized by the need to have some shared or common information seen by all users and some that is private to individual users. Depending on the skills and backgrounds of the users, there may also be a need to display the shared information in different ways to different users.

Within this domain, we have chosen to concentrate on graphical, direct manipulation interfaces. We want the users to be able to manipulate applications with simple gestures like clicking and dragging, and with a minimum of menu selection. We would also like to have a rich graphical environment, both in terms of the number of shapes available and the number of parameters of the shapes that may be manipulated. For performance and cost reasons, however, we are concentrating on 2-D monochrome graphics.

We are developing a tool called MEL[1], which is in the same general class of tools as User Interface Management Systems (UIMS), to support the development of these interfaces. Unlike many UIMSs, MEL is not designed to allow non-programming user interface designers to build interfaces. We felt that this would severely restrict the range of interfaces that could be built with MEL. Instead, MEL is a special purpose programming language and environment (specifically, an extended LISP), that is optimized for the development of multi-user graphical interfaces. Later, when we know more about what makes a good multi-user interface, we hope to build tools for non-programmers on top of MEL.

MEL is a very powerful and flexible tool, so to help programmers use it effectively, we are developing generic run-time architectures and definitions of standard classes that will be needed in multi-user applications. Without this guidance and assistance, programmers using MEL would have to re-invent a usable architecture and set of classes for each new interface. We believe that the architecture and basic set of classes is sufficiently generic that they can be designed once and then used in a wide range of interfaces.

This chapter concentrates on the graphics aspects of MEL. It is an object-oriented graphics system that uses constraints to control graphical properties and maintain both graphical and structural consistency. MEL has been heavily influenced by the Sassafras [Hill, 1986] and Tube [Hill and Herrmann, 1989] UIMSs, as well as other object-oriented UIMSs and graphics systems, most notably Grow [Barth, 1986], Coral [Szekely and Myers, 1988], Lapidary [Myers et al., 1989], and Pogo [Tarlton and Tarlton, 1989].

This chapter is organized as follows: In Section 2 the requirements placed on the graphics system by the needs of MEL are presented and illustrated with examples. In Section 3, the tools and technologies used to meet these requirements are discussed. Section 4 briefly describes the current implementation and gives the implementation of the graphics for an interface built with MEL. Section 5 presents some important lessons we have learned about the combination of object-oriented graphics and constraints that we have used in MEL. Finally, Section 6 summaries the chapter and outlines our future plans.

2. Requirements of the Graphics System

We began from the assumption that the graphics system must be based on an object-oriented approach, with two key structures:

- a class hierarchy — a static hierarchy of classes of graphical objects that relies on inheritance to simplify the specification of classes, and

---

1 MEL is an acronyms of acronyms for the three major components of MEL. M — Maintained Variable System, a simple one-way constraint system, E — Event-Response Language, a simple rule based language, and L — Local Event Broadcast Method, a light weight process mechanism with message passing. MVS was developed for MEL. ERL and LEBM are borrowed, with extensions, from Sassafras [Hill, 1986]

- a display structure — a form of part hierarchy, that is a dynamic run-time structure that collects and organizes graphical objects that define an image visible on a display.

Given these basic assumptions, we identified six key requirements for the graphics system which we list here. The remainder of this section expands on these requirements.

Structural Parallelism
: The structure of the implementation of the user interface (or interactive graphics) should be parallel to or consistent with the users' model of the interface.

Composition of Graphical Objects
: The graphics system should provide support for composite objects — complex graphical objects that are constructed by combining simpler objects.

Communication
: The display structure should be a data structure that is shared between the graphics system and the user interface.

Responsiveness
: The display structure should support fast picking, and fast redraw.

Hierarchy
: The display structure must be hierarchical, but more general than an *n*-ary tree.

Abstraction
: The detailed graphical layout of the display should be separable from the abstract structure of the display structure.

These concrete requirements are the result of the distillation of more abstract requirements. Several of these abstract requirements will be illustrated with examples in the following discussions.

2.1. Structural Parallelism

It is generally agreed that programming is difficult, and the implementation of graphical, direct manipulation interfaces is particularly difficult. We believe that one cause of difficulty is the need to translate problems and solutions between the user's view of an interface, and the implementation of the interface. We believe that the tasks of programming and maintaining graphical interfaces can be simplified by making the structure of the implementation closely parallel the structure of the user's view of the interface. Object-oriented programming (with careful selection of classes) is one step towards achieving this parallelism. But it is important to ensure that the run-time organization of the object is consistent with the users' view of the interface. Hence, some flexible means of structuring the objects at run-time is also needed. This structuring mechanism should provide an organization for the computational objects that is analogous to their real-world counterparts and/or their organization on the display.

2.2. Composition of Graphical Objects

The use of composite objects simplifies the creation of complex displays. For example, a bar graph class can be defined in terms of other objects such as rectangle and text. This requirement is not specific to multi-user interfaces, but is generic to interactive graphics, and is met, for example, by PHIGS [PHIGS, 1988]. Because of the dynamic nature of the interfaces we want to build, it is important that it be easy to alter a composite object at run-time (say, by adding an extra bar to a bar graph, or an item to a menu). This, together with the next requirement, implies that the graphics system must provide some mechanism to support composition at run-time.

2.3. Communication

Graphics systems such as GKS [Hopgood et al., 1986] and CORE [CORE, 1979] tend to treat the display list as a data structure to be built and then sent to the graphics system for processing. If the display is to be changed, the application or user interface can modify a retained copy of the display list, or generate a new display list. In either case, the new display list (or a copy of it) must be sent to the graphics system for processing. Unless the graphics system retains the old display list, and can infer the necessary display updates from the difference between the lists, it will have to completely rebuild the display.

If the display list is a shared data structure, and the graphics system monitors all operations that change it (rather than inferring changes by comparing old and new versions), the graphics system can, with relative ease:

- detect when a redisplay is needed, and
- redisplay only those parts of the display that have changed.

By using the shared display structure as a medium for communications between the user interface and the graphics system, this communication can be made very rich, reducing the amount and complexity of programming required by shifting a lot of the burden to the graphics system.

2.4. Responsiveness

We are building graphical direct manipulation interfaces with MEL. These interfaces require a lot of picking (selection of graphical objects), and frequent updates of the graphics for feedback. If the system is to feel responsive to the user, these must both be done quickly.

Picking will be used in two primary ways:

Discrete Picking

A user points to an object on the display, and signals that some command is to be applied to the object (usually by clicking a mouse button). This requires quickly determining which objects (if any) are being pointed to when the command signal is received.

Continuous Picking

In some interfaces, there is no explicit signal to indicate when picking must be done. Instead, the interface must be continuously checking to see which objects are being pointed to. This could be used to provide feedback when the pointer is over a selectable item (by highlighting the item or the pointer), or to show interactions between dragged and stationary objects (e.g., on the Macintosh desk-top interface, dragging a file icon over the printer icon causes the printer to highlight, as the file can be dropped on the printer, causing meaningful work to be done).

Both of these types of picking impose strict performance requirements: discrete picking must have low latency to ensure rapid feedback, and continuous picking must have low overhead so as not to interfere with dragging performance.

Rapid display update, the other key to responsiveness, can be achieved by only redrawing those parts of the display that have changed. To do this, there must be a way to search the display structure quickly for objects that overlap with the regions to be redrawn. This search for intersecting regions is similar to the point-inside-region search required for picking.

2.5. Hierarchy

There are two key motivations for the use of a hierarchical display structure:

- provide run-time support for composite (or complex) objects as sub-hierarchies, and
- facilitate the use of logarithmic searching algorithms for picking and redraw.

Similar motivations encouraged the use of hierarchies in earlier systems, such as Andrew [Palay et al., 1988; Borenstein, 1990] and Tube [Hill and Herrmann, 1989].

An *n*-ary tree meets our fundamental requirements, but is not sufficiently general. *N*-ary trees are good for supporting ordered lists at each level of the tree, but some interface constructs, such as tables and spreadsheets, are not easily represented as lists. Implementations of tabular structures, like these, that are based on lists tend to be biased against either column or row operations. What is needed is a representation that supports a two-dimensional array of cells.

2.6. Abstraction

The display structure provides a mechanism for collecting and organizing descriptions of the graphical objects. We call this the abstract structure. We would like to be able to impose different graphical layouts on given abstract structures. For example, organizing a list of options buttons either vertically or horizontally, or centred verses right justified. By keeping the graphical layout separate from the abstract structure, we can easily change the layout without touching the abstract structure or the objects in it.

3. Enabling Technologies and Techniques

The above requirements have been met in MEL by combining a variety of technologies and techniques. We list here, and explain below, the four most important:

- Heterogeneous tree structure for the display structure.
- Simple, fast constraint-maintenance system.
- Separation of graphical layout from abstract structure.
- Dynamic inheritance and synthesis.

These technologies are described in detail below.

3.1. Heterogeneous Tree Structure

It is clear that the display structure must be a hierarchy in order to support logarithmic searching algorithms for picking and redraw. The basic structure modification operations must also be standardized so that a set of core structural operations can be applied to any graphical object in the display structure. These requirements led us to choose a form of tree — all objects have a unique parent (except the root, which has no parent), and must have a method to return (a possibly empty) list of immediate children[2]. Except for these restrictions, the organization of the child nodes at each level in the tree is completely free. In particular, the child nodes need not be organized as a flat list, but can be stored as a matrix, or some other structure. Different organizations for child nodes can be used at different points in the tree.

This heterogeneous tree is implemented by having each graphical object have a pointer to its sub-structure, which is a structure object that collects and organizes the children. In addition to the obvious parent and sub-structure pointers which each graphical object must have, they also have pointers into their super-structure (the sub-structure of their parent) that provide information that permit structure specific operations. For example, graphical objects may require access to their neighbours. To do this, they need to know where they are in the structure of their super-structure (e.g., *n*-th element of the list of children).

Although there is a great deal of freedom with structure objects, we expect that most interfaces will need only two basic types: an ordered list (implemented as a doubly linked list, making it easy to ask for next and previous siblings) and an *n*-dimensional array.

We have chosen to implement the sub-structure of each object as a separate object. This allows us to make major changes to the structure of the display structure at run-time by

---

2 We also require that the order in which objects appear in this list remain unchanged, unless the objects are explicitly moved in the structure. This allows us to provide limited support for 2.5D graphics by using the order in which objects appear in these lists as a full ordering by depth, where the last object is closest to the viewer Incremental redisplay is implemented by first clearing the area to be updated, and then redrawing every object that intersects the region that must be redrawn. These objects are drawn in order, from back-most to front-most, and under a mask so that only that area to be update is affected by the drawing operations

simply replacing sub-structure objects. Figure 1 illustrates the basic structure of the heterogeneous tree, showing how instances of (sub-classes of) GraphicalClass are linked together by OrderedList and Matrix structure objects.

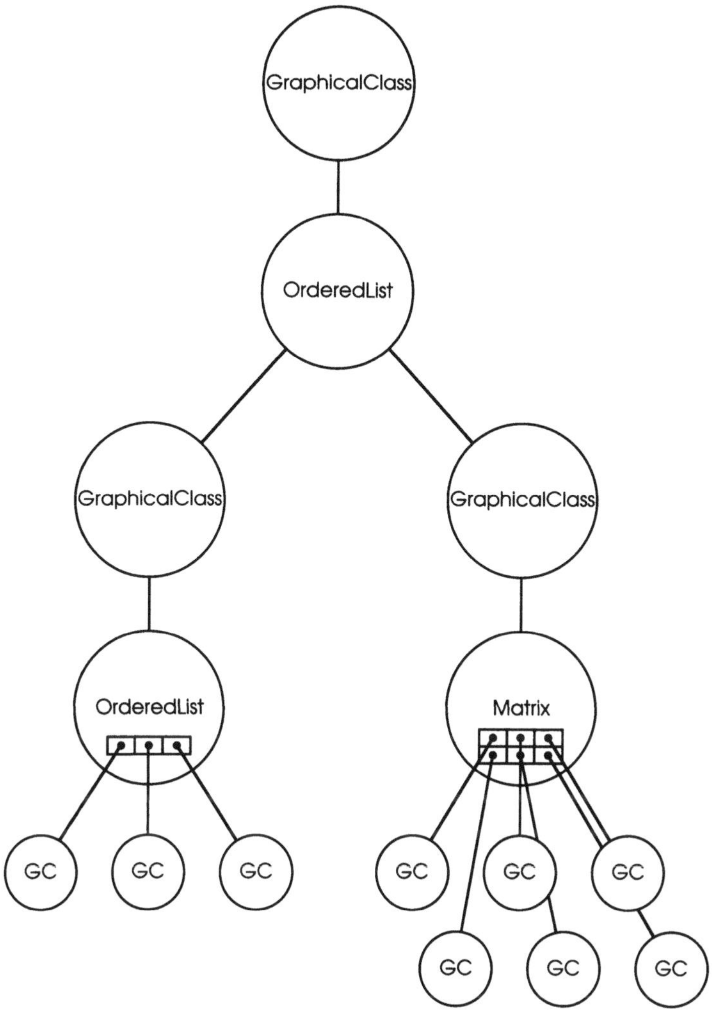

Figure 1: Basic structure of heterogeneous tree.

Requirements met: The use of the heterogeneous tree structure is important to almost all requirements. It is important to supporting: structural parallelism (by being a fairly general structure), composition (by providing different structuring mechanisms for the components of composite objects), and responsiveness (by being hierarchical). This approach is a hierarchy that is more general than a simple tree, and supports tabular displays.

3.2. Constraints

Within MEL, we have implemented a constraint maintenance system known as the Maintained Variable System (MVS)[3]. MVS is used extensively in MEL, and it is probably the single most important factor in determining the structure and capabilities of MEL. Constraints are used to control the relationships among the objects on the display, to connect the graphical objects to the application, and to maintain consistency of the display structure, the constraint graph, and the relationship between the display structure and the constraint graph.

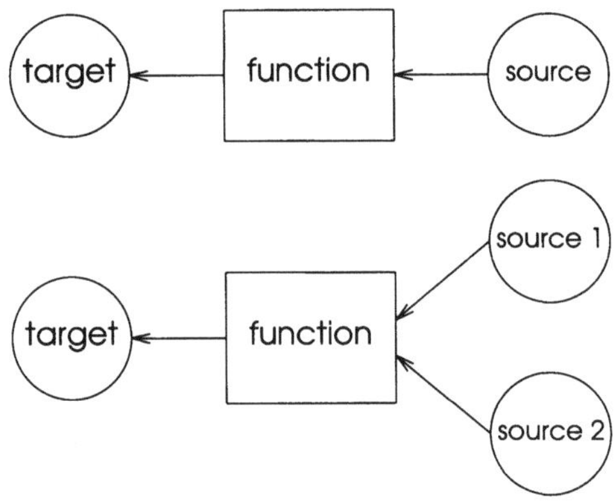

Figure 2: One-way constraints with one and two sources.

MVS is essentially a mechanism for maintaining one-way constraints among arbitrary values, and is similar in spirit to the constraint systems used in Coral [Szekely and Myers, 1988], Apogee [Hudson, 1989], Tube [Hill and Herrmann, 1989], and Grow [Barth, 1986]. In MVS, the programmer specifies the variable to be updated (the target), a set of variables whose values the target depends on (the sources), and a function to be called to compute the new value for the target whenever one of the sources changes (Figure 2)[4].

3 Here, we will provide only an outline of the capabilities of MVS, the full details of its capabilities and implementation are the subject of another paper, in preparation.

4 It is tempting to think that the sources could be determined by extracting variable references from the function. This is usually true. Unfortunately, using our current constraint maintenance algorithm which is based on local propagation, this will not always give the desired result Consider three variables, A, B and C, with the constraints B ← A - C and C ← A - B. Now, if A changes, the final values for B and C are determined by which of the two constraints is evaluated first. This non-determinism is undesirable in general. This problem can be solved by retaining the functions just defined and stating that B is re-computed when A or C changes, and that C is re-computed only when B changes. Now, there is no ambiguity about which order the constraints must be evaluated in. In the specific example this comes from this is exactly right — A is the absolute position of an object, and B and C are the absolute and relative positions of a child, respectively. The relative position of the child (C) is *computed* from the absolute position of the parent (A) and and the absolute position of the child (B), but does not change simply because the parent has moved (i.e., A changed). The absolute position of the child (B), changes whenever the parent's absolute position (A) changes, or the child's relative position (C) changes.

Like some earlier systems, MVS allows two one-way constraints to be installed between a pair of values, one in each direction (Figure 3).

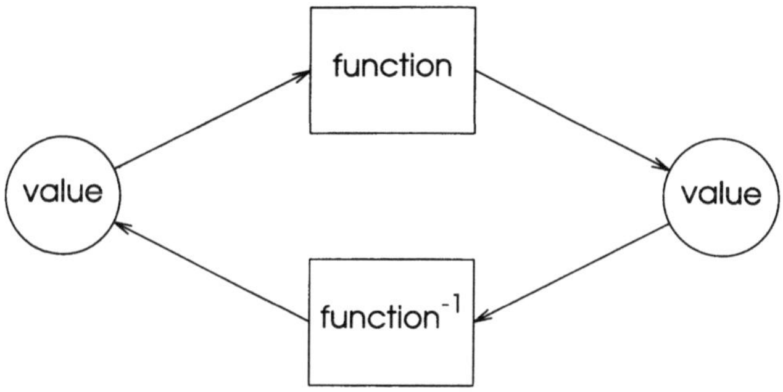

Figure 3: Two one-way constraints, one in each direction.

If MVS were to install these inverted dependencies automatically, it would have to be able to invert the functions used to compute the new values, which is beyond the scope of the current project.

Allowing the values of two variables to be bound in both directions provides a great deal of programming convenience, but is not equivalent to a two-way constraint system. A two-way constraint system must also allow multiple constraints to update a value (Figure 4).

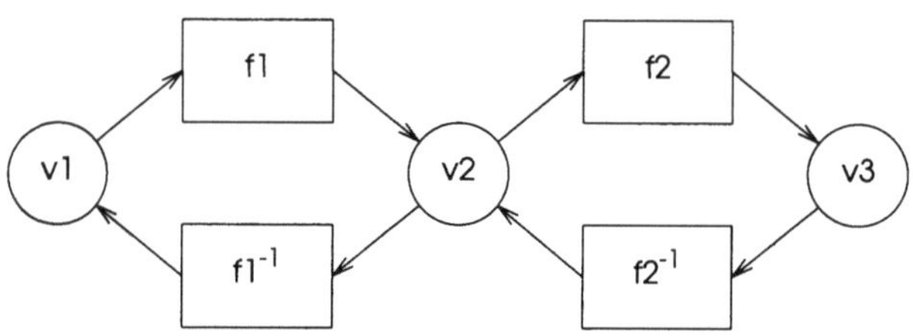

Figure 4: General two-way constraints.

MVS allows the creation of a constraint graph where multiple constraints update a single value (as seen in Figure 4), but makes no special effort to ensure that the constraints can be solved. It simply attempts to solve the constraints via a form of local propagation, and reports an error at run-time if it cannot. Because of the architecture and design philosophy imposed by MEL, typical MEL programmers have no need to write complex constraints, and are unlikely to create a constraint graph that cannot be solved by MVS.

An important additional feature of MVS is that it supports higher-order constraints. Higher-order constraints are constraints that modify constraints [Leler, 1988]. By creating constraints whose sources are structural elements in the display structure, and whose targets are constraints in the constraint graph, MVS is used to maintain consistency between the display structure and the constraint graph (see Dynamic Inheritance and Synthesis below, for one application of this). This use of higher-order constraints allows the programmer to modify the display structure without need to worry about updating the constraints, significantly reducing the programming effort needed to implement both MEL and interfaces in MEL.

One final feature of the constraint system is that a constraint need not have a target. In this case, when any of the sources change, the function is executed for side effect. In MEL, target-less constraints are used to trigger display updates, and recomputation of the layout of objects (see, Pluggable Layout, below). The result is a declarative feel to control of the redraw and layout operations: the MEL programmer *declares* when objects must be redrawn by creating a constraint with no target, the sources set to the slots of the object that are important to the display, and a standard function used in all such constraints.

Requirements met: Constraints, by themselves, do not aid in meeting any of our requirements. They are, however, important enablers of all the following technologies and techniques that do address our requirements.

3.3. Separation of Graphical Layout from Abstract Structure

As was done in Pogo [Tarlton and Tarlton, 1989], we use layout objects to maintain a separation of graphical layout from abstract structure (geometry and topology in Pogo terminology). This separation allows different graphical layouts (e.g., vertical list and horizontal list) to associated with a portion of the display structure (the abstract structure of the composite objects).

Separation is implemented by allowing each structure object to have a layout object associated with it. A layout object provides a method that updates the graphical attributes of the children of the structure object it is associated with, and some retained data used in the calculation of the graphical attributes. For example, the VerticalList layout object can be associated with ordered list structure objects. It modifies the position slots of the children such that they are arranged vertically, possibly with space between them. The retained data for the current VerticalList class is simply the amount of space to leave between objects. Future versions will retain mode flags that control justification of objects and other layout parameters. A typical configuration of graphical objects, with structure and layout objects is shown in Figure 5.

In general, the only restriction on the objects being laid out is that they be instances of sub-classes of GraphicalClass (the root class for all graphical objects), but this same restriction applies to all graphical objects in the display structure. It is reasonable, however, to develop special purpose layout functions that work only with certain classes.

Layout objects can be attached to and detached from structure objects at run-time. The constraint system is used to invoke the layout function whenever necessary. Thus, to change a set of buttons from a vertical layout to a horizontal layout, one simply changes the layout object associated with the structure object for the set of buttons. Hence, the graphical layout is separate from the abstract structure and can be easily changed.

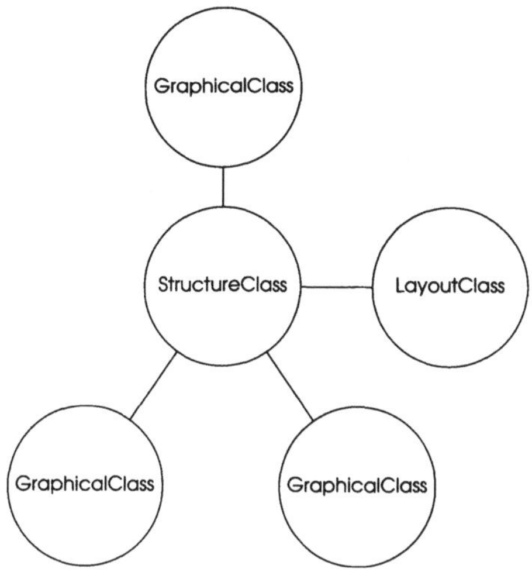

Figure 5: Relationship of structure objects and layout objects.

Layout objects keep the constraints and functions that control the graphical layout of a related set of objects in one place. Collecting these constraints, particularly those that may relate graphical aspects of two or more objects, is good software engineering practice and aids modification and maintenance. Also, there is the problem of changing these inter-object constraints when the structure of the display structure changes. If this is not done correctly — and it can be quite tricky — strange behaviour that is difficult to debug may result. Graphical objects in the structure do not have full access to knowledge of the structure necessary to update the constraints (ideally, for portability and generality, they neither require nor have access to this knowledge). The layout objects, however, by virtue of being connected to the structure objects, have full knowledge of this information and are in a good position to maintain the layout when the structure of the display structure changes.

Finally, the layout object may be implemented in a variety of ways. It can install a set of constraints to do the layout, or it can take the opposite extreme and do the layout procedurally whenever necessary. The programmer implementing the layout object is free to choose either extreme, or any point between. This flexibility is important because there are some things that are better done with constraints and others that are better done procedurally.

Requirements met: The use of layout objects supports abstraction by separating the specifics of graphical layout from abstract structure.

3.4. Dynamic Inheritance and Synthesis

In an hierarchical object-based graphics system like MEL it is useful to inherit values at run-time through the display structure. For example, in MEL the positions of graphical objects are determined by adding the relative position of each object to the absolute position of the parent object. This implies that if the parent is moved, the child is moved. Dynamic inheritance of graphical properties is used in Tube [Herrmann and Hill, 1989], and we adopted this approach in MEL.

In Tube and MEL, graphical properties are also synthesized; that is, they are inherited *up* the display structure. For example, picking in MEL is based on a tree search of regions. Each graphical object has two slots: self-pick-region, the region occupied by this object, and pick-region, the region containing all objects in the sub-tree of the display structure rooted at this object. The pick-region slots are synthesized from the children's pick-regions by taking the union of the object's self-pick-region and the pick-regions of all its children.

These two examples are standard forms of run-time inheritance and synthesis supplied by default in MEL. MEL programmers can also specify inheritance and synthesis that may be specific to their application, for example, inheriting fount information from a menu into each of the menu items, to ensure consistency of fount.

MEL implements inheritance and synthesis with constraints[5]. Because an object's inheritance constraints must change when the object's parent changes, MEL generates higher-order constraints (usually second-order, but sometimes third-order) to modify the constraints when the structure of the display structure changes. For example, the inheritance of position information requires a constraint that includes the parent's position as a source. If the parent changes, the position inheritance constraint must be changed to have the new parent's position as a source, and not the old parent's position. MEL generates a higher-order constraint that has the object's parent as a source, and the list of sources of the position inheritance constraint as a target. This higher-order constraint ensures that the position inheritance constraint is consistent with the structure of the display tree. Similarly, higher-order constraints (usually second order because of intricacies of the heterogeneous tree) are generated to maintain synthesis constraints are changed when the children change.

Note that graphical objects are not allowed to attach constraints to arbitrary objects. They may only request that MEL install constraints that implement inheritance and synthesis with respect to its parent and children. This minimizes violation of the principle of object-oriented programming that states that objects do not directly access the slots of other objects, and allows the object and constraint system to combine forces to keep the inheritance and synthesis constraints consistent with the display structure as it changes.

Requirements met: Run-time synthesis is used by the picking and redraw algorithms to maintain the information needed for logarithmic searching. Inheritance is used to link the positions of child objects of composite objects to the position of the composite object. Thus, run-time inheritance and synthesis are important to fast pick and redraw, and to the support of composite objects.

5 Simple dynamic inheritance could also be implemented with delegation, but we felt that using the constraint system would result in simpler code, greater flexibility (the inherited value can be a function of several values) and improved performance, as the constraint system would minimize unnecessary recomputation, and would ensure correctness when the display structure is changed.

4. Implementation and Example

4.1. Implementation Environment

MEL is implemented in Common Lisp [Steele, 1984] and uses the X Window System™ [Scheifler et al., 1988] for graphical input and output.

We chose to implement our own object system rather than use CLOS [Bobrow et al., 1986] or some other standard object systems. There are two key reasons for this:

- Existing CLOS implementations are not fast enough to support real-time graphics operations like dragging, while other object systems are not likely to be portable nor well supported in the future.
- We wanted to modify the object system extensively to support constraint inheritance, run-time inheritance and synthesis, and several other features necessary to the behavioural control aspects of MEL. We felt that it would be just as hard to modify an existing object system to provide seamless integration of these features as it would be to start from scratch.

Our object system is built on top of the Common Lisp structure facility, and relies on the single inheritance mechanism of structures to support single inheritance of methods, slots, constraints, rules and sub-structure. MEL object specifications are simply compiled into Common Lisp structures and a large number of methods. Methods include the name of the class in the method name, for example the access method to get the absolute positions (abs-position) of an instance of the class GraphicalClass is GraphicalClass-abs-position. Limited polymorphism is supported in that methods can be applied to any sub-class of the class they are defined on. For example, GraphicalClass-abs-position can be applied to an instance of the class Circle (a sub-class of GraphicalClass).

Currently we find our performance adequate for demonstration purposes, using Franz Allegro Common Lisp on Sun 4 workstations and SPARCstations™. Our philosophy has been to emphasize generality, not speed, on the assumption that it is easier to tune for performance (if necessary) than to significantly extend functionality (without impacting performance). We attribute our current good performance to careful choice of algorithms:

- Searching for drawing and picking use algorithms that search the display hierarchy and are logarithmic in the number of objects.
- Constraint evaluation is done via a partially lazy algorithm that attempts to minimize the sum of unnecessary recomputation and overhead in minimizing recomputation. Typically, only a very small part of the constraint graph is recomputed in response to a change.

4.2. Classes and Class Definition

GraphicalClass is the root class of all graphical objects. It provides all the basic structural and graphical slots and constraints needed by graphical objects. The current implementation of GraphicalClass has twenty slots. Of these ten have to do with graphical attributes, picking and redrawing (e.g., position, line width, regions occupied on the screen, etc.). Five slots are concerned with the display structure (e.g., parent, substructure, etc.). The remaining four slots are used for record keeping, debugging and system information. GraphicalClass also defines ten constraints and higher-order constraints. Most of these constraints are used to support dynamic inheritance of graphical information, and dynamic synthesis of regions used for picking and redraw.

Our current library of primitive graphical classes includes: NullGraphic, Text, Line, Circle, Rectangle, Bitmap, Button, and PopUpWindow. Because so much information is embedded in GraphicalClass, the definition of these graphical primitives is relatively simple. For example, the definition for the class Circle is included in Figure 6. In addition to the defClass to formally define the sub-class with its slots, default values, and dependencies (our term for one-way constraints), two functions must be defined to: draw the circle in a window, and determine if a point is inside the Circle.

Looking at the code in detail, only one slot is defined, it represents the radius of the circle, defaults to 10, and its type is an integer greater than, or equal to, zero. Two defaults are defined; they assign functions to slots (the functions are discussed later). If the MEL object system were truly polymorphic, this might not be necessary, but this currently is the only way that functions walking the display structure can access class specific methods. Finally, two dependencies or constraints are specified. Dependencies are specified in four parts: name, target, sources and function. The name is used in the specification of sub-classes to override inherited dependencies. The other parts are as discussed for constraint specification above. The first dependency is called Circle-self-region and sets the self-region, an inherited slot whose value is a region that is a bounding box for the area occupied by this object on the display. Self-region is used for picking and redrawing, and must be defined. The sources for this constraint are the radius, line-width and absolute position (abs-position) of the object. When any of these changes, the expression is evaluated to compute the new self-region. The second dependency has no target, has radius a9 the source, and the standard MEL function redraw-trigger-function as the function. This dependency causes the function redraw-trigger-function to be called with the current object as a parameter whenever the radius changes. This will cause the circle to be redrawn.

In Figure 6 the function Circle-redraw-function is shown as a stub, as it only calls the xlib function to draw a circle. (Because of the complexities of dealing with X, this requires 18 lines of code including four calls to xlib routines, and several type conversions!) The Circle-inside-p function simply returns *t* if the given position is inside the circle. This is used by the picking algorithm as a detailed check on picking.

The three biggest tasks in developing a new primitive are: learning how to draw it with X, writing an expression to compute its bounding box, and writing a function that can determine if a point is inside it. The first of these is not difficult for experienced X programmers, but can be frightening for beginners because of the size of the X documentation. The difficulty of the latter two are largely determined by the complexity of the figure being drawn. Both are easy for simple figures like circles, but more difficult for

```
(defClass Circle
  :super-class GraphicalClass
  :slots ((radius 10 :type (integer 0 *)))
  :defaults ((inside-p-fun #'Circle-inside-p)
          (redraw-fun #'Circle-redraw-function)
          )
  :dependencies ((Circle-self-region
              self-region
              (radius line-width abs-position)
              (let* ((r (+ radius (ceiling (/ line-width 2)))))
                (make-region
                 :left (- (position-x abs-position) r)
                 :top (- (position-y abs-position) r)
                 :width (* 2 r)
                 :height (* 2 r))))
             (Circle-redraw nil (radius) redraw-trigger-function)
             )
  )

(defun Circle-redraw-function (object window)
  "redraw a Circle."

  (declare (type Circle object)
        (type window window))

  ;; xlib calls to draw a circle.....
  )

(defun Circle-inside-p (object p)
  " returns t if p is inside the Circle."

  (declare (type Circle object)
        (type position p))

  (let ((abs-pos (Circle-abs-position object)))
     (<= (+ (* (- (position-x abs-pos) (position-x p))
             (- (position-x abs-pos) (position-x p))
             )
           (* (- (position-y abs-pos) (position-y p))
             (- (position-y abs-pos) (position-y p))
             )
           )
         (* (Circle-radius object)(Circle-radius object))
         ))
  )
```

Figure 6: Definition of Circle class.

complex figures like arbitrary closed polygons. As the next example suggests, however, most new displays or interfaces, are created not by creating new primitives but by subclassing and composing existing graphical objects. This is a simpler task than defining a new primitive.

4.3. Bar Graph Example

Figure 7 shows a screen dump of one of the test applications we have developed. It shows a form of bar graph, with five pairs of bars. The length of each bar is attached (with constraints) to a parameter in a simulation (written in MEL)[6]. As the simulation computes new values, the bar lengths are updated. The black bars are anchored at their right end, the white bars at their left end. The MEL class definitions to implement this display are included in Figure 8, and the display structure is illustrated in Figure 9.

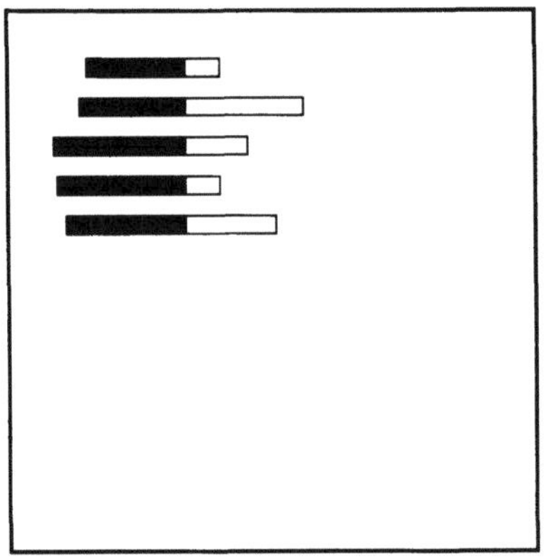

Figure 7: Screen dump of bar graph demonstration.

Specific points to note about this application are:

- The top two layers of the display structure (TwoBars, DistanceBars and SizeBars) are made up of instances of sub-classes of NullGraphic. NullGraphic is a sub-class of GraphicalClass that has no visible representation on the display. These objects are needed to build up a convenient topology in the display structure. Without them, the display structure could not have the structure that it does, which is clearly analogous to the display, and simplifies the use of layout objects.
- The sub-structure specifications in DistanceBars and SizeBars include calls to map-car to generate and return the five child bars. This code is executed at creation time and is inherited by sub-classes of DistanceBars and SizeBars.
- All the bars are given an initial position to set their horizontal position. The layout objects sets their vertical position.
- The Rectangle class (the super-class of SizeBar and DistanceBar) allows the anchor point for each instance to be specified. The anchor point is the point in the frame of reference of the rectangle that corresponds to its position. Thus, by setting a rectangle's anchor to *upper-left*, and its position to 100, 100, the upper

6 The architectural rules that determine the structure of the connection to the application, are discussed in [Patterson et al, 1990]. The specific tools and techniques available in MEL for implementing the simulation, and other applications, are topics for another paper.

```
(defconstant *bar-height* 10)

(defClass DistanceBar
 :super-class Rectangle
 :defaults ((fill-p t)
        (delta-y *bar-height*)
        (anchor *upper-right*)))

(defClass SizeBar
 :super-class Rectangle
 :defaults ((delta-y *bar-height*)
        (anchor *upper-left*)))

(defClass DistanceBars
 :super-class NullGraphic
 :defaults ((sub-structure
        (create-OrderedList
         :children
         (mapcar #'(lambda (n)
                 (create-DistanceBar
                  :rel-position (make-position :x 100 :y 25)))
               '(1 2 3 4 5))
         :layout (create-VerticalList :vGap 5)))))

(defClass SizeBars
 :super-class NullGraphic
 :defaults ((sub-structure
        (create-OrderedList
         :children
         (mapcar #'(lambda (n)
                 (create-SizeBar
                  :rel-position (make-position :x 100 :y 25)))
               '(1 2 3 4 5))
         :layout (create-VerticalList :vGap 5)))))

(defClass TwoBars
 :super-class NullGraphic
 :defaults ((sub-structure
        (create-OrderedList
         :children
         (list
          (create-DistanceBars)
          (create-SizeBars))))))
```

Figure 8: Class definitions for bar graph demonstration.

left corner of the rectangle will be placed at 100, 100. The anchor feature relies heavily on constraints for its implementation, and makes it easy to control the direction of growth of the bars in this example.

- Although the running interface includes 70 constraints, no constraints are explicitly defined in these class definitions. They are all inherited from the superclasses. The large number of constraints implies a great deal of flexibility, while the fact that they are all inherited suggests that the programming cost of having this flexibility is low.
- There is no explicit provision for connection to the application in these classes. To connect the application to the graphics, constraints are attached to the delta-x

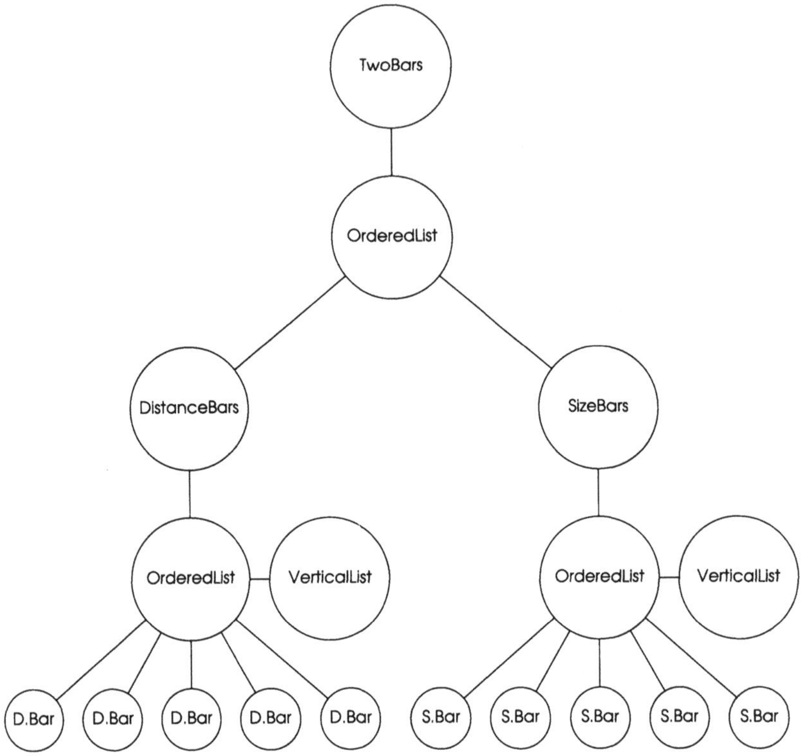

Figure 9: Display structure for bar graph example.

slots of the bars. These constraints are connected and maintained by an instance of a special class, known as a link[7].

- The organization used is two columns of five bars. An equally valid organization would be one column of five pairs of bars. The choice is up to the designer of the implementation based on the specifics of the interface and application.

4.4. Running Interfaces Created with MEL

To start and run a user interface created with MEL, one simply calls the MEL function start-and-run-view passing it the root object of the display structure and a window to display the interface in. For example, to create and run an instance of our bar graph example:

```
(start-and-run-view (create-TwoBars)
          (create-window <window-creation-parameters>))
```

7 Link classes and their use are described in detail in a paper describing our generic architecture for multi-user interfaces, in progress.

One must also create and install any links between the application and graphics.

Start-and-run-view starts a light-weight process to run the user interface. This process repeats this basic loop:

check for and process any user input
re-evaluate any layout functions that need to be re-evaluated
erase the displays for any objects that have been deleted
re-display any objects that need to be redisplayed

This process is careful to share the processor with other light weight processes running other interfaces or applications. It retains some information necessary to connect to the X Window System and to control scheduling, but the vast majority of the information it manipulates is in the display structure.

At run-time, constraint maintenance is interleaved with normal program execution. The constraint system is invoked, as needed, whenever constrained values are updated or accessed. The constraints used to keep the display consistent with the display structure are special. Rather than re-computing layouts or updating the display as soon as there is any change, a list of graphical objects needing to be redisplayed, and a list of structure objects whose layout must be re-evaluated, are maintained for each user interface. The layouts are re-computed and the objects (and any objects they overlap) redisplayed whenever there is no user input to process. This is a good compromise between immediately updating the display to give immediate feedback, and making many wasteful screen updates, that will immediately be overwritten by the next update.

4.5. Some Other Examples

Figure 10 shows screen dumps of some other graphical representations we have built for the simulation. All can be active, and interacted with, at the same time, while connected to a single instance of the simulation application.

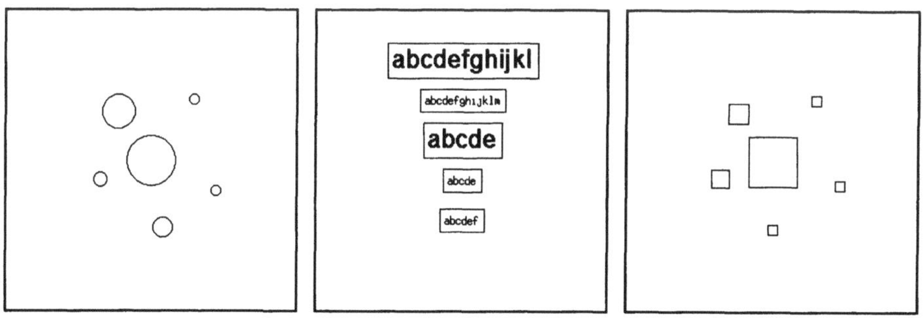

Figure 10: Some other graphical representations built for our simulation.

In the graphical representations with circles and squares, the positions of the smaller circles and squares represent distance (the black bars in the bar graph) and their size represents size (the white bars in the bar graph). The text representation uses centred text strings as bar graphs. The length of the strings represents the size parameter. (The founts can be changed to test the fount software.) All views active at a time change in unison. For example, moving a small circle in the circular representation moves the corresponding square, and changes the length of the corresponding black bar.

We have also built a Tic-Tac-Toe game. There are three representations for this game, an X player, an O player, and an observer. There must be one X and one O player to play a game, but there may be any number of observers. Figure 11 shows a screen dump of this interface. The X and O in the bottom left corner indicate that this is the X player's representation and it is O's turn to play.

Figure 11: X player's view of Tic-Tac-Toe.

5. Lessons

The lessons we have learned from our development and use of MEL fall into three broad categories:

- Constraints.
- Special Cases.
- Sub-classing, Composition, and Integration.

5.1. Constraints

Based on experience with Tube [Hill and Herrmann, 1989], and from reports in the literature (e.g., Coral [Szekely and Myers, 1988], Grow [Barth, 1986]) we started out with the belief that a constraint maintenance system would be a powerful and useful tool for controlling graphical presentation. Hence, we began by implementing a simple but general constraint maintenance system. As time went on, we discovered more and more uses for the constraint system. In general, we use constraints anywhere there is a need to maintain state. We have used constraints heavily in all of our test applications (which drive our graphics), to connect the applications to the graphics, to control graphics, to support run-time inheritance and synthesis, to initiate layout and redisplay, to maintain consistency of back pointers in the display structure, and to maintain state information in the constraint system itself. We continue to find new uses for the constraint system, and have never regretted the initial effort required to make the constraint system quite general.

The use of the constraint system to maintain its own run-time state makes it easy to support higher-order constraints. Higher-order constraints are implemented by replacing standard state maintenance constraints in the constraint system with the constraints supplied by the MEL program. Support for higher-order constraints in MVS (MEL's constraint system) is crucial to the broad use of constraints in MEL. Programmatically, the most intricate parts of systems implemented in MEL are those parts that maintain consistency of the display structure, and between the display structure and constraint graph. This results from our need to change the display structure quickly and easily at run-time to update the display. Since we are interested in interfaces with lots of graphical feedback, we must alter the display structure frequently. Altering the display structure can have far reaching effects, both rippling through the display structure, and on the constraint graph. Because MVS supports higher-order constraints, it is possible to maintain the necessary consistencies entirely with the constraint system. The necessary constraints were written once (and debugged!) and are now automatically installed by MEL. The use of higher-order constraints simplified the work of the programmers implementing MEL and will simplify the work of programmers using MEL.

5.2. Special Cases

It is often tempting to treat graphically intensive operations such as dragging and rubber-banding as special cases, to be implemented differently from regular graphical update, to improve performance. We have adopted the philosophy that there should be no special cases that avoid the normal graphical update procedure. There are several reasons for this:

- We intend MEL to be an open-ended system. As such, new, graphically intensive operations will frequently be added. Writing and maintaining the code for all of these special cases would be time consuming, and ensuring that there are no undesirable interactions between them would be almost impossible.
- We want to use MEL to build interfaces that will have lots of different forms of graphical feedback and update (e.g., highlighting, pop-up menus, animations). We want these forms of feedback to be fast. It seemed that the best way to do this is to concentrate on improving the general purpose graphics update algorithms, rather than just the special cases, so that all graphics could benefit.
- In most environments, if the user is dragging a circle with the mouse, the interface can be sure that the mouse is busy, and is not going to pop-up a menu and change the circle to a square. Thus, it is safe to optimize the dragging based on

the assumption that the circle will not change. This is not true of the multi-user applications we are building with MEL. The fact that one user is dragging an object does not prevent another user (or the application) from changing the object. Consistent with the general What-You-See-Is-What-You-Get (WYSIWYG) philosophy of direct manipulation, and the What-You-See-Is-What-I-See (WYSIWIS) philosophy of multi-user interfaces, if the dragged object is changed while it is being dragged, it should change right away, not when it is finally placed. Our experience with MEL tells us that the only way to support both WYSIWYG and WYSIWIS is to adopt the philosophy: *No Special Cases!*

The implication of the no special cases philosophy is that regular graphical update must be fast. Hence, as discussed in the previous section, we have been careful to design the basic structures and algorithms of MEL to facilitate rapid update. The key thing that we have done is make graphics update automatic. By building it into MEL, it becomes worthwhile to expend extra effort on algorithms that many programmers may not always use. In MEL, we are careful to only redraw things that must be redrawn, and use logarithmic (or better) algorithms wherever possible. The constraint system helps us here, making it easy to keep track of information that is needed by these algorithms.

5.3. Sub-classing, Composition and Integration

MEL is intended to be a tool for *constructing* interfaces as much as it is a tool for *programming* interfaces. By constructing interfaces, we mean assembling from existing components wherever possible. Object-oriented systems can facilitate construction in two ways: sub-classing and composition.

The MEL object system supports inheritance of constraints in addition to the traditional slots and methods. This greatly enhances the utility of inheritance in MEL. Because so many aspects of MEL graphical objects are controlled by constraints, the inheritance of constraints means that very little effort is required to produce new objects that are very rich in graphical properties and malleability.

MEL also goes to great lengths to support the construction of complex objects and (to a lesser extent) classes, by combining several simpler objects or classes. The main features of MEL that facilitate composition are:

Run-time inheritance and synthesis of values

Because the inheritance and synthesis mechanisms do not depend on the number of children nor the classes of the parents and children, it is easy to combine components of different types to produce a wide range of complex objects, and to experiment with subtle changes.

Explicit layout objects

The use of explicit layout objects that can be easily and dynamically changed, makes it easy to combine and modify sub-structures (topologies) and graphical layouts (geometries).

Inheritance of sub-structure

Specifications of sub-structure are inherited through the class hierarchy, making it possible to sub-class composite classes. Thus, the powers of both sub-classing and composition can be combined when defining new classes.

The ease of use and utility of sub-classing and composition in MEL rely heavily on the seamless integration of *all* MEL features in the object system. The specific features mentioned above are just artifacts of this seamless integration. The constraint system, techniques like run-time inheritance and synthesis, and sub-structure specification are all an integral part of the MEL object system, not warts attached to the side. This means that all of the parts of MEL can work together harmoniously, so that the utility of the whole is greater than the sum of the utilities of the parts. This harmonious mixing of powerful tools is the key to the usability and utility of MEL.

6. Summary and Future Work

MEL is a large ongoing project that is focussed on the problems of developing multi-user graphical interfaces. Only the parts of MEL dealing with object-oriented graphics have been discussed in this chapter. Other aspects have to do with controlling interactive behaviour, design of conceptual architectures for multi-user applications, and design of generic sets of interactive graphical objects for use in multi-user computer mediated games.

Work on the graphics aspects of MEL is largely complete; future work will concentrate on multi-media presentation, and usability and utility issues:

- We wish to expand MEL so that it can be used to develop interfaces that include audio and video objects, in addition to graphical objects.
- We plan an informal study of programmers building and modifying multi-user games in MEL. From this we hope to learn if ordinary development programmers can learn to use non-traditional tools like constraint-based object-oriented graphics.
- At the same time we will build several large scale, graphical multi-user interfaces to prototype communications systems being developed at Bellcore.
- Finally, based on our experience with the previous two activities, we will explore ways to make MEL more usable. This could include development of non-programming techniques (e.g., direct manipulation and programming by example) for building interactive graphical objects. Peridot [Myers, 1987a; Myers, 1987b] shows one way of doing this, but we would like to produce techniques that are more general. In particular, we want to make all of the power of MEL, including the distinction between graphical layout and abstract structure, available to the non-programming interface developer. Techniques like those used in the Mode Composer [Shan, 1990] may prove effective.

Based on our experience so far, we believe that the combination of constraints and object-oriented graphics is a powerful tool for the implementation of graphical user interfaces. But to be truly useful more is needed:

- Seamless integration of all features into the object system so that everything possible is inherited through the class hierarchy.
- Relatively general, shared display structure, so that the structure of the display structure can match the structure of the graphics of the interface, and can be modified without rebuilding the display list.
- A constraint maintenance system, with support for higher-order constraints, that almost eliminates the often complex code needed to maintain structural consistency.

We currently have these features in MEL, and will be soon be testing their usability and utility when applied to the development of multi-user user interfaces of realistic size and complexity.

Acknowledgements

Scott Meeks implemented the initial version of the Tic-Tac-Toe program. Steve Rohall implemented several graphical primitives and interfaces to the simulation program. Scott Meeks, Steve Rohall, John Patterson and Wayne Wilner have all contributed to the design and direction of MEL, and to the improvement of the presentation in this chapter. Nathaniel Borenstein and Laurie Reuter provided many suggestions for improving this chapter.

References

Barth, P.S. (1986) "An Object-Oriented Approach to Graphical Interfaces," *ACM Trans. On Graphics*, vol. 5, no. 2, 142-172.

Bobrow, D.G., Kann, K., Kiczales, G., Masinter, L., Stefik, M., and Zdybel, R. (1986) "CommonLoops: Merging Lisp and Object-Oriented Programming," *SIGPLAN Notices*, vol. 21, no. 11, 17-29. (OOPSLA '86 Conference Proceedings, September 29-October 2, 1986, Portland, Oregon.)

Borenstein, N.S. (1990) *Multimedia Applications Development with the Andrew Toolkit*, Prentice Hall.

CORE (1979) "Status Report of the the Graphics Standards Planning Committee," *Computer Graphics*, vol. 13, no. 3.

Herrmann, M. and Hill, R. (1989) "Abstraction and Declarativeness in User Interface Development Systems — The Methodological Basis of the Composite Object Architecture," *Proceedings of the XIth World Computer Congress.* (San Francisco, California, August 28-31, 1989.)

Hill, R.D. (1986) "Supporting Concurrency, Communication and Synchronization in Human-Computer Interaction — the Sassafras UIMS," *ACM Trans. on Graphics*, vol. 5, no. 3, 179-210.

Hill, R.D. and Herrmann, M. (1989) "The Structure of Tube — A Tool for Implementing Advanced User Interfaces," *EuroGraphics'89*, 15-25. (Proceedings of the European Computer Graphics Conference and Exhibition, Hamburg, Federal Republic of Germany, Sept. 4-8, 1989.)

Hopgood, F.R.A., Duce, D.A., Gallup, J.R., and Sutcliffe, D.C. (1986) *Introduction to the Graphical Kernel System (GKS)*, Academic Press.

Hudson, S.E. (1989) "Graphical Specification of Flexible User Interface Displays," *Proceedings of the ACM SIGGRAPH Symposium on User Interface Software and Technology*, 105-114. (Williamsburg, Virginia, November 13-15, 1989.)

Leler, W. (1988) *Constraint Programming Languages*, Addison-Wesley, Reading, Massachusetts.

Myers, B.A. (1987a) "Creating Dynamic Interaction Techniques by Demonstration," *Proceedings of CHI+GI 1987*, ACM, New York, 271-278. (Toronto, April 5-9.)

Myers, B.A. (1987b) *Creating User Interfaces by Demonstration.* Ph.D. Thesis, Department of Computer Science, University of Toronto.

Myers, B A., Zanden, B. van der, and Dannenberg, R.B. (1989) "Creating Graphical Interactive Application Objects by Demonstration," *Proceedings of the ACM SIGGRAPH Symposium on User Interface Software and Technology*, 95-104. (Williamsburg, Virginia, November 13-15, 1989.)

Palay, A.J., Hansen, W.J., Sherman, M., Wadlow, M.G., Neuendorffer, T.P., Stern, Z., Bader, M., and Peters, T. (1988) "The Andrew Toolkit — An Overview," *Proceedings of the USENIX Winter Conference*, 9-21.

Patterson, J.F., Hill, R.D., Meeks, W.S., and Rohall, S L. (1990) "Rendezvous: An Architecture for Synchronous Multi-User Applications," *Proceedings of CSCW '90*, Los Angeles.

PHIGS (1988) "Information processing systems — Computer Graphics — Programmer's Hierarchical Interactive Graphics System functional description," ISO/IEC 9592:1.

Scheifler, R W., Gettys, J., and Newman, R. (1988) *X Window System*, Digital Press.

Shan, Y.P. (1990) "An Object-Oriented Framework for Direct-Manipulation User Interfaces," In: E. Blake and P. Wißkirchen (ed) *Advances in Object Oriented Graphics*, Springer-Verlag, Berlin.

Steele, G.L. (1984) *Common Lisp: The Language*, Digital Press, Bedford, Massachusetts.

Szekely, P. and Myers, B. (1988) "A User Interface Toolkit Based on Graphical Objects and Constraints," *Sigplan Notices*, vol. 23, no. 11, 36-45. (OOPSLA'88 Conference Proceedings, September 25-30, 1988, San Diego, California.)

Tarlton, M.A. and Tarlton, P.N (1989) "Pogo. A Declarative Representation System for Graphics," In: W. Kim and F.H. Lochovsky (ed.) *Object-Oriented Concepts, Databases, and Applications*, Addison-Wesley, Reading, Massachusetts, pp 151-176.

Part II

Modelling and Design

6

Persistent Graphical Objects

Chris Laffra and Peter van Oosterom

Persistent objects are objects whose contents may outlive the execution time of the program. This chapter describes the process of introducing persistent objects in the object-oriented programming language Procol. The strength of persistent objects in an object-oriented programming language is the integration of a database system with a programming language. Persistent objects make program development easier, because the programmer does not have to implement the explicit loading and saving of data. Besides the general functional aspects, special attention is paid to graphical applications in order to deal with their specific geometric requirements. For example, it must be possible to find, in an efficient manner, all graphical objects that fall within a given region. These issues, persistent objects and their geometric requirements, have not yet got the attention they deserve in the literature covering object-oriented graphical systems where modelling and functional aspects dominate.

---

1. Introduction

The fact that the object-oriented approach is so successful in computer graphics, is mainly due to the system modelling capabilities that the object-oriented paradigm offers. The specialization relationships which exist between the graphical objects in a system can be modelled with inheritance or delegation which are present in many object-oriented development environments. Geometric data types, such as points, vectors and matrices may be implemented by abstract data types using object classes [Blake and Cook, 1987; Cox, 1986; Dietrich et al., 1989; Meyer, 1988]. However, in practice this modelling power is not enough when implementing CAD systems or Geographical Information Systems (GISs) which deal with large data sets. Integrated database facilities are required to support the graphical application in an efficient manner.

In this chapter we describe a solution that is based on the introduction of *persistent* objects in the object-oriented programming language called *Procol.* A short introduction to Procol is given in [Laffra and van den Bos, 1990], also contained in this book. A detailed functional description of the C-based language Procol can be found in [van den Bos, 1989] and some implementation aspects in [van den Bos and Laffra, 1989]. The resulting system is also extendable with new (persistent) types and operators. In itself this approach is not new and has been described by several other authors [Atkinson and Buneman, 1987; Richardson and Carey, 1989; aw et al., 1989], but we also tried to make the system suitable for highly *interactive and graphical* applications. This goal is achieved by putting emphasis on both time-efficiency (offering techniques such as: navigation, index structures, and parallelism) and the recognition of multi-dimensional data. As an example, not only one-dimensional, but also multi-dimensional index structures are provided in Procol. The emphasis in this document is on the inclusion of persistent graphical objects in the syntax and semantics of Procol and on its implications for the technical realization; e.g., how Procol deals with problems such as referential integrity and associative searching.

We will state the problem area in Section 2 and define our general requirements for persistence in an object-oriented language in Section 3. Our first attempt to introduce persistence in Procol and comparisons with several other systems are described in Section 4. Building on this experience the following topics are discussed in more detail: referential integrity, (multi-dimensional) search problems, Procol extension alternatives and object instances of different sizes in Sections 5 through 8, respectively. In Section 9 we present the solution as chosen in Procol. In nearly all the sections the requirements of graphics play an important role. The discussions are illustrated with examples based on graphical systems. Finally, Section 10 indicates some topics where further research is required.

2. The Need for Persistence

The computer science research in the area of programming languages emphasizes programming constructs and data structures. One of the most popular paradigms is that of Abstract Data Types (ADTs). Object-Oriented Programming Languages (OOPLs) encapsulate this paradigm in an elegant manner using object types to describe the ADTs. Access from outside to the data inside an object instance is only possible through the methods or procedures defined for that object type. In this document we will use the term *object type* to indicate a class of objects and the term *object* to indicate one instance. In case more emphasis is needed we use the term *object instance* explicitly.

The data stored in data structures (or objects) of a running program are in general volatile, that is, as soon as the program stops, the data are lost. However, in many applications the data themselves are very important. An obvious solution is to save the data in a file with explicit write statements. The next time the program is started it first reads the data from file into the volatile data structures. Persistent objects make the program development more efficient, because the programmer does not have to be concerned with the reading and writing of data from and to disk. The structure of the data file may also become quite complex, resulting in possibly intricate parsing. Moreover, for large quantities of data this "file" solution becomes cumbersome during the execution of the program. Consider as an example an information system that registers bank accounts. A characteristic of this and many other information systems is that the objects are well structured, quite passive and occur in large quantities. Passive objects are objects that hardly ever send messages to other objects (except for replies): they only react to messages from outside. In the bank account example, an account object replies with its current amount when requested, and updates it when told so by a message from an authorized object.

Database Management Systems (DBMS) have been developed to deal with the large amounts of data mentioned above. DBMSs concentrate on the information representation and tackle related problems such as, integrity, security, redundancy, consistency, efficient searching, query formulation and concurrency control. A major drawback is that the DBMSs of the current generation are not extendable with new data types and operators. This makes the use of these DBMSs inconvenient in non-standard applications that need support for other data types.

The database research community has recognized this deficiency and is now trying to design systems that are more open [Egenhofer and Frank, 1989a; Stonebraker and Rowe, 1986; Wolf, 1989]. At the other side the OOPL research community has recognized the need for persistent objects. These two worlds are now meeting. In some cases these encounters result in conflicts because of very different and incompatible principles. For example, explicit (navigation) links amongst instances are considered harmful by the database community, because they are hard to maintain. However, these same links form the backbone in representing complex objects in OOPLs. On the other hand, sometimes the combination of the two research communities result in a nice symbiosis. An example of this is that the concurrency control problem in the database is solved by the model of an object that accepts messages one by one (as in Procol).

We are interested in interactive graphical applications, such as: CAD systems, VLSI Design, and Geographic Information Systems (GISs). Common aspects in these systems are: interactivity, graphics, and large amounts of data. In [van Oosterom and van den Bos, 1989] we showed that the object-oriented approach offers a good data modelling and design environment for GIS applications. In the same paper the need for persistent objects in our object-oriented programming language Procol, was identified.

3. Our Wish List

This section briefly discusses the major requirements for persistent objects in Procol. Some will be elaborated in one of the later sections, for those the relevant section is given here. Note that these requirements may neither be orthogonal nor independent of each other.

1. *Upward compatible.* Persistent objects have to be introduced with a minimal change to Procol. This implies that existing Procol programs do not have to be changed in order to be compiled by the new version of the Procol compiler.

2. *Transparent persistent objects.* Persistent objects are treated in the same manner as volatile objects by the application. Perhaps except for incompatible database facilities; for example, associative searching, that is object searching based on the contents or value of instances. [Atkinson and Buneman, 1987] refine this by recog-

nizing the following principles for persistent data (they assume several levels of persistence):

1. Persistence independence: the persistence of an object is independent of how the program manipulates that object. So, it has to be possible to call a procedure of which the actual parameters are sometimes persistent objects and other times volatile objects.

2. Persistence data type orthogonality: all objects are allowed the full range of persistence. This means that no matter how complicated the type is, its instances can still become persistent.

3. *Complex objects*. This provides the system with sufficient modelling power, e.g. *part-of hierarchies*. In Procol complex object types are defined by means of links (or references) to other object types that together define the complex object. The complex objects are static in terms of the object type structure and dynamic in the sense of the object instances.

4. *Extendibility with new ADTs*. This wish might be a trivial one in the context of OOPLs or object-oriented databases, but certainly not in the context of the traditional DBMSs. The definitions of the new persistent ADTs also have to be stored somewhere, if we want to be able to manipulate its object instances in a sensible manner.

5. *Efficient handling of large amounts of objects*. Long-lived systems allow time for data to accumulate. This, combined with the fact that we aim at developing interactive systems, justifies this efficiency requirement to be even more important than in other systems. Not only efficient retrieval by object id (which is very important in OOPL and object-oriented databases, as used in navigation links) is required, but also efficient associative searching has to be possible. This is realized, as usual, by indexing techniques such as B-trees [Bayer and McCreight, 1973; Comer, 1979] or hashing.

6. *Object instances of different sizes*. A polyline or polygon has to be stored with a minimum of overhead, because of the required time (and space) efficiency in interactive systems. This implies that different instances of the same object type may have different sizes. To treat an object instance as a *unity* means that it is stored in a contiguous part of memory. This may seem to be an implementation issue, but it is very important and by putting it in our wish list we emphasize this. This topic is further discussed in Section 8.

7. *Highly interactive and graphical applications*. The previous two wishes actually are part of this more general wish to make Procol suitable for this kind of applications. It has to be kept in mind that multi-dimensional data sometimes require other approaches than the data types encountered in traditional DBMSs. Also, the fact that Procol is designed as a parallel programming language should be exploited.

8. *Exchangeable objects.* It should be possible to exchange object instances between different systems. Object instances created by one system must be directly usable by other systems.

9. *Deal with referential integrity in a satisfactory manner.* This is well-known problem in database and programming language research. The topic will be discussed in depth in Section 5.

4. The First Attempt

In this section we will give an example of a Procol object. Then we describe our first (and quite simple) attempt to provide a mechanism for persistent objects, without trying to satisfy all the wishes of our list. The problems we encountered give some insight in the complexity of introducing persistent objects. In the last subsection we briefly compare our first attempt with the approaches taken in some other systems.

4.1. A Procol Object

A characteristic Procol feature is the "protocol". The protocol regulates access to an object by ordering the incoming messages which activate the actions and by checking the identity of the senders. In our example the protocol happens to be simple. An example is the object type MUNICIPALITY described in Procol:

```
OBJ      MUNICIPALITY (string name, polygon geom, PROVINCE parent);

Declare  ... local declarations ...

Protocol ANY -> Display        +
         ANY -> RetrieveData   +
         ANY -> ChangeData

Init     parent.AddMUN;

Actions  Display      = ......
         RetrieveData = ......
         ChangeData   = ......

EndOBJ   MUNICIPALITY.
```

In Procol, as usual, an object consists of a data-part and an operation-part. In a Procol object the data-part consists of: the attributes (in OBJ section) and the local data (in Declare section). The state of the object is determined by the data-part and the current status of the protocol. The operation-part contains: the local functions (in Declare section) and the Init, Protocol, Actions and Cleanup sections. In order to have persistence, the operation-part has to be stored once for each object type and the state has to be stored once for each object individual instance.

4.2. Introducing Persistence

Normally, object instances are only present when the program is executing. Data will have to be loaded from a file or a database system into the (new) objects when the program is initialized. Just before the program stops, the data have to be saved again. This is, as argued in Section 2, an inconvenient method, especially in the case of applications with huge amounts of data that are not entirely needed in each session. An object-oriented step in the right direction is to store the state of objects themselves. This can be compared with making a *core dump* of a single object. When an object is saved, a "snapshot" of the object instance is made. Changes made after the save operation are not propagated to this snapshot.

The suggestion to store the objects themselves is not as simple as one might expect. This is because objects usually contain references (in attributes or local variables) to other objects. A reference to an object is an *id* (identification of the proper type), assigned to that object by the operating system when it was created with the Procol primitive *new*. In some situations it is useless to save an object without also saving the related objects.

4.3. Comparison with Other Systems

The "snapshot" method is used in several other OOPLs. In systems offering multiple inheritance the object type that also has to be persistent, inherits this property from a general object type with methods to save and load the object. Egenhofer and Frank [Egenhofer and Frank, 1989b; Frank, 1988] suggest the object type *db_persistent* with methods *store, delete, retrieve* and modify. ET++ [Weinand et al., 1989] has an object hierarchy with the object type *object* in the top of this hierarchy. The object type *object* has methods called *PrintOn* and ReadFrom which enable transfer to and from disk. These solutions work fine as long as the object types contain no references to other objects but only simple attributes, such as for example an array of coordinates describing a polygon.

The persistent data in PS-algol [Atkinson and Buneman, 1987; Morrison et al., 1986] are organized into one or more databases. Each database has its own root and may contain values of different (complex) data types. The data are "imported" into a program with the *open.database* procedure which returns a pointer to the root. The root has the form of a name-value table in which the value is usually a pointer to another data structure. The actual data are accessed by following these pointers and it is assumed that the programmer has to know the structure of the database (though this is nowhere stated in the PS-algol papers). Once imported, the data can be manipulated in the same manner as volatile data. The procedure *commit* propagates the changes made so far to the database, if it was open for writing. Everything that is accessible from the root is stored. This means that values may change and data (structures) be added or removed.

In the OOPL Eiffel [Meyer, 1988] an object type that inherits from the object type *STORABLE* gets this kind of behaviour by means of the methods *store* and *retrieve*. If the method *store* is invoked in object instance x , the whole object structure starting at x is dumped (in a special format) to a file, even if the referenced object types in x do not inherit from *STORABLE*. Depending on x and the object structure of the application, it is possible to store the whole object structure, or just a part of it. Basically, this solution has two drawbacks. First, the application programmer has to indicate when to save or load the objects explicitly. So, if the program is stopped before the save, the latest data are lost. Second, updating one object in an object structure can become very expensive if all related objects have to be saved also, even if they did not change.

5. Referential Integrity

What happens if an object is deleted by its creator while other objects are still referring to this deleted object? A dangling reference is not a problem specific to persistent objects, it is a problem in the case of volatile objects too, but it manifests itself in a severe manner in combination with persistent objects. Assume, a persistent object contains a reference to a volatile object and the program is stopped. The next time the program is started, the reference to the volatile object is not valid any more (though it has not been deleted). Of course, dangling references can also occur in non-OOPL. For example, in C it is possible to have pointers to deleted data structures, which may be the cause of some severe errors in a program. Some systems guarantee *referential integrity*. An associated problem is that of an "unreachable" object, that is an object to which the last reference is lost. There are a number of possible approaches towards these problems:

- If we want to guarantee referential integrity, we at least have to be able to detect whether the integrity is damaged by the deletion of an object. This can be achieved by associating a reference count with each object instance. If the reference count has a value greater than zero, the object will not be deleted and the creator is notified of this fact. The reference count mechanism introduces overhead, because the counters have to be updated in each assignment to an object variable. Problems are introduced by cyclic data structures.

- A slightly different approach, but also based on a reference count, is followed in *O_2* [Bancilhon et al., 1988]. The object deletion is not refused but postponed until the value of the reference count is zero. The creator does not have to worry about trying to delete the object another time.

- Dangling references can not occur if we prohibit the deletion of objects. This approach is taken in for example GemStone [Penney and Stein, 1987]. In order to avoid congestion of the system, *garbage collection* has to be performed. Two well known methods for this are:

    1. Using a reference count: when the count becomes zero, the associated object instance is automatically deleted by the system.

    2 Performing a sweep through the object space (a directed graph) in order to detect which objects are unreachable. A disadvantage is that the sweep is performed periodically and during this operation the system can not be used by the applications. This can be avoided by using an incremental version of the sweep algorithm.

- The maintenance of the reference count introduces overhead; both memory usage and execution time increase. Clearly, it is more efficient to omit a reference count and directly delete the object at request. However, in this case the system is not allowed to reuse the *id's* of deleted objects for new objects. So, if a message is being sent to a deleted object, the system can detect this, and the sender will be notified. This strategy implies that the address of an object can not be used as its id, because when the object is deleted we want to be able to reuse that part of the memory space for new objects.

It may be clear by now that we are biased towards the latter approach. In the context of Procol, dangling references are probably programming errors and the detection of the illegal use of dangling references during run-time is an adequate solution. Finally, it is interesting to note that PCTE+ [IEPG, 1988; IEPG, 1988] offers links both with and without referential integrity. This is probably done for efficiency reasons. It is not stated in the PCTE+ documents how the referential integrity is maintained.

6. Object Management

In order to solve the administrative problems associated with the use of object id's, there is a need of an Object Management System} (OMS) that takes care of the (persistent) objects. One of the responsibilities of the OMS to keep the references in the object system consistent. To be more precise, an object system is consistent iff[Khoshafian and Copeland, 1986]:

- No two distinct objects have the same identifier (unique identifier assumption). In other words, the identifier functionally determines the type and the value of the object.
- For each identifier present in the system there is an object with this identifier (no dangling identifier assumption).

6.1. Object Identity

A uniform object identification mechanism has to be developed, capable of dealing with objects shared by multiple programs, multiple users or even multiple computers (in a network). There should be a mechanism to indicate in which persistent objects one is interested, so one is not bothered by non-interesting objects of others. One possible method could be to organize the object instances in "datasets" which are put in the normal hierarchical file system. This limits the scope and makes the task of finding the right communication partner easier for the OMS.

In relational databases [Codd, 1970] an identifier key is formed by one or more user-supplied attributes. Value based matching is a transparent technique for expressing relationships. However, it provides no support for referential integrity at all. By contrast, OOPLs support the notion of object identity which is independent of the attribute values [Paton and Gray, 1988, Khoshafian and Copeland, 1986]. describe several techniques for implementing object identity and they conclude that using so called *surrogates* is the best technique. Surrogates are system-generated, globally unique identifiers, completely independent of the physical location and data contents of an object.

6.2. Searching

The objects presented so far are not suited for associative search operations. That is, searching based on the contents of an object instead of using the object id to find an object. This is especially useful for a program that wants to use objects created by other programs, because the id's are unknown and have no semantic meaning. All that a program(mer) knows is about: object types (the kind of data he wants to use) and attribute values (restriction of instances).

Another use of associative searching is to solve the query: "How many inhabitants has the municipality with the name attribute 'Leiden'?". We have to look at all the instances of the municipality object type until we have found the proper one. This is an $O(n)$-algorithm. However, this problem can be solved with an $O(\log(n))$-algorithm, if a binary search is used. In a relational database, efficient search is implemented by a B-tree [Bayer and McCreight, 1973; Comer, 1979] for attributes on which an *index* is put. The B-tree has many useful properties, such as: it stays balanced under updates, it is adapted to paging (multiway branching instead of binary) and has a high occupancy rate.

The B-tree solution in an object-oriented environment is established by a set of auxiliary (system) objects. These objects do not contain the application data, but contain tree structures with references to the objects with the actual data. This B-tree has to be part of the OMS and, if possible, transparent to the "application" objects. Note that the OMS itself can be implemented in Procol as a set of objects.

There is some friction between the concepts behind the ADTs and the idea of associative searching, because associative searching requires knowledge of the internals of other objects. An object has to specify his query in terms of data-part that are inside other objects. To limit the damage, only so called *visible* attributes may be used in the query. These visible attributes become part of the specification of an object type (together with the actions of course), in contrast to the non-visible data-part which belong to the implementation. Note that an index may be put only on a visible attribute of an object type.

6.3. Multi-dimensional Data

The searching problem also applies to the graphic or geometric data. If no spatial structure is used, then queries such as "Give all municipalities within rectangle *X*" are hard to answer. A spatial data structure which is especially suited for the object-oriented environment is the R-tree [Guttman, 1984]. This is because the R-tree already deals with objects; it only adds a minimal bounding rectangle (MBR) and then it tries to group the MBRs which lie close to each other; see Figure 2. This grouping process is reflected in a tree structure, which in turn may be used for searching. Several test results [Faloutsos et al., 1987; Greene, 1989] indicate that the R-tree is a very efficient spatial data structure.

Not all known spatial data structures [van Oosterom, 1988] are suited for this purpose. For example kd-trees [Bentley, 1975], quadtrees [Samet, 1984], R+-tree, bsp-trees [van Oosterom, 1989], cell-tree [Günther, 1988] and gridfiles, are more difficult to integrate in

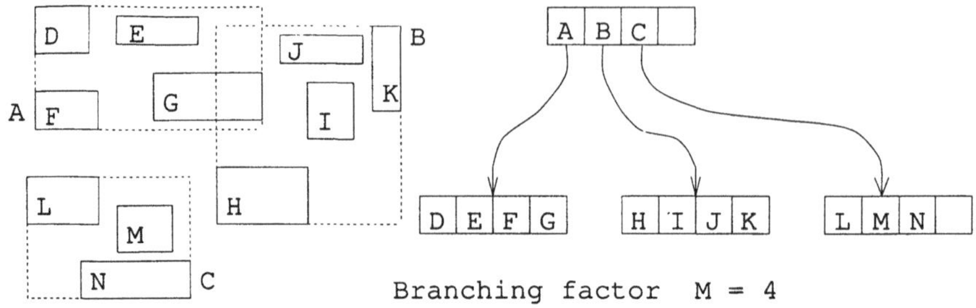

Figure 1: The R-tree

the object-oriented environment because they cut the geographic objects into pieces. This is against the spirit of the object-oriented approach, which tries to make complete "units," with meaning to the user. The Field-tree [Frank and Barrera, 1989], KD2B-tree and the Sphere-tree [van Oosterom and Claassen, 1990] are good candidates for integration in an object-oriented system, because they do not split the objects. Each of the spatial search structures has its own strengths and weaknesses, so if several alternatives are offered by the system, an application can use the structure that fulfills its needs the best.

In Procol, trees can be implemented in two different ways. The first method stores the entire tree in one single search object. The second method stores each node of the tree in a separate instance of the search object. The latter introduces an overhead by creating a lot of search objects (nodes). However, it has the advantage of being suited to parallel processing in Procol because the search objects can run on parallel processors. This is useful for range queries: "Give all municipalities with more than 10 000 and less than 20 000 inhabitants." Appendix A contains a part of the Procol implementation of the R-tree. In this implementation each node is a separate object. In the case of the R-tree this is a reasonable choice, because there is a fair amount of work in each node. The same would be valid for B-trees, but not for binary trees. In any case, for practical reasons, there has to be a separate search tree (index) for each attribute for which efficient searches are required. This has to be made clear to the OMS before the queries are posed.

It is possible that the value of an attribute changes, after the search tree has been created for that attribute. In that case, the tree may have become incorrect or inconsistent. This can be solved by sending an (implicit) message to the search tree object(s) in the OMS, just after the attribute has changed. Upon receipt of this message the search tree adjusts itself.

7. The Procol Extension

This section presents some issues concerning the syntax and semantics of the constructs which might be added to Procol for the support of persistent objects. This is done here without worrying how this can be achieved in our implementation of Procol. From the users point of view, this extension should be as small and simple as possible. First, we have to decide how to indicate that an object is persistent. Some alternative possibilities are:

- *On the fly:* Make a volatile object instance persistent by applying a new Procol primitive *persistent*. Assume the variable *x* holds the id of an object instance; then this instance is made persistent by: *persistent x*. Note that there is a difference with the *save* operation of Section 4, because the values (states) of a persistent object are always guaranteed to be up-to-date.
- *Per Object Instance:* At the moment an object is created, it is decided whether it will be persistent or not. A convention can be made that objects created with the *new* primitive are volatile and the ones created with the *persistent* primitive are persistent.
- *Per Object Type:* At the moment the object type is defined it is specified whether all instances of this type are persistent or not. A modified keyword *OBJ* could indicate this: PERSISTENT_OBJ.

A combination of these approaches is also possible. In the language E [Richardson and Carey, 1989] the programmer has to indicate per type (class) that instances are optionally persistent. The programmer has to decide per instance if it is really a persistent object instance.

The advantage of persistence per object type is that only once, during the object type definition, is there a difference for the application programmer between persistent and volatile objects. In the other solutions it is required to indicate that the object is persistent for each object instance. The major drawback of the latter choice is that two different types have to be defined if we want to use both the volatile and the persistent variants of basically one object type. In the case of strong type checking this means that we can not freely interchange the use of volatile and persistent objects as arguments in messages and procedure calls.

In order to get hold of persistent objects with unknown id, Procol will be extended with the *retrieve* primitive. Perhaps it is better to take the following approach towards the primitives new, delete, and retrieve: consider them as messages to the object types themselves ("class methods"). These are system objects (partly) responsible for the OMS tasks. These system objects have to maintain index structures if requested by sending them an create_index message.

The *retrieve* primitive has some resemblance to the *new* primitive, because it also assigns the id of an object to a variable of the proper type. Unlike *new*, retrieve will not execute the Init section, because that already happened when this object was created for the first time. The protocol (expression) of the object regulating access to the object is matched starting at the current (saved) state.

A *discrimination condition* can be used, because the object type information may not be specific enough. Of course only visible attributes can be specified in the condition. A retrieve returns the id of the object of the proper type for which the discrimination condition evaluates to "True". If there is more than one object satisfying these criteria, only one is returned. If there is no object satisfying these criteria, a *NULL* object is returned.

It is a small step from the *retrieve* primitive to the associative search operation. In fact, it could be considered as an iteration over the retrieve operation. If fast replies are necessary, then in the case of large set of objects, an index has to be used. This index could be a spatial index structure; e.g., needed for efficiently solving a "rectangle" query. There are several options for returning the answer of a search:

- Return one big set that contains the id's of all objects that satisfy the query. In case of large answers, a lot of temporary memory is required and it may take quite a while to generate the complete answer.
- Another strategy is first to state the query and then retrieve the answers one by one (or perhaps in buffers of a fixed size). The first part of the answer will probably be ready sooner than the complete answer would be. This promotes parallelism and is also quite important in an interactive application, because the end-user can see something early on.

The problem with the second solution for returning a search result is that other objects might interfere with the set of objects that belongs to the queried object type. "Third-party" objects could change values and add new instances or delete existing ones. We still have to investigate whether this can be solved by applying the right protocols in the system (OMS) objects. This has to be solved before we decide on the syntax of a search query.

8. Object Instances of Different Sizes

In Section 3 we saw that the wish to store a polyline or polygon with a minimum of overhead, implies that different instances of the same object type may have different sizes. So for example, the pure relational solution, presented by van Roessel [Roessel, 1987] is not acceptable, because a polyline is scattered over several tuples in a table and first has to be aggregated before it can be used again. In [van Oosterom et al., 1989] a solution in the context of the relational data model is presented.

Different sizes have an (enormous) impact on the implementation of persistent objects. In *CO_2*, the C implementation of *O_2* [Bancilhon et al., 1988], it was decided to prohibit object instances of different sizes. In contrast we would even like to have persistent objects whose sizes change dynamically. For example, to make it possible to remove points from or add points to a polyline. However, this would even further complicate the implementation. A decrease of the size of an object is not too hard, but an increase of object size means that an object does not fit in its (contiguous) part of memory and the memory after this object is probably occupied by another instance. The object will have to be moved to another larger place, because we want to treat an object as a unity and do not want to split it. This would have been impossible if the id of the object is its address. However, this was already disapproved of because of reasons discussed earlier. In any case, growing persistent objects could introduce a lot of overhead, e.g. requiring the moving of objects.

A more feasible situation is that after the Init section, the size of an object may not vary any more. It is still possible to deal with dynamic problems. For example, use a pointer (id) to an object of type linked list. This object type has an "application" data-part and a pointer to the next list element. Each instance represents one list element and they all have the same fixed size. We can extend this approach and simplify our implementation of Procol, if we only allow the following data types as attributes: *Basic types* (int, char, float, ...), *References* (or links) to other objects, and *Arrays* with fixed size after the Init.

9. Persistent Objects in Procol

The question of how to implement persistent objects in Procol can be divided into two sub-questions. The first is how to adapt the languages features (the external implementation). The second is how to implement this on the underlying platform (the internal implementation).

9.1. External Implementation

Our decisions according the external implementation of persistence in Procol included the introduction of the following new keywords:

1. **persistent** <object-id>
   in <dataset-key>
   With this statement a volatile object instance identified by <object-id> can be made persistent by coupling it to a dataset identified by <dataset-key>.

2. **volatile** <object-id>
   With this statement an object instance (identified by <object-id>), that has been made persistent before, can be made volatile. The result of this statement is that the persistent object instance is removed from its dataset.

3. **retrieve** <object-id>
   from <dataset-key>
   where <discrimination-string>
   and
   next <object-id>
   With this statement we can retrieve an instance of the same type of <object-id> from the dataset with identifier <dataset-key>, that satisfies the <discrimination-string>. If the dataset in question contains more than one instance of the required type, only one will be returned in <object-id>. Any successive execution of the **next** statement, will retrieve the *next* instance of the required type until all required instances have been retrieved from the dataset.

In general, <dataset-key> will be a string. This string can then be used to compose the filenames of the necessary dataset files. An example use of the provided persistence in the Declare section of an object type using the object DRAWING:

```
Declare

    object DRAWING drawing;

    allocate_drawing(char *name)
    {
        new drawing;
        persistent drawing in name;
    }
    read_old_drawing(char *name)
    {
        retrieve drawing from name;
    }
    erase_drawing(char *name)
    {
        retrieve drawing from name;
        volatile drawing;
    }
    move_drawing(char *name1, *name2)
    {
        retrieve drawing from name1;
        volatile drawing;
        persistent drawing in name2;
    }
    copy_drawing(char *name1, *name2)
    {
        retrieve drawing from name1;
        persistent drawing in name2;
    }
```

9.2. Internal Implementation

We will now motivate our design decisions for the internal implementation. Procol has been developed and implemented on a network of Sun workstations running under SunOS Release 4. Five possible implementations of the extension of Procol with persistent objects were considered, (compare with [Tsichritzis and Nierstrasz, 1988]):

1. *Bare* implementation: The problem of persistent objects is deferred to the kernel of Procol. Procol stores and manages these objects in (one or more) files, by using the Unix OS-interface calls: open, close, read and write. The advantage of this method is that it is very portable. Disadvantages are: a lot of work, relatively inefficient because of the many read/write calls that have to be made. We also have to implement the memory management aspects (within each file), such as: allocation, deallocation, gaps, fit strategies, and so on.

2. *Shared mapped memory* (virtual files) implementation: A file is mapped directly by the Unix OS on the address space of a process. A major advantage is that there is no difference between the "stored" object instances and their "running" counterpart, at least not at the level of the Procol kernel. At OS level there is a difference and this is the same as the difference between virtual memory pages that are in main-memory and the ones that are swapped on disk. We expect this implementation to be very efficient. In order to gain some experience we are currently converting a local application that uses explicit read and write statements, into a mapped memory implementation. First test results indicate that the elapsed times decrease by about 40% in applications with a lot of read and write statements. A

disadvantage of the mapped memory approach is that we still have to do the memory management ourselves.

3. *INGRES* [Sun, 1987] (or other relational DBMS) based implementation: The memory management is now done by database system. Also, all kinds of other useful DBMS features are provided. Wiederhold [Wiederhold, 1986] suggest the use of *view-object generators* to reconstruct objects from relations and view-object decomposers/archivers} for the inverse operation. However, there are several disadvantages. Object types can not (always) be mapped on a relation in which each tuple represents one object instance. For example, objects with polylines have changing instance sizes. Another disadvantage is that there is a difference between the "stored" object instance and its "running" counterpart, as observed by the Procol kernel. Of course, not from the point of view of the application program.

4. *POSTGRES* [Stonebraker and Rowe, 1986] (or other extendable DBMS) based implementation: New data types can be defined, so it should be possible to have a one to one relationship between tuples in a relation and the objects. Still, the difference between stored and running parts of objects remains. Another disadvantage is that a DBMS implementation is probably less efficient that the mapped memory implementation.

5. *PCTE+* [IEPG, 1988; IEPG, 1988] based implementation: The Portable Common Tool Environment PCTE+ offers a powerful OMS derived from the *Entity-Relationship Model* of Chen [Chen, 1976]. The objects in PCTE+ are not (complete) encapsulations of ADTs. An advantage is that the OMS of PCTE+ is already distributed amongst workstations in a network. It has to be investigated if it is possible to manipulate multi-dimensional data in an efficient manner. A disadvantage of a PCTE+ based implementation is that we have to switch completely to the PCTE+ concepts and will be tied to these concepts. Finally, the availability of PCTE+ may be a problem. It is not in the *public domain* and therefore we expect problems with the distribution of Procol.

We have decided to use the mapped memory approach for the prototype implementation of persistent objects in Procol. The main reasons were the expected efficiency of the approach and the provided synchrony between "stored" and "running" object instances.

An object instance is identified by a *surrogate* [Khoshafian and Copeland, 1986]. That is, the object id is not the actual address in memory but we need an indirection [Straw et al., 1989] to locate the object. See Figure 2 for a graphical demonstration of the process. Each surrogate contains an indication of whether the object instance is volatile, persistent or deleted. When, during the execution of a Procol program, an object is referenced, we have to check the first part of the surrogate. If the object instance is volatile, the surrogate contains a key than can be used to retrieve the memory address of the instance variables. If the object instance is persistent, the surrogate contains a dataset identifier, and a key. With this dataset identifier and the key, the OMS is able to retrieve the actual memory address of the instance variables of the persistent object in question.

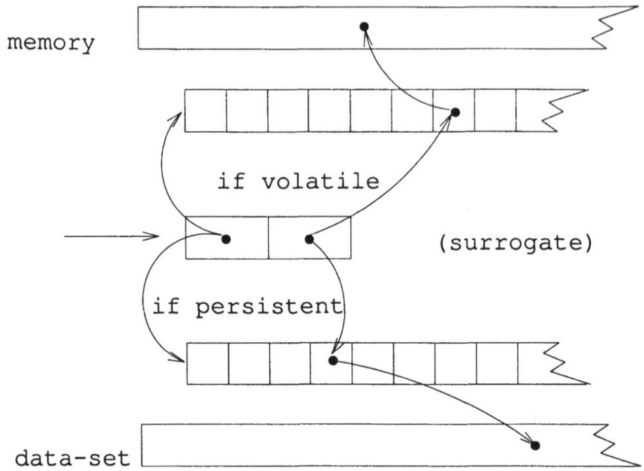

Figure 2: Object Reference with Surrogates

The disadvantage of surrogates is that there is an extra indirection. However, surrogates have several important advantages. They enable objects to be switched between volatile and persistent state, by modifying a part of the surrogate. We decided, based on the advantages and disadvantages mentioned in Section 5, that the control of referential integrity is not required in Procol. However, the use of illegal references is signalled at run-time. This is done by inspecting the surrogate and taking the appropriate measures.

If a persistent object contains a reference to a volatile object, this volatile object is not saved automatically. The proper way to program this case is to make the other object also persistent, if the referenced object is still needed in the future. The state of each object instance is stored as a unity, that is in contiguous memory. Instances of different sizes are no problem. The state also contains some additional data, for example the creator. The application programmer decides whether instances of the same object type are "stored together" without instances of other types in one dataset or if a dataset contains instances of different types. The later is advantageous for representing complex objects in an efficient manner, because the instances of the different types that define a complex object are stored close together.

10. Further Research

Procol is both an object-oriented programming language and a parallel programming language. It is possible that the objects run in parallel on multiple processors. We have only used this in a few examples. Clearly, this topic deserves more attention and more research is needed in the context of highly interactive and graphical systems.

It is a small step from one single user Procol program with persistent objects to a system with multiple users. At least conceptually, because each object has its own protocol which regulates the communication. It should not matter from which program a message originates. However, we will have to reconsider some of the concepts.

The query facilities provided are very limited; with *retrieve* it is only possible to get hold of one "starting" object id of a specified type or to perform the selection of instances from one set (object type) at a time. More complex queries have to be programmed into the objects (the Procol program). Attention has to be paid to prevent object types from becoming too specific. That is in contradiction with one of the basic principles of databases of data being independent of applications. More research in this area is necessary.

Appendix — The R-tree in Procol

This appendix contains the Procol code of the objects *R-TREE* and *R-NODE*, which together implement a persistent multi-dimensional index structure; see Section 6. In the case of a GIS with attributes such as points, lines and regions in the plane the dimension of the R-tree is two. A CAD system with solid objects, for example a polyhedron, will need a three dimensional R-tree. Higher dimensional R-trees are also possible, because in some applications it is beneficial to interpret a combination of *k* scalar attributes as one *k*-dimensional point attribute on which range queries may be formulated.

Not all the code is given here. This is indicated by three dots (...). Especially, some intricate parts of the insert and delete algorithms are omitted, but can be found in [Guttman, 1984]. The code is non-trivial because the tree has to be kept in balance under the insert and delete operations. The purpose of this appendix is to show how the R-tree is implemented in an object-oriented manner. We only showed one query type: the box select (in two dimensions
that is, a rectangle select), which returns the id of every object in the R-tree that overlaps the search box *sbox*. The result is sent back to the original object *sid* by invoking the action *InRegion* with the id of the found (graphical data) object. This happens once for each object that is found.

Note that we implemented a parallel or distributed version of the tree by using the object *R-NODE*. During the search operation several nodes can work in parallel on different processors. There is quite a bit of work in each node, because a typical value for *M* (maximum number of entries) is 100. This solution would probably not be very efficient for binary tree, because the overhead introduced by sending messages to other processors may require more time than the time that is gained by the parallel execution. Besides the search operation, the delete and insert operations might also benefit from parallel execution in case of node overflow and node underflow respectively. This is not shown in the code below.

```
#define DIM 2                                          /* or any other value > 1 */
#define LENGTH 256

typedef struct{
   ANY        id;                                      /* R-NODE or graphical object */
   float      box[DIM][2];
} EntryType;

----------------------------------------------------------------------------

OBJ            R-TREE (int m, int M, char dataset[LENGTH]);

Description    In R-tree literature m and M are the minimum and
               maximum number of entries per node. The tree is suited
               for DIM dimensions.
               Assumed is that just after the creation of the R-TREE,
               it made persistent by its creator in 'dataset'.

Declare        R-NODE         root, node;
               float          box[DIM][2], sbox[DIM][2];

Protocol       /* Assumption: The Add and Delete actions are          */
               /* invoked by the (graphical data) objects themselves and   */
```

```
              /* they send their correct minimal bounding box in box.      */
              ANY (box)   -> Add      +
              ANY (box)   -> Delete   +
              ANY (sbox)  -> Select

Init          root = NULL;

Actions       Add = {
                 if (root==NULL) {
                    new root(m, M, true);
                    persistent root in dataset;
                    root.EntryAdd(sender, box);
                 } else {
                    ...
                    new node(m, M, true);
                    persistent node in dataset;
                    ...
                 }
              }
              Delete = {
                 ...
                 /* If a (persistent) node is deleted, then this also      */
                 /* implies removal from the dataset                       */
                 ...
              }
              Select = { root.Search(sender, box); }
EndOBJ        R-TREE.

-----------------------------------------------------------------------------

OBJ           R-NODE (int m, int M, boolean leaf);

Description   m and M have same meaning as in R-TREE.
              If leaf has value true, then this node is a leaf,
              else this is an internal node.

Declare       float         box[DIM][2], sbox[DIM][2];
              ANY           id, sid;
              EntryType     entry[M];
              int           NrOfEntries, i;
              R-NODE        next;

Protocol      (NrOfEntries < M): R-TREE (id, box) -> EntryAdd    +
              (NrOfEntries > m): R-TREE (id, box) -> EntryDelete +
              R-TREE (sid, sbox)                  -> Search      +
              R-NODE (sid, sbox)                  -> Search      +
              R-TREE ()                           -> Full

Init          NrOfEntries = 0;

Actions       EntryAdd = {
                 /* Assumption: R-NODE is not full */
                 entry[NrOfEntries].box  = box; entry[NrOfEntries++].id = id;
              }
              EntryDelete = { ... }
              Full = { sender.(NrOfEntries==M); }
              Search = {
                 for (i = 0; i < NrOfEntries; i++)
                    if (overlap(sbox, entry[i].box)
                       if (leaf)
                          /* Return found object */
                  sid.InRegion(entry[i].id);
                  else { /* Propagate search to lower level */
                        /* This part of the code causes the parallelism */
                  next = entry[i].id;
                          next.Search(sid, sbox);
                       }
              }
EndOBJ        R-NODE.
```

References

Atkinson, M P and Buneman, O.P. (1987) "Types and persistence in database programming languages," *ACM Computing Surveys*, vol. 19, no 2 (June), 105-190

Bancilhon, F., Barbedette, G., Benzaken, V., Delobel, C., Gamerman, S., Lècluse, C., Pfeffer, P., Richard, P., and Velez, F. (1988) "The design and implementation of O2, an Object-Oriented database system," In *Advances in Object-Oriented Database Systems, 2nd International Workshop on Object-Oriented Database Systems*, Bad Munster am Stein-Ebernburg, FRG, pp. 1-22.

Bayer, R. and McCreight, E. (1973) "Organization and maintenance of large ordered indexes," *Acta Informatica*, vol. 1, 173-189.

Bentley, J.L (1975) "Multidimensional binary search trees used for associative searching," *Communications of the ACM*, vol. 18, no. 9 (September), 509-517.

Blake, E.H. and Cook, S. (1987) "On including part hierarchies in object-oriented languages, with an implementation in smalltalk," In: *ECOOP '87*, pp. 41-50.

Bos, J. van den (1989) "PROCOL· A protocol-constrained concurrent object-oriented language," *Information Processing Letters*, vol 32, no September, 221-227.

Bos, J van den and Laffra, C. (1989) "PROCOL - A parallel object language with protocols," In· *OOPSLA '89*, New Orleans, pp 95-102.

Chen, Peter Pin-Shan (1976) "The entity-relationship model - toward a unified view of data," *ACM Transactions on Database Systems*, vol. 1, no. 1 (March), 9-36.

Codd, E.F (1970) "A relational model of data for large shared data banks," *Communications of the ACM*, vol. 13, no. 6 (June), 377-387.

Comer, D. (1979) "The ubiquitous B-Tree," *ACM Computing Surveys*, vol. 11, no. 2 (June), 121-137.

Cox, B J (1986) *Object-Oriented Programming - An Evolutionary Approach*, Addison-Wesley, Reading, Mass..

Dietrich, W.C. (Jr.), Nackman, L.R., Sundaresan, C.J., and Gracer, F. (1989) "TGMS: An object-oriented system for programming geometry," *Software - Practice and Experience*, vol 19, no 10 (October), 979-1013.

Egenhofer, M. and Frank, A. (1989a) "Panda: An extensible DBMS supporting object-oriented software techniques," In. *Database Systems in Office, Engineering, and Scientific Environment*, Springer-Verlag, New York.

Egenhofer, M.J. and Frank, A.U. (1989b) "Object-oriented modeling in GIS· Inheritance and Propagation," In. *Auto-Carto 9*, Baltimore, pp. 588-598.

Faloutsos, C., Sellis, T., and Roussopoulos, N (1987) "Analysis of object oriented spatial access methods," *ACM SIGMOD*, vol. 16, no. 3 (December), 426-439

Frank, A U. (September 1988) "Multiple inheritance and genericity for the integration of a database management system in an Object-Oriented approach," In· *Advances in Object-Oriented Database Systems, 2nd International Workshop on Object-Oriented Database Systems*, Bad Münster am Stein-Ebernburg, FRG, pp. 268-273.

Frank, A U. and Barrera, R. (1989) "The fieldtree. A data structure for geographic information system," In: *Symposium on the Design and Implementation of Large Spatial Databases*, Santa Barbara, California. July

Greene, D (1989) "An implementation and performance analysis of spatial data access methods," In. *IEEE Data Engineering Conference*, pp. 606-615.

Günther, O (1988) "Efficient Structures for Geometric Data Management," *Number 337 in Lecture Notes in Computer Science*, Springer-Verlag, Berlin.

Guttman, A. (1984) "R-trees: A dynamic index structure for spatial searching," *ACM SIGMOD*, vol. 13, 47-57.

IEPG, Independent European Programme Group - Technical Area 13 (IEPG TA-13) (1988) *PCTE+ C Functional Specification*, vol. Issue 2.

Khoshafian, S.N. and Copeland, G P. (1986) "Object identity," In: *OOPSLA '86*, pp 406-416

Laffra, C. and Bos, J van den (1990) "A layered object oriented model for interaction," In: E.H. Blake and P. Wisskirchen (ed.) *Advances in Object Oriented Graphics I*, Springer-Verlag, Berlin.

Meyer, B. (1988) *Object-oriented Software Construction,* Prentice Hall, London.

Morrison, R., Florianis, A.L., Dearle, A., and Atkinson, M.P. (1986) "An integrated graphics programming environment," *Computer Graphics Forum,* vol. 5, 147-157.

Oosterom, P. van (1988) "Spatial data structures in Geographic Information Systems," In: *NCGA's Mapping and Geographic Information Systems,* Orlando, Florida, pp. 104-118. September

Oosterom, P. van (1989) "A Reactive Data Structure for Geographic Information Systems," In: *Auto-Carto 9,* Baltimore, pp. 665-674. April

Oosterom, P. van and Bos, J. van den (1989) "An object-oriented approach to the design of Geographic Information Systems," *Computers & Graphics,* vol. 13, no. 4, 409-418.

Oosterom, P. van and Claassen, E. (1990) "Orientation insensitive indexing methods for geometric objects," In: *4th International Symposium on Spatial Data Handling,* Zürich, Switzerland. July

Oosterom, P. van, Hekken, M. van, and Woestenburg, M. (1989) "A geographic extension to the relational data model," In: *Geo '89 Symposium,* The Hague. October

Paton, N.W. and Gray, P.M.D. (1988) "Identification of database objects by key," In. *Advances in Object-Oriented Database Systems, 2nd International Workshop on Object-Oriented Database Systems,* Bad Münster am Stein-Ebernburg, FRG, pp. 280-285. September

Penney, D.J. and Stein, J. (1987) "Class modification in the GemStone Object-Oriented DBMS," In: *OOPSLA'87,* pp 111-117

Richardson, J E and Carey, M J (1989) "Persistence in the E language: Issues and implementation," *Software - Practice and Experience,* vol. 19, no. 12 (December), 1115-1150

Roessel, J.W. van (1987) "Design of a spatial data structure using the relational normal forms," *International Journal of Geographical Information Systems,* vol 1, no. 1, 33-50.

Samet, H. (1984) "The quadtree and related hierarchical data structures," *Computing Surveys,* vol. 16, no. 2 (June), 187-260.

Stonebraker, M. and Rowe, L.A (1986) "The design of POSTGRES," *ACM SIGMOD,* vol. 15, no. 2, 340-355.

Straw, A., Mellender, F., and Riegel, S. (1989) "Object management in a persistent smalltalk system," *Software - Practice and Experience,* vol. 19, no. 8 (August), 719-737.

Sun Microsystems Inc. (1987) *SunINGRES Manual Set.*

Tsichritzis, D.C. and Nierstrasz, O.M. (1988) "Fitting round objects into square databases," In: *ECOOP '88,* pp 283-299. August

Weinand, A , Gamma, E., and Marty, R (1989) "Design and implementation of ET++, a seamless object-oriented application framework," *Structured Programming,* vol. 10, no. 2, 63-87.

Wiederhold, G. (1986) "Views, objects, and databases," *IEEE Computer,* no. December, 37-44.

Wolf, A. (1989) "The DASDBS GEO-Kernel, concepts, experiences and the second step," In: *Symposium on the Design and Implementation of Large Spatial Databases,* Santa Barbara, California.

7

Retrospective Creation of Virtual Alternative Hierarchies

Jan Rogier and Daan Otten

In this chapter we present an object-oriented strategy to support the creation of *geometric models*. These models are represented as *part-whole hierarchies* of objects. Creation of new models is done by copying and modifying previously existing models or parts of them. Past models are stored in the system's database and serve as *prototypes* for the new models. To support the selection of an appropriate prototype the system provides a view on its database presenting an *is-a hierarchy* of *object type definitions* that depends on:

- the currently available models in the system's database,
- a *functional specification* that represents the designer's intentions, and
- a set of *definitions* that are used by the system to interpret a functional specification.

From the hierarchy the user can either select an object type definition that might serve as a *template* for a new part or select one of the past models from which an object type definition originates. Since the 'is-a' hierarchy of object type definitions only exists virtually, is moreover directly controlled by the user and is highly flexible, as well as providing alternative hierarchies presenting alternative views on the system's database, we call our approach 'Virtual Hierarchies Creation in Retrospect'.

1. Introduction

We are currently developing a design system as part of a research project on intelligent CAD [Veth, 1987]. The feature that will be discussed in this chapter concerns the structure and use of the database of our design system for the reuse of existing models. The system's database has a twofold purpose. Firstly, it is used to make models persistent, i.e., to store models and their relations which last beyond a program session. Secondly, it provides a mechanism to browse through the models in the database. Selected models can be used to create new models. The basis of our design system is a strategy called *extensional decomposition* [Rogier, 1991] and the use of *standard vocabularies* and *standard components*. Essentially, extensional decomposition is a design strategy that views every object as a set of components which are also objects in themselves. This is elaborated in Section 3.1. As regards the first purpose of our database, the system's database stores and maintains models as part-whole structures that result from the use of extensional decomposition. For the second purpose of the database, selected models from the database are organized in an 'is-a' hierarchy of object type definitions. From this hierarchy the user can select a single definition, modify it and use it as template [Lieberman, 1986] for creating or detailing the new model. Comparison of models is based on their extensional decomposition structure and the use of standard vocabularies and standard components.

The creation of an 'is-a' hierarchy of object type definitions is based on i) the models in the database, ii) a description of what the user wants concerning the object to be designed (called a *functional specification*), and iii) a set of definitions that are stored in the system and are used for the interpretation of a functional specification. The user has three means to influence the organization of object type definitions in a hierarchy:

a. Modification of the functional specification. Based on the functional specification the system selects a set of models that minimally meet the specification. All extra data with each model can be considered to be the specialization of the functional specification and is used to form the hierarchy of object type definitions.

b. Manipulation of the set of definitions used by the system to interpret both functional specification and past models. We make a distinction between two types of definitions: i) *categories*, being sets of standard components, and ii) *scenarios*, being sets of requirements for object types. The total set of definitions that is applied by the system is manually controlled by the user by declaring which definitions are 'active'. The current set of definitions will influence the interpretation of the functional specification and therefore influence the order of the hierarchy.

c. Controlling the effect of the constraints over properties. Scenarios also include constraints on physical properties of objects. These properties are organized in so-called *aspects*. Controlling the effect of constraints by making it possible to ignore, that is, deactivate, aspects will influence the contents of the selected set of past components. In turn this will influence the hierarchical order in the object type definitions.

The chapter is organized as follows. Section 2 describes the background to our system and gives a short description of the design strategies of the group of designers we are aiming at. In Section 3, the basis of our system, viz. extensional decomposition, standard vocabularies and standard components, is elaborated. Section 4 describes the architecture and the basis elements of our system. In Section 5, the way the system works is explained. It describes the selection of prototypes and the creation of the virtual hierarchy and template. In Section 6, a comparison with class-based object-oriented systems is made. Section 7 contains a summary and conclusions.

2. Background

The current generation of design systems take generic characteristics of specific classes of design objects as a basis for the structure of the system. They use a fixed reference model for a certain type of design object. This reference model is created by the designer of the system instead of by the user. Apart from the fact that it introduces a problem of miscommunication between system designer and user, this approach ignores the fact that i) generalization of characteristics is based on concrete examples and ii) reference models evolve in time. The limitations of such a system can only be removed by changing it fundamentally. The main reason is that the reference model forms an integral part of the system's structure. Instead of being of use as a supporting tool, systems that use a fixed reference model as an integral part of their structure dictates their view on a class of objects to a user. As a result a user can only work within the boundaries set by the system.

According to Bijl's view on a system's role in design [Bijl, 1987], a system should not specify the boundaries within which a user has to design. The user should be free to use the system to design anything he wants with it. For this reason we took an approach where the user can create his own reference models based on what was previously designed with the system.

We identify three approaches taken by the user in which past models play an important role in the design process. These approaches are based on the identification via context, association and generalization.

a. With the first approach a user identifies a prototype based on its *context*. Identification takes place by referring directly to a past model. This approach is adequate as long as the number of models in the system is relatively small. It is often taken by users who do not have much experience or practice in a broad application field. Identification from context is supported by our database structure. No special tools are required to apply this approach. Applying it in fact results in copying and modifying an existing design object description. Due to the limitations of currently available design systems, this approach is often practiced manually.

b. The second identification approach is based on *association*. In this case the user wants to associate the current design problem with a previous one, but does not know exactly which previous model. First, he builds a functional specification of the current design problem. Then this specification is applied to all past models and produces a set of comparable models. From this set the user selects the most appropriate model which will serve as a template for the specification of the new model. According to Yoshikawa [Yoshikawa, 1981] this approach forms the basis of the design process.

c. The third approach is comparable to the previous one. However, in this case the user does not select a single model from a set but uses the whole set to construct a template. The template describes all generic properties of a certain type of object based on what the designer has stored in the system's database.

Our system aims at users that apply the following design strategy.

1. The user creates an initial functional specification.
2. The user specifies the criteria which should be applied by the system to interpret the functional specification in order to compose a set of comparable past models.
3. The user gets the database to search for past models that match the functional specification and to organize them based on their extra data. As a result a hierarchy is created that has the initial functional specification as the root and contains all selected models as specializations.
4. The user looks for a specialization in the hierarchy that will help him further detail the functional specification until he gets one that fully meets his intentions.
5. The user then repeats the steps from step 2.

3. The Basis of the Design System

The basis of our design system is extensional decomposition and the application of standard vocabularies and standard components.

3.1. Extensional Decomposition

Extensional decomposition is a design strategy that views every object as a set of components which are objects themselves. With the term *extensional* we want to emphasize that every component has two different identities. It has an identity as a unique entity and it has an identity as a set of components. These two identities have to be viewed independently. The essence of this twofold identity is explained with an example.

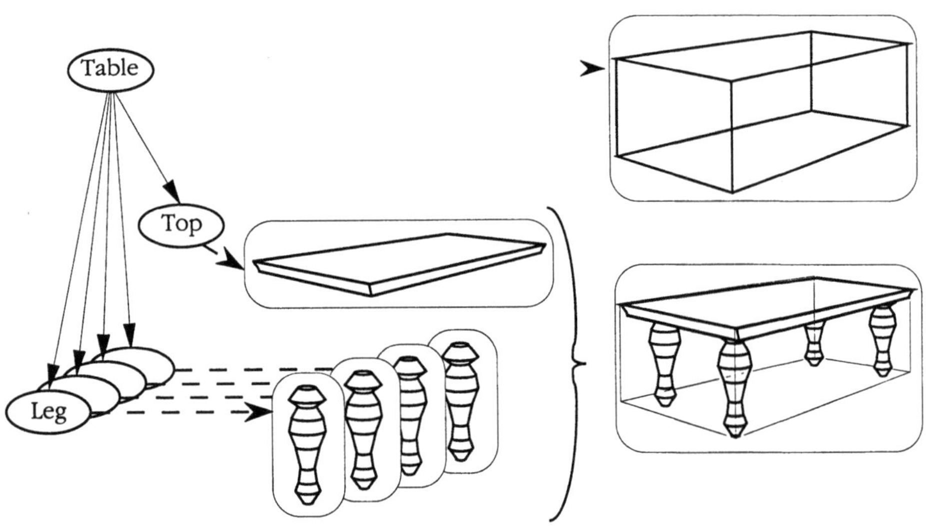

Figure 1: Twofold identity of a component

Figure 1 gives a rough impression of what we mean with a twofold identity. The table has a geometry that on its own level describes its rough shape as a block form, with a height, a width and a length. This shape describes the space that is occupied by the table. Apart from this, it has a shape that is a composition of the shapes of its components. Although the shape of both identities are probably related, they in fact exist independently. The height of a table may be defined as a value that should be equal to the sum of the length of its leg(s) and the thickness of its top. From a declarative point of view however, the height of a table may be the actual intended height. The other two values may be derived from descriptions of standard parts. Extensional decomposition puts the emphasis on the *incompatibility* of these values. This incompatibility between an attribute of a model and the attributes of its components are observed by the system. However in contrast to expert systems, the system does not change the functional specification but only notifies the user.

3.2. Standard Vocabularies

Standard vocabularies are sets of terms used to define aspects of an object (compare Wilson and Kennicot [Wilson and Kennicot, 1987]). They are used i) to support the process of declaring different aspects of an object, ii) as an intermediary to exchange data between different external applications, and iii) as a basis for comparison of models based on their properties.

3.3. Standard Components

Standard components are the primitive objects which define the lowest level of detail considered by a designer. Standard components are categorized. For instance, for an architect building a house, categories might be doors, windows and walls. For a construction engineer a wall itself is built up from more detailed components and is therefore not a standard component.

4. The Basic Elements of Our System

4.1. The System's Environment

The architecture of our design system is one that contains a kernel modeller that communicates with a number of external, independently operating, special purpose applications (see Figure 2).

Data exchange between the kernel and applications is simplified by using standardized languages for different aspects. Such languages are vocabularies of terms. In our approach we make these vocabularies independent entities and establish explicit links between the terms in the model and the terms in these vocabularies. This approach has the advantage that both vocabularies and models can easily be extended.

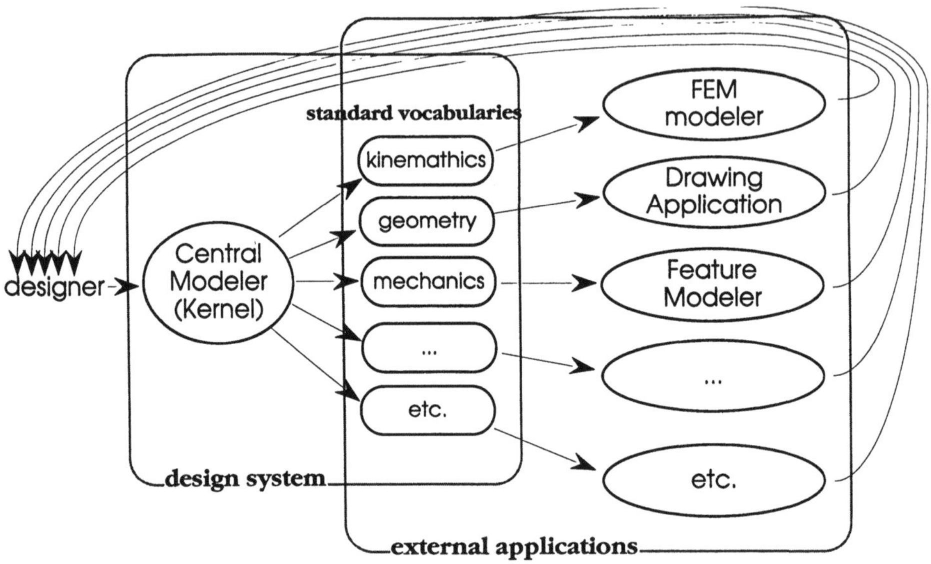

Figure 2: The kernel modeller in its environment

4.2. Basic Primitives

Applying extensional decomposition leads to a part-whole structure of component descriptions. For the description of each single component we use the same basic primitive. Each object is described with a *set of attributes* (see Figure 3). Values of attributes can be of three different types. Firstly, they can be *constants*, e.g., when one wants to describe the height of an object. Secondly, they can be *references to other components*. These attributes are used to describe the 'has-part' relations between objects. Thirdly, they can be *references to mathematical expressions*.

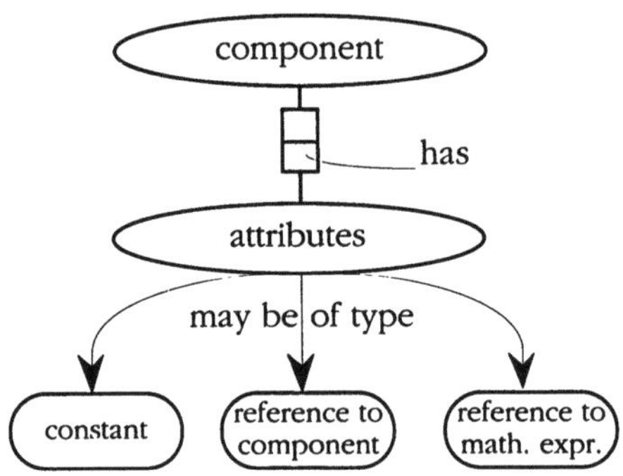

Figure 3: Basic data structure

References to mathematical expressions are used to describe the dependency relations between constants. They contain a reference to a *term* and a *mapping list*. A term is part of a *standard vocabulary*. The mapping list describes the mapping between each of the local attributes of a term and local attributes of the component. A standard vocabulary itself contains all terms used to describe an *aspect* (see Figure 4).

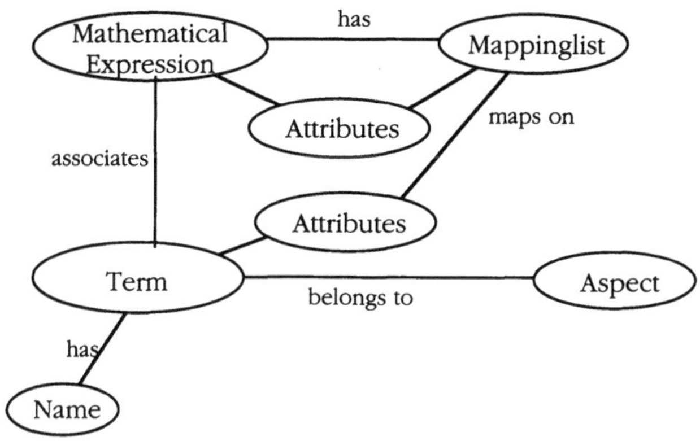

Figure 4: Basic data structure of dependency reference

4.3. Aspects, Categories and Scenarios

Aspects, categories and scenarios are the implementational counterparts of vocabularies of terms, sets of standard components and functional specifications, respectively. Categories may be specified as sets of other categories. Scenarios use the names of aspects and categories or other scenarios to define the requirements of object types. These requirements constrain the number of parts or the physical properties of an object.

5. The System's Operation

The system uses a functional specification to select and organize a part of the database. A functional specification is described by a scenario. It has a twofold purpose. On one hand, it is used to describe the user's intentions with the new object being designed. On the other hand it is used to select and organize items in the system's database. These two roles may be in conflict. The simplest example is when a functional specification is so accurate a description of the new object being designed that no items in the database meet all requirements. However, the second purpose of this functional specification is to collect as much data as possible from the system's database to simplify the declaration process. Although components may not exist that fully meet the constraints specified by the functional specification, there may be enough items that will partly meet them and contain valuable information. To facilitate identification of these components, modifying the functional specification itself is not allowed since this is in conflict with its first purpose.

For its second purpose the functional specification should be interpreted more globally. This requires mechanisms that control the interpretation of functional specifications.

One mechanism will interpret the functional specification to *select* a set of appropriate components in the database. The other mechanism serves to *organize* object type definitions into a hierarchy. Because these hierarchies present merely a view on the database, we call them virtual hierarchies.

5.1. Virtual Hierarchies

We define a virtual hierarchy as one that is generated according to a functional specification applied to models in a database. A virtual hierarchy serves to create a template for the specification of a new component that will become part of the current model. Such a template describes a type of object, and includes all generic properties of a small set of comparable past models.

An object type definition is written in a scenario. Such a scenario contains rules that constrain the number of parts of specific types and the boundaries of other properties. To identify an object we say that an object belongs to a type if it at least meets the constraints in the scenario. Although an object may not exceed the boundaries set by the scenario it may however contain properties which are not mentioned in such a scenario. So if a table is an object that has a single top with at least one and at most four legs, a desk is 'a-kind-of' table because it meets these constraints even though it has drawers.

5.2. The Creation of a Virtual Hierarchy

The process of creating a virtual hierarchy of object type definitions (see Figure 5) is subdivided into two steps.

1. A set of components is selected that meets the functional specification as interpreted according to the selection criteria.
2. This set is transformed into a hierarchy of object type definitions based on the data about extra parts. Objects with different numbers of the same type of parts result in subtypes at the same specialization level, extra parts result in object types at a lower specialization level. In our example the desk is a subtype at a lower specialization level of the table because it contains extra parts not mentioned in the object type definition of a table.

We shall now discuss the steps in more detail.

5.2.1. Step 1

Selection of a set of appropriate components is done with a functional specification which is interpreted by the system using certain criteria. All components in the database that minimally meet the constraints in this functional specification are selected. A functional specification is a scenario. It contains two types of constraints: constraints on physical properties and constraints on part properties.

a. Constraints on physical properties set boundaries for values of attributes of components. They are specified by i) a link with a term in an aspect vocabulary, and ii) constraining the local attributes of the term. When a constraint is applied to a past model the system will first look for the term linkage and then, based on the

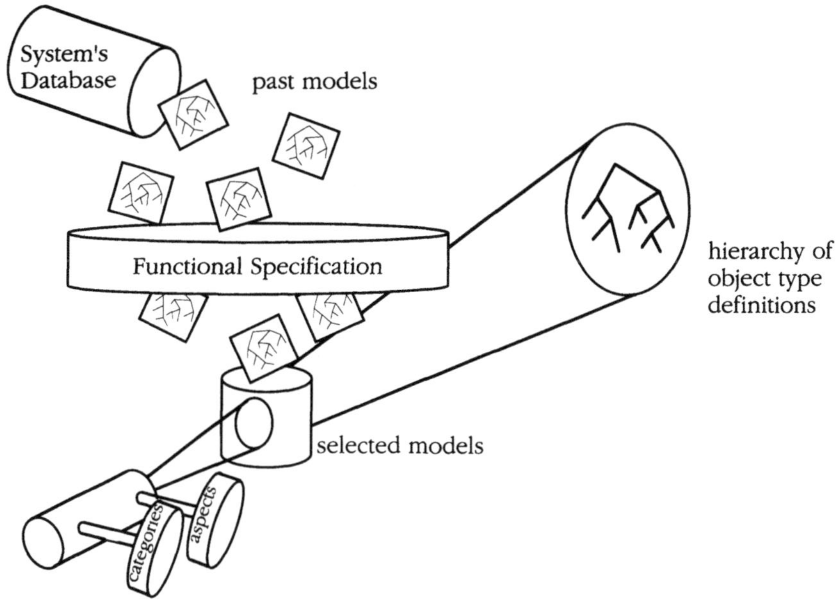

Figure 5: Creation of a virtual hierarchy of object type definitions

mapping list that is associated with this model, compare the value of a model attribute with a range that is specified in the constraint.

b. Constraints on part properties specify the type of a part and set boundaries on the number of parts of this type. The type is specified by using names of categories or object type definitions (other scenarios). Therefore, to evaluate whether a component belongs to a certain type, it requires a process which evaluates whether its parts belong to the types in the scenario. This is a recursive process of type checking that boils down to verifying whether standard component parts belong to mentioned categories — the predefined sets of standard components.

The interpretation of the functional specification is controlled by activation of aspects and categories. Deactivating an aspect leads to constraints on physical properties in object type definitions being ignored. This results in the selection of a larger set of components that meet the requirements of object type definitions. The relevance of this possibility can be illustrated with imagining a situation whereby a doll's house should play a role in detailing a floor plan for a real house. A doll's house will probably not meet the measurement requirements of a real house. Making the aspect 'geometrical-measurement' inactive however will make the doll's house selectable.

Deactivation of categories will lead to a more global interpretation of them. When a scenario (i.e., an object type definition) refers to a category that is marked 'inactive', the system will collect all standard components that belong to those categories that refer to this inactive scenario. For instance, we want to make a functional specification on a dwelling with one study and one bedroom. Assume beds and desks, which distinguishes studies from bedrooms, are subcategories of a category furniture. Deactivating the category desks, will make the scenario of a study able to select a bedroom. This will make a house with two bedrooms meet the constraints in the functional specification.

5.2.2. Step 2

A hierarchy of object type definitions is based on the comparison of all extra data with respect to the functional specification of the set of selected components. The comparison is based on the identification of the type of these parts. As more than one type can match a part, identification of the type results in a set of appropriate types. The system will then look for the type of part that is referenced by most models. This type is used to subdivide the set of selected models into subsets based on the number of parts of this type. This type defines the first level in the subtype hierarchy. Each subtype is then further subdivided. The process stops when the description of all elements in a subset matches in detail or when a subset contains a single element.

5.3. Use of the Virtual Hierarchy: Creation of a Template

Selecting an object type definition in the virtual hierarchy by the user results in the creation of a template. The process of creating a template is subdivided in the following steps.

1. All components that has led to the creation of the selected type definition are first collected.
2. A template is created that contains the initial part-whole structure as described by the selected type definition. It uses default names for all parts (names of attributes only have a local purpose and can always be modified by the user).
3. This template is extended with the attributes mentioned in the scenario, e.g., attributes like the height, width and depth of our new table.
4. It is also extended with the terms mentioned in the scenario, e.g., the block shape of the table.
5. All attributes linked to the selected terms will next be added, with arbitrary names (a composition of all the names of attributes as used in the different items in the selected set). For instance, any block has a volume and surfaces. Therefore when these are mentioned in one or more of the selected models, they will be added to the template.
6. As the attributes added in (5) might be used to refer to other aspects in a model, the terms in these aspects will also be included in the template.

   After this, step 5 and 6 will be re-executed until the sets of attributes and terms are not longer extended. For instance, when the length and width of a model are used for strength calculation then terms concerning kinematic aspects are added.

Note that the template stays interactive in a sense that removal of parts or attributes will lead to removal of dependencies.

6. Relation with Object-Oriented Systems

Object type definitions in our system can be compared with classes in class-based object-oriented systems [Borning, 1986; Lieberman, 1986]. Both systems provide a method to modularize and organize data and to support the creation of new objects. However, there are some major differences:

a. In class based object-oriented systems there is a notion that enough information is available beforehand to define a class for a group of objects. Each individual object can be created by instantiation of the class. In our system, every instance is an autonomous entity whose properties might become part of an object type definition. The reason to apply this approach is that in our case the object is defined incrementally so that an object type definition cannot be given beforehand.

b. Class based systems assume that it is possible to create a unambiguous specialization/generalization hierarchy of classes. In our system, it is not possible to define a single specialization/generalization hierarchy. Firstly, the hierarchical order is dependent on an evolving database. Secondly, it is based on a functional specification whose interpretation is controlled by the user and therefore can lead to several alternative hierarchical organizations. The reason we took this approach is that the hierarchical order plays an important role in the identification of the intended object type.

c. In class based systems, the use of subclassing determines which properties of the superclass are inherited. In our system we decided that the user should choose which properties of the object type definition are actually inherited. The reason for this choice is that, even in the case where the system provides a suitable object type definition, this might not completely reflect the users intentions. It must therefore be modifiable.

7. Summary and Conclusion

In this chapter we discussed a method for creating an 'is-a' hierarchical view on a set of elements in a database that has a part-whole structure. The reason for creating such a view is that we would like to use an 'is-a' hierarchy to identify objects according to their type. In our view this plays an important role in design. Our design system supports a design strategy based on extensional decomposition. As a result the system's database has a part-whole structure. An essential item in applying a design strategy based on extensional decomposition however, is the selection of prototype objects based on a functional specification. The appropriateness of our design strategy can be deduced from a diversity of other design theories. There is the work of Yoshikawa [Yoshikawa, 1981] on his general design theory, and the work of Gielingh [Gielingh, 1988] on Product Modelling. Design strategies as described by Alexander [Alexander, 1964], Eastman [Eastman, 1987], Gero [Gero et al., 1985] or Brown and Chandrasekaran [Brown and Chandrasekaran, 1985] also contain elements that justify our strategy.

We identified a functional specification with an object type definition. Type definitions however can be structured in 'is-a' hierarchies rather than 'part-whole' hierarchies of object data. Considering the structure of our database this made us look for a mechanism to transform a 'part-whole' hierarchy into an 'is-a' hierarchy for the purpose of supporting the declaration of elements which should become part of a 'part-whole' hierarchy. This chapter described the mechanism we have developed to this purpose. Using Yoshikawa's terminology we make a distinction between a functional (constraint based) and a attributive (product based) specification. Our system transforms existing attributive specifications into prototype attributive specifications by means of a functional specification as an intermediary.

On the basis of a functional specification we make a selection from a set of components that belong to the system's database. Based on their part-data, these components are generalized to object types. The set of types is organized into a hierarchy. The structure of this hierarchy is controlled by the user who manipulates the interpretation criteria of the system. From a hierarchy of object type definitions the user selects a single one. This leads to the creation of a template that is used for a prototype attributive specification.

The transformation of a part-whole hierarchy into an is-a hierarchy takes place *virtually*. We only present a view on an existing database with components which are existing objects. This view also only exists for the purpose of creating a single template and exists only during this process. This makes it *volatile*. To select the most appropriate template the user is free to manipulate the interpretations of the functional specification that lies above the hierarchy of object type definitions. He is able to create a number of *alternative* hierarchies based on the same specification. We call our approach 'Virtual Hierarchies Creation in Retrospect'.

References

Alexander, C. (1964) *Notes on the synthesis of form,* Harvard University Press, Cambridge, Massachusetts.

Bijl, A. (1987) *Strategies for CAD,* pp. 2-19, Springer Verlag, Berlin.

Borning, A.H. (1986) "Classes versus prototypes in object-oriented languages," In: H.S. Stone and S. Winkler (ed.) *1986 Proceedings Fall Joint Computer Conference,* IEEE Computer Society Press, Washington, D.C., pp. 36-47.

Brown, D.C. and Chandrasekaran, B. (1985) *Expert system for a class of mechanical design activity,* pp. 17-19, North Holland, Amsterdam, The Netherlands.

Eastman, C M. (1987) "Prototype integrated building model," *Computer Aided Design,* Butterworth-Heinemann, vol. 12, no. 3, 115-119.

Gero, J S., Radford, A.D., Coyne, R., and Akiner, V.T. (1985) "Knowledge-Based Computer Aided Architectural Design," In· Gero, J.S (ed) *1984 Proceedings of IFIP WG 5 2 Working Conference on Knowledge Engineering in Computer Aided Design,* North Holland, Amsterdam.

Gielingh, W.F. (1988) "General AEC Reference Model (GARM)," Report by TNO-IBBC, Rijswijk. October

Lieberman, H. (1986) "Using Prototypical Objects to Implement Shared Behavior in object- oriented Systems," In: Meyrowitz, N (ed.) *Object-Oriented Programming Systems, Languages and Applications,* ACM Press, New York, pp. 214-223.

Rogier, J (1991) "A Component Class for Design," In: Veerkamp P. and Ten Hagen P. (ed.) *Intelligent CAD systems 3 Practical experience and evaluation,* Springer-Verlag, Berlin. forthcoming

Veth, B (1987) "An Integrated Data Description Language for Coding Design Knowledge," In: Ten Hagen, P.J W. and Tomiyama, T. (ed) *Intelligent CAD Systems I: Theoretical and Methodological Aspects,* Springer Verlag, Berlin.

Wilson P. and Kennicot, P.R (1987) *STEP/PDES Testing Draft,* St Louis Edition 4 1.2, St Louis, U.S A..

Yoshikawa, H. (1981) "General Design Theory and a CAD System," In: Sata, T. and Warman, E. (ed.) *Man and Machine Communication in CAD/CAM,* North Holland, pp. 35-57.

8

Coordinate Frames and Geometric Approximation in Graphics Object-Oriented Programming

John R. Rankin and Jonathan Burns‡

Coordinate transformations and coordinate systems are introduced as an object class. Finite point sets are considered as objects with internal constraints, communicating through point identifications. A geometric approximation algorithm for curve intersection based on a generic nearest-point method for curves is explored. The method is guaranteed to find an intersection point or nearest approach, depending on the starting point and specified precision. Convergence properties of the algorithm have been proved, and demonstrated in implementation. Intersection problems are thus made independent of object type, without the need for explicit algebraic solutions.

1. Topics Addressed

In this chapter we attempt to apply the concepts of Object-Oriented Programming to geometric problem solving. The principal geometric classes involved are coordinate systems and constrained systems of points or real variables. These classes hide the algebraic details of their implementations from the caller. The first practical result of this is a polymorphic intersection method relying on the possession of a generic nearest-point method by a general class of curves.

1.1. Object-Oriented Design

We begin by recognizing four identifiable levels of structure:

1. Bodies
2. Geometric figures

---

‡ This chapter combines work towards a Ph.D. by Burns with practical results by both authors.

3. Systems of equations

4. Discrete data structures

Entities on each level are *represented* by entities on levels below. Within a level, entities are related by *inheritance* (the 'is-a' relation) and *composition* (the part-whole relation).

Procedural and stream programming concepts are appropriate to the pipelined nature of graphic display, and we should also leave the way open to relational (that is, equational and logic) programming. The Smalltalk concept of a message protocol should also be expanded to include special-purpose mini-languages which may be inherited in a class hierarchy. Plurality and structure will then be expressed by replacing abstract collection classes with functional mini-languages which operate on collections at all levels.

1.2. Constraints

Geometry (inferential and analytic) includes *constructions*, which are geometric functions, and *theorems*, which are identities between constructions. The critical distinction is between constraints, i.e. equations, which imply no direction of dependency between variables, and procedures, in which dependency is explicit. We need a semantics for constraint programming in which constraints are imposed and released on collections of objects, and interrogated for specific controlflow directionality. Abelson and Sussman [Abelson and Sussman, 1985] discuss this in the context of Scheme.

Constraint programming has been put to use in geometric modelling. For instance we have Zeltzer's dissertation [Zeltzer, 1984] on the animation of articulate skeletons. Alan Borning's ThingLab shows the usefulness of constraints in constructing interactive computer graphics [Borning, 1981; Borning, 1979].

1.3. Continuity and Approximation

Some questions are: what general properties of constraints can be encapsulated in a general constraint class? Can a compound figure preserve its significant internal relations at run-time by tracking its constraints? How much of the tracking process must be performed at run-time, and how much can be compiled?

Our current work investigates the efficiency of simple geometric approximations in finding intersections of curves, which may generalize to n-dimensional space. Since a constraint in a continuous system is a surface in the system's configuration space, this suggests a general constraint satisfaction method which need only be primed with a few geometric algorithms to track constrained systems for which there is no hope of closed-form parameterization.

1.4. Coordinate Systems

Geometric figures are represented algebraically by assigning a coordinate tuple to the figure configuration. Tuple-to-tuple functions realize figure-to-figure transformations (active transformations), or change of coordinate frame (passive transformations). Generally, tuple, figure, and frame form a triad in which any of these elements can be fixed, allowing a second to be expressed as a function of the third.

Using this notation as a language for representations, we can encapsulate the triad. So for instance, a point-constellation contains a frame reference which can be inherited by derived instances of the same class, or a new frame can be derived from a body moving with respect to an existing frame. This provides a useful basis for articulated-figure systems and user interface mechanisms.

2. Classes of the Present Design

The original intention of this work was "to design a geometry-oriented language" for the succinct expression of geometric algorithms. This led to designing geometric figure classes as abstract data types, with their coordinate representations mostly hidden as method implementations. At present, the following classes are contemplated.

2.1. Body Classes

Bodies are specialized entities to be packaged for different high-level purposes: CAD, animation etc. They will not be discussed further here.

2.2. Geometric Classes

Geometric objects denote geometric figures. We should be able talk about a point instance P as if it were the true point which it denotes. Geometric functions and identities can thus be invariant while representations and coordinate frames change. They constitute a body of reusable software for generating new calculations.

2.3. Collection Classes

A 'Collection class' in say Smalltalk, is an abstract data type which hides the type of objects in the collection, leaving a protocol for adding, deleting and extracting members. We propose that collection protocols be Lisp or APL functions, passed to an interpreter. These functions will operate on collections, producing new collections.

Having defined basic storage and retrieval methods for a collection, one can build functions to read or rewrite it in many different ways: reversed, or for a matrix transposed, or for a tree in preorder or postorder. Likewise, a collection function may take as argument a function to be applied to the element type, to implement masking, mapping and so on. This substitutes in many cases for clumsy ways of specifying iteration and recursion.

2.4. Coordinate Frame Classes

Coordinate frames are the primary mechanism of algebraic representation, relating geometric figures to real variable sets (tuples). Frames defining point coordinates are the most obvious kind, since most other figures are developed from points. But the degrees of freedom of compound figures define their configuration spaces, and these can also be given frames.

To see how frames connect the geometric and algebraic levels, consider the following notation:

x represents a numeric tuple

f represents a frame

x/f represents the point which in f has coordinates x

p represents a point

$f \cdot p$ represents the coordinates of p in f

By definition,

$$f \cdot (x/f) = x$$

$$(f \cdot p)/f = p$$

Given two frames f and f',

$$p = x/f = x'/f'$$

so that:

$$x' = f' \cdot (x/f),$$

which we will write as $f' \cdot x/f$ (no meaning is imputed to the expression $f' \cdot x$).

Define f'/f as the function:

$$f'/f := x \rightarrow f' \cdot x/f$$

This defines a passive transformation: the passive role is taken by the coordinates, the active by the frame, while the point is neutral or pivotal.

Likewise, for the same two frames,

$$x = f \cdot p = f' \cdot p'$$

$p' = (f \cdot p)/f'$, which we write as $f \cdot p/f'$

Define $f//f'$ as the function

$$f//f' := p \rightarrow f \cdot p/f'$$

The coordinates of p' in f are given by

$$f \cdot p' = f \cdot (f//f' p)$$

$$= f \cdot (f//f' x/f)$$

This defines an active transformation: the coordinates in the respective frames are unchanged, but the point moves with the frame. But the coordinates of the new point in the old frame are different.

It is easy to prove existence of identity and inverses, and associativity for f'/f and $f//f'$ functions by composition. So we get:

$$\begin{aligned} f \cdot p' &= f \cdot ((f \cdot p)/f') \\ &= f/f' f \cdot p \\ &= f/f' x \end{aligned}$$

Thus the coordinates of the new point in the active transformation are derived by a function f/f' which is the inverse of the passive transformation f'/f.

We can now denote:

frames, e.g.

C for a base cartesian point frame

transformations

$\mathbf{T}_a = \mathbf{x} \rightarrow \mathbf{x} + \mathbf{a}$ for a translation

frames as 'products' of frames and transformations

$$\mathbf{C}_a = \mathbf{T}_a \mathbf{C}$$

transformations as 'quotients' of frames

$$\mathbf{T}_a = \mathbf{C}_a / \mathbf{C}$$

This allows considerable flexibility. For instance, for the active transformation which rotates all points an angle 5 about a point a, we can write

$$Rotate(\mu, a) = T(-a) \cdot C/P \cdot \left[(r, \phi) \rightarrow (r, \phi + \mu) \right] \cdot P/C \cdot T(a)$$

where $T(a)$ is a translation and P is the polar coordinate system on the same origin as C.

The development so far is functional; storage has not entered the picture. What storage attributes, methods and protocol should we expect of a frame object?

We have attempted to answer this by making a class of transform objects in C++, which package functions of type f'/f with their inverses. Tuple objects, of type x, are simply lists of reals. A frame object f consists of pointers to a parent frame f' and a transform f/f'. A point object is a tuple x plus a pointer to a native frame f.

Frames thus comprise a tree, the root being a base frame with no parent. There is a path through the tree between any two frames, so the non-native coordinates $f' \cdot p$ of any point can be calculated by successively evaluating transforms along the path.

Transform instances generally have instance variables parameterizing the transform, e.g., the vector **a** for a translation $T(\mathbf{a})$. Frames may be moved relative to their parents by changing the parameters. We have thus left the functional description above in favour of one which is partly assignment-based; so that the value of an expression such as $f' \cdot p$ depends on the assignment history of the frames along the path.

Regrettable as it is to forfeit referential transparency, this leads to a very practical system. Points are effectively attached to their native frames; we can move them by reassigning their coordinates, and also move the frames to which they are attached. It is then easy to model rigid bodies and mobile camera objects as frames, with cameras mapping between their parent frames and the screen. The commonest kind of frame is (or rather derives from the base frame as) a set of cartesian axes along a set of orthonormal base vectors. It is endowed with methods for translation and rotation relative to its parent. For practical purposes it is the equivalent of a Logo turtle: a point with orientation and a local scale.

An immediate benefit is the encapsulation of vector and matrix calculations. Rather than instantiating vectors and matrices to perform a geometric calculation, one instantiates frames and asks them for point coordinates. This makes for succinct programming, as we have found by writing out some standard geometric algorithms using frames. These include: the Graham scan for convex hull of a set of points in two dimensions; the usual inside-outside test for simple polygons; and the 'concavity tree' for a simple polygon, which makes the inside-outside test more efficient. With frame objects stationed along the edges of a polygon or spline, collision warning and detection are simple extensions of the above. The algorithm returning the nearest point on a polyline to a given point, crucial for the Rankin intersection method discussed below, is also elegantly expressible with cartesian frames.

In the present system, frames are created, and interrogated for point coordinates, at run time. There would be great gains in efficiency however, if a frame tree could be compiled and the consequent composition of transforms optimized, before binding the total transformation to a stream of input point data. To do this, the transform programming needs to be lifted from its present situation as C++ source to a symbolic algebra system.

In summary, transform objects are the algebraic entities mentioned above, from which we create geometric representations.

2.5. Finite Defining Point Set Objects

In designing the relation between entities in graphics images, the objects representing the entities can be thought as black boxes. Lines in and out of object boxes carry point data, evoked by methods. For example, the design shown in Figure 1c corresponds to the schematic in Figure 1d. If an entity has a fixed control point then this is represented as an output only from its object box. Thus entity 1 in Figure 1c is assumed to be fixed in space in this example, and therefore its vertices, A, B, C, D, and E are outputs from its box in the schematic. For entity 2, once the centre point F is given, there are no further degrees of freedom for the entity, and F is the only input to its object box. For entity 3, if endpoint G is given an input line to its object box) then endpoint H is determined (i.e. is an output from its box) under the assumption that no rotation information is input to the entity. Representing the design in Figure 1b by a schematic requires a technique for handling intersections which is discussed in the next section.

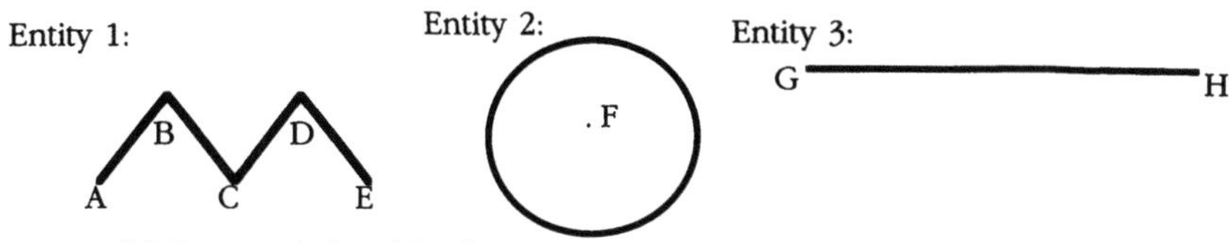

(a) Entities defined by finite point sets

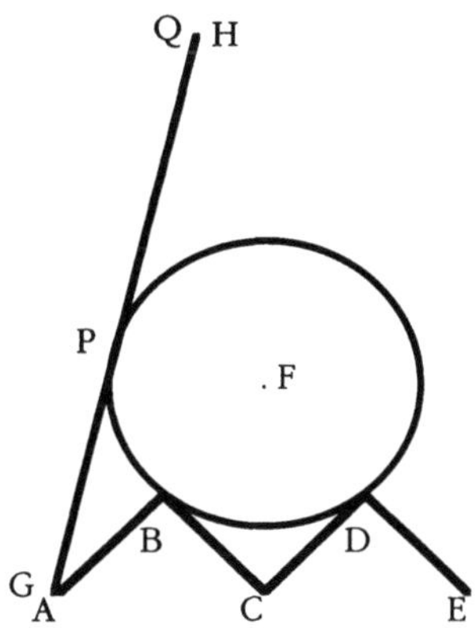

(b) The construction of points P and Q based on the intersection of three different shapes.

(c)

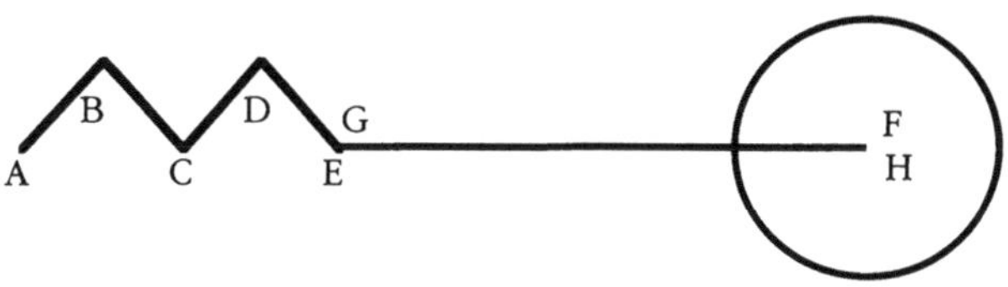

(d)

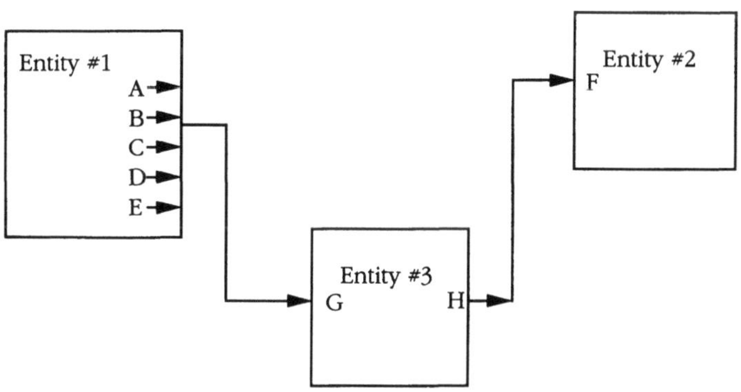

A block schematic diagram showing how to link the OOP objects together to produce (c).

Figure 1: Dataflow schematics for point-set objects

The schematic operations (drawing boxes, connecting inputs to outputs and so on) are polymorphic methods, applying to all geometric figure classes. Particular classes, such as circles, determine the boundary and interior of the figure as a function of the defining points.

2.6. Constraint Objects

Figures may be dependent on co-moving frames, on parametric variables, on contact and joint constraints etc. The dependencies can be presented explicitly as functions, or implicitly as constraints. We would like to define constraints geometrically, and have them operate numerically, as systems of equations, with dataflow directionality determined subsequently.

In Borning's ThingLab, entities to be constrained are parts of a compound object, which contains: a test for constraint satisfaction, and multiple methods for satisfying it. For instance

```
Class MidPointLine
        Superclasses
                Geometric Object
Part Descriptions
        line_segment: aLine
        midpoint: aPoint
Constraints
        midpoint = (line point1 + line point2)/2
                midpoint ← (line point1 + line point2)/2
                line point1 ← midpoint * 2 - line point2
                line point2 ← midpoint * 2 - line point1
```

For each possible dependence of one point on the other two, a function has been put in by hand, although in this case a solution of the constraint equation is simple.

Also note the constructions such as 'line point1'. This is a direct reference to internal data of the line object, not a message passed to line. It would have been possible to express the code in terms of 'get-point1' and 'set-point1' messages; but it makes the syntax much more readable when objects are in some cases allowed to export access paths to their parts. This allows ThingLab to implement 'message plans' in the form:

```
midpointline point1 moveby: 10@0
```

This class of line-segment has the schematic shown in Figure 2. The message plan makes point1 an input. The line-segment object will then select a satisfaction method which makes one of the other points the output. The methods may be taken in source order as a default, but this might be overridden by a prior message to hold one or the other point fixed. Graphically, the same message can be issued by drawing a connection to the point1 input of the box.

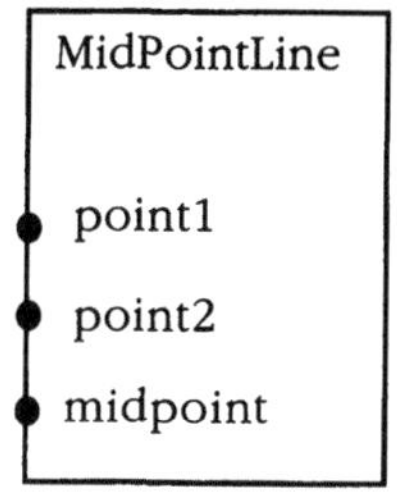

Figure 2: Schematic for MidPointLine class

A triangle object may be implemented as:

Class Triangle
    Superclasses
        Geometric Object
Part Descriptions
    line: line1,line2,line3
Constraints
    line1 point 2 = line2 point1
        line1 point2 ← line2 point1
        line2 point1 ← line1 point2
    line2 point2 = line3 point1
        ... etc
    line3 point2 = line1 point1
        ... etc

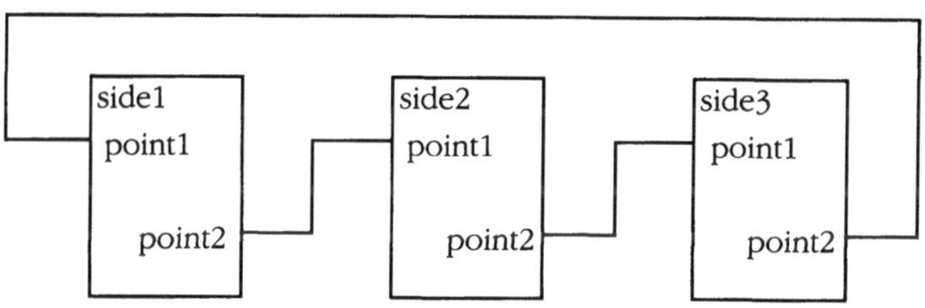

Figure 3: Schematic for Triangle object.

The schematic is shown in Figure 3. A message plan is compiled into a series of messages to parts of the triangle by a general method which determines which other parts must be moved (e.g. (triangle side3 point2)) to keep all constraints true.

This satisfier relies on three methods, which are called in sequence until one succeeds or all fail. These are:

1. Propagation of degrees of freedom, in which a part is found which can be moved so as to satisfy all its constraints. The part's appropriate function is selected, and the satisfier proceeds. In our case, the satisfier notes that 'line3 point2 = line1 point1' has been invalidated, and that (line3 point2) has no other constraints on it. The dependency direction (line1 point1) → (line3 point2) is therefore selected.

The search continues for constraints invalidated by changes in either (line1 point1) or (line3 point2), but none are found.

2. Propagation of known states, in which parts are marked as constant for present purposes. Other parts involved in constraints with these are inspected to see whether they can also be proved constant. The system is thus reduced to those parts which are still free.

3. Relaxation, in which each part's values are changed in turn so as to minimize an error measure.

The parts involved in the greatest number of constraints are addressed first. According to Borning, relaxation need only be tried in case of circularity. A special relaxation method is compiled by approximating each constraint to a linear equation in the remaining variables, and finding a least-squares fit to the equations.

This can all be viewed as a navigation and marking exercise in a table of constraints versus degrees of freedom. The full constraint set for Triangle is tabulated in Table 1. In this case the entire triangle is free: any movement of points which displaces (side1 point1) as required and holds the sides together at their vertices is a satisfaction.

Variables		Constraints 1	2	3
side1	point1			X
	point2	X		
side2	point1	X		
	point2		X	
side3	point1		X	
	point2			X

Table 1: The constraint set for Triangle. Each **X** marks a free variable involved in a constraint.

The message plan mentions only (side1 point1), so we mark it as the only independent variable. We find it involved in constraint 3 with (side3 point2), so mark that as dependent (see Table 2). Both rows are free of other constraints, so we have a minimum-change satisfaction.

A configuration like that show in Table 3 is already fully determined (unless the constraints are degenerate), and any attempt to alter either variable must fail. The configuration presents us with a circularity: a job for the relaxation technique.

A final note: in the Triangle example, each point variable comprised two reals. The one satisfaction applied equally to the x and y coordinates of the points, which were independent. If for any point they had been coupled, say by constraining the point to some curve, we would have had to consider the problem in terms of 12 reals, rather than 6 points.

Variables		Constraints 1	2	3
side1	point1			1
	point2	X		
side2	point1	X		
	point2		X	
side3	point1		X	
	point2			2

Table 2: The constraint set for Triangle. Each **X** marks a free variable involved in a constraint, **1** marks an independent variable, and **2** marks a dependent variable.

Variables	Constraints 1	2
1	X	X
2	X	X

Table 3: A fully determined configuration

The number of ways to satisfy a constrained system grows combinatorially with the number of variables. Borning has his satisfier techniques select the first simple satisfaction they can find. But the variety of satisfactions is an opportunity rather than a problem, offering many different behaviours for the one configuration, as long as we have a simple means to determine constants and free variables.

A graphic display is a nice tool for this purpose. For the Triangle example, we only need a 'pin icon' which we can attach to vertices on screen, to impose constancy. As easily, we can provide interface gimmicks for constraining a point to a curve, a line to a slope, or a line to pass through a point. Some other conditions, such as tangency of curves, may take more imagination.

Packaging constraints as Borning does allows us to bridge a gap between declarative and functional statements at the geometric and algebraic levels. The ideal is to have our users talk to the system geometrically, and have numeric functional programs compiled accordingly.

2.7. Comparison of Constraint Programming Techniques

Introducing frames and transformations as programming elements adds nothing to the general problem of solving arbitrarily constrained systems, except in manifesting certain dependencies as parameterized degrees of freedom (e.g. the angle coordinate of a pivot). Fertey et al. [Fertey et al., 1990] sum up the general problem: "Solutions are either mundane, due to rigidity of rules, or unexploitable, due to combinatorial explosion."

Under the heading of constraint systems, the following have been discussed by various authors:

- Fixed dependencies: i.e. the program determines which variables are independent and which are derived from them.
- Variable dependencies: the direction of dataflow between variables may vary between program modes.
- Omni-directional dependency: all free variables of the system are modified together, by tracking a simultaneous set of constraints incrementally.

The system discussed above is basically of the fixed-dependency type; native-frame coordinates and transform variables being independent, all others being derived. The advantage of our system is the flexibility with which we can define output values as functions of the inputs. Hill's MEL [Hill, 1990] is also a fixed dependency system, though potentially extendable to two-way constraints.

An example of variable-dependency programming is the triangle discussed above. Borning's ThingLab provides a general framework for such mechanisms. Unavoidably it is dominated by special cases, and it is not clear whether it offers practical reusability. Transform and point-set objects at least provide a sound infrastructure for building variable-dependency objects.

Rule-based programming has two roles in variable-dependency systems: within an object definition to determine the calculations which manifest a specific dependency direction, and in the larger context to specify the directionality itself. The first is the method of algebraic solution systems like TKSolver. The second appears in systems like that of Fertey et al. [Fertey et al., 1990], and in the constraint-satisfier methods of ThingLab. Although these systems are practical, one does not have the sense of being able to plug reusable components together with simple connectors such as point identifiers, pivots etc.

Gleicher and Witkin's "Snap Together Mathematics" [Gleicher and Witkin, 1990] contains an omni-directional mechanism for tracking multiple variables incrementally. Where other systems (such as ours) have objects return values, this system has them calculate the values of their derivatives, so that an evaluation tree implements the Jacobian of a desired set of output variables with respect to all inputs. This allows a far more modular and reusable set of mechanical components. Connecting them by point identification implements the Lagrangian dynamics of the compound system, with the bulk of computation consisting in the inversion of the Jacobian matrices.

3. A Geometric Approximation Method

3.1. Curve Intersection by Nearest-point Iteration

For most of the curves of interest in Computer Graphics, no general closed form solution for intersections exists. The intersection of polynomial curves such as Bézier curves for example can lead to a polynomial equation of degree higher than four which cannot be solved in closed form. Curves which are piece-wise polynomial, such a splines, introduce further complexities. In any case we would need an algebraic solution for the intersection of every pair of types of curve. The following algorithm however is polymorphic.

We require a **nearest_point** method for all curve classes. Given a in space, a call to this method returns a point on the curve which is closest to the given point. Intersection of two curves proceeds via the algorithm illustrated by the schematic in Figure 2. The algorithm is iterative and starts from a seed point x_0. The nearest point to x_0 on the first entity is found by a call to its **nearest_point** method resulting in point x_1, the next approximation to the intersection point. The point x_1 is then used in a call to the method **nearest_point** for the second entity to return x_2, the nearest point on the second entity to x_1. The separation of successive approximations, x_i and x_{i+1}, is constantly monitored, and if this distance, d_i, falls below a prescribed epsilon value then the iteration is terminated and the final point is taken as the point of intersection. The algorithm is shown in its simplest form in Figure 4.

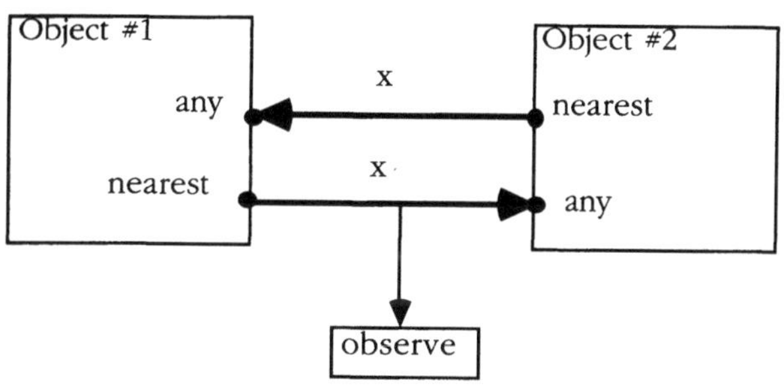

Figure 4: Illustration of the geometric intersection algorithm.

Figure 5 shows an infinite line intersecting a circle. In this case there is one point of intersection, and any point in the plane will converge by this method to the intersection point. The algorithm shows very strong convergence properties which will be investigated further in the next section. In the next case (Figure 6) there is no point of intersection. The behaviour of the algorithm is again the same for all points in the plane: the sequence of points oscillates between the closest points between the circle and the line. This case of no intersection is therefore easily detected by the failure of the successive separations d_i to decrease.

The final case shown in Figure 7 has all points to the left of the normal NN' to the line which passes through the centre of the circle C converging strongly on the intersection

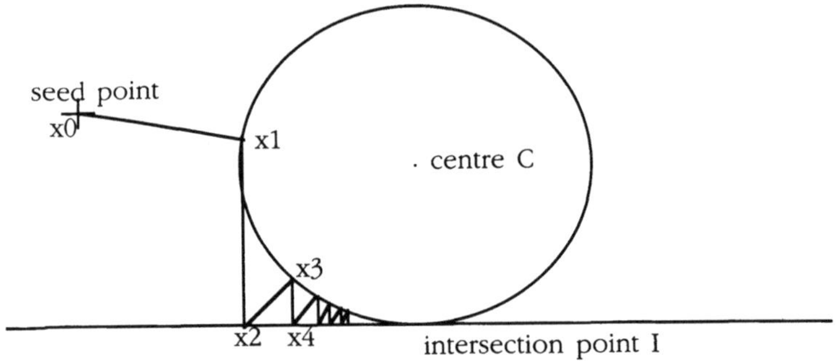

Figure 5: The sequence x0, x1, ... converges to the point of intersection.

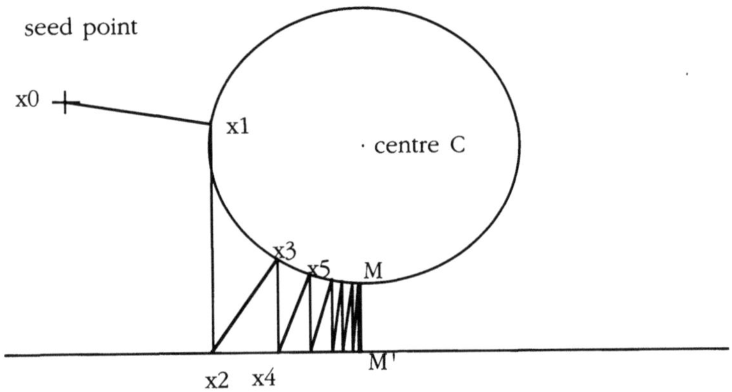

Figure 6: The sequence x0, x1, ... approaches oscillation at a local nearest approach.

point

I_1, all points to the right of NN' converging strongly on intersection point I_2, and all points on the line NN' oscillating between the point M on the line and the point M' on the circle. The region to the left of NN' is a basin of attraction for the point I_1, and the region to the right of NN' is a basin of attraction to the point I_2. The seed points in the border line NN' have unstable behaviour because any slight error or disturbance in the coordinate values will put the point into either the basin of attraction for I_1 or the basin of attraction for I_2. It follows that the algorithm always succeeds in finding an intersection point or indicating the lack of one.

The line-circle intersection is dominated by the recurrence relations:

For n even:

$$x_{n+1} = C\cdot x + \frac{r}{\sqrt{1+\left((y_n - C\cdot y)/(x_n - C\cdot x)\right)^2}}$$

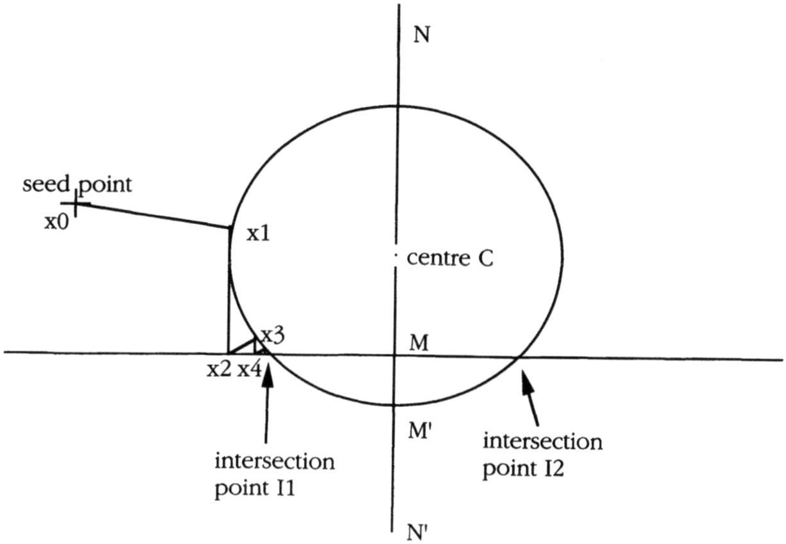

Figure 7: The sequence x0, x1, ... converges on one of two intersection points or oscillates midway between them.

$$y_{n+1} = C \cdot y + \frac{r}{\sqrt{1 + \left((y_n - C \cdot y)/(x_n - C \cdot x)\right)^2}}$$

For n odd:

$$x_{n+1} = x_n$$

$$y_{n+1} = b$$

where the equation of the line is $y = b$ and the equation of the circle is $(x - C \cdot x)^2 + (y - C \cdot y)^2 = r^2$.

This can be compared with the standard methods in numerical analysis for finding the roots of equations. Three iterative methods are the Newton approximation method, the function iteration technique (and for higher-dimensional problems) the method of steepest descent. Consider for instance using the Newton algorithm for the problem in Figures 3 to 7. The iteration formula is:

$$x_{i+1} = x_i - \frac{f(x_i)}{f'(x_i)}$$

where f must be taken as the equation of the lower half of the circle. The possibility of multiple roots and slopes for an entity is thus an immediate problem for the Newton method. The seed point for the Newton algorithm should be chosen as some point on the line (which is taken to be the x-axis). For seed points between $C \cdot x - r$ and $C \cdot x + r$ in Figure 3 where r is the radius of the circle, and C its centre point, the Newton method also rapidly converges to the intersection point I. For seed points outside of this range the Newton method fails because f and f' are undefined. In the case of Figure 4 the Newton algorithm fails for all choices of seed point since even if $C \cdot x - r \leq x \leq C \cdot x + r$ the closer the sequence gets to the oscillation points M, M' the smaller the slope f' is ultimately throwing the iteration point out of the range for which f and f' are defined. For the case of Figures 5 to 7, the Newton method will converge to I_1 if $C \cdot x - r \leq x < C \cdot x - r * d$ where d is a small positive factor that ensures that the tangent does not send the iteration point out of the range where f and f' are defined:

$$d = \frac{r^2 - (r - z)^2}{r^2 + (r - z)^2}$$

where $z = |MM'|$.

Similarly if x is in the range $C \cdot x + r * d \leq x \leq C \cdot x + r$ then convergence to I_2 is assured. These ranges are too restrictive and indicate that the Newton method is highly likely to fail for this kind of problem.

3.2. Nearest-point Functions

For a straight line $ax + by + c = 0$ the nearest point to (x_0, y_0) is given by

$$x = x_0 + aE$$

$$y = y_0 + bE$$

where

$$E = -\frac{ax_0 + by_0 + c}{a_2 + b_2}$$

The same line is given if the coefficients are multiplied by a common factor, so there is no trouble with small denominators in E.

For a circle, in vector notation:

$$\mathbf{x} = \mathbf{centre} + \frac{\text{radius}}{|\mathbf{x}_0 - \mathbf{centre}|}(\mathbf{x}_0 - \mathbf{centre}).$$

For a general implicit curve $f(x,y) = 0$ the feet of normals passing through x_0 are given by solutions of this equation simultaneously with $f_x(x,y)/(x - x_0) = f_y(x,y)/(y - y_0)$.

where f_x and f_y are the partial derivatives. Systems like this tend to be algebraically complex; for instance a parabolic curve gives a cubic equation for x, while a cubic curve gives quintics. The foot of a normal may be a furthest point from x_0 rather than a nearest.

For a general parametric curve $\mathbf{x} = \mathbf{f}(t)$, the feet of normals are given by $\mathbf{f}_t \cdot (\mathbf{f} - \mathbf{x}_0) = 0$ where $\mathbf{f}_t$ is the derivative with respect to t. This may or may not lead to simpler algebra than the implicit form. If the curve is defined for just a finite interval $t_{min} \leq t \leq t_{max}$, solutions with t out of the range would be set to the minimum or maximum.

It is easier, and may be faster, to treat the curve as a spline, finding the nearest point on each chord and taking the nearest of those. If an intersection between the curves exists, there will be an intersection of chords nearby. This can be improved by refining the spline-sections to smaller segments and repeating the process. It is not even necessary for the endpoints of the segments to lie on the spline, so long as they continue to approach the spline at each refinement.

A modification of the algorithm is to examine the first pair of chords found, which will either intersect or not, and in the latter case to find the nearest pair of endpoints directly. This avoids having to calculate a succession of nearest points, which would lead to the same result.

We have a simple proof by monotonicity that the nearest-point method converges to an intersection or a mutual normal, in two dimensions. We have not found a similar proof for higher dimensions; nonetheless, the method appears to work. For higher-dimensional nearest-point methods, we can borrow a trick from Gouraud shading, linear interpolation of normal vectors across a surface patch. Thus we have a basis for sampling surface intersections in three dimensions, though we cannot characterize the intersection curves algebraically.

4. Summary

One can get a sound basic set of geometric data structures and operations by integrating point set objects with transform and coordinate frame objects; including polygon convexity operations and curve intersections. Compound objects can be connected by identifying points, with dependencies which are one-way at any given time but may be reversed in the manner of ThingLab constraint objects.

References

Abelson, H. and Sussman, G.J. (1985) *Structure and Interpretation of Computer Programs*, MIT Press. ISBN 0-262-01077-1 (MIT Press), ISBN 0-07-000-422-6 (McGraw-Hill)

Borning, A.H. (1979) "ThingLab — A Constraint-Oriented Simulation Laboratory," Ph.D Dissertation, Dept. Computer Science, Stanford University, Stanford, Cal..

Borning, A.H. (1981) "The Programming Aspects of ThingLab, a Constraint-Oriented Simulation Laboratory," *ACM Transactions on Programming Languages and Systems*, vol. 3, no. 4.

Fertey, G., Peroche, B., and Zoller, J. (June 1990) "Creating 3D scenes with constraints," In: *Technology of Object-Oriented Languages and Systems (TOOLS).* Proceedings of the Second International Conference, PARIS 1990

Gleicher, M. and Witkin A. (1990) "Snap together mathematics," In: E.H. Blake & P. Wisskirchen (ed.) *Advances in Object Oriented Graphics I*, EurographicSeminar Series, Springer-Verlag, Berlin.

Hill, R.D. (1990) "A 2-D graphics system for multi-user interactive graphics based on objects and constraints," In: E.H. Blake & P. Wisskirchen (ed.) *Advances in Object Oriented Graphics I*, EurographicSeminar Series, Springer-Verlag, Berlin.

Zeltzer, D. (1984) "Representation and Control of Three-Dimensional Animated Figures," Ph.D. dissertation, Dept. Computer Science, Ohio State University.

9

A Direct Manipulation Environment for Conceptual Design of Three-Dimensional Objects

Maarten J.G.M. van Emmerik

The conceptual design of a three-dimensional model can be regarded as a cyclic process in which a global scheme is gradually refined into a detailed specification of components. The system presented in this chapter demonstrates how an object-oriented approach in combination with an interactive graphical environment facilitates the elaboration of a design concept during the different stages of the design process. A model is described as a part-whole hierarchy in which components are represented as interrelated graphical objects with an internal representation. Objects can be grouped bottom-up into more complex objects, or alternatively, their internal representation can be decomposed top-down into other objects. An interactive graphical interface allows the designer to view and edit both the geometric and the hierarchical organization of the model by direct manipulation.

Keywords: user interface, direct manipulation, constraints, object-oriented graphics, visual programming, part-hierarchies.

1. Introduction

A design process can be described as the top-down refinement of a schematic concept into a more detailed result. In an early stage of the design process a product is defined as an assembly of vaguely specified components (Figure 1). Each component is in fact a black box which is worked out in subsequent stages of the design process. A graphical representation of assemblies in the conceptual design stage is essential to oversee the complexity of the conceptual scheme, and to evaluate the global geometric and topologic organization of the model. The actual geometric representation in the conceptual design stage is relatively unimportant, as long as it gives some indication of the global shape and shows how components are connected to each other. Once the designer has specified the global organization, the black boxes in the schematic concept are decomposed into sub-assemblies and parts. Lastly, all leaves in the assembly hierarchy are materialized (i.e., reified or supplied with specific physical properties) by predefined standard parts, or alternatively, by newly designed parts. It is essential that components are interchangeable so that alternative materialization options can be evaluated.

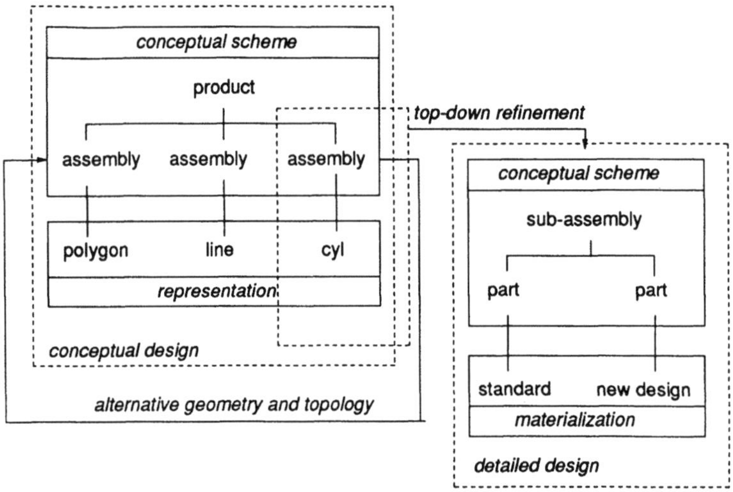

Figure 1: Top-down refinement of a conceptual scheme.

An object-oriented approach is well suited to modelling the design concept and to support the elaboration of the design during the different design stages. The complexity of an assembly hierarchy can be managed by representing (sub-)assemblies as graphical objects with an internal geometric and topologic organization and an interface to the outside world. The interface enables the user to specify the dimension, position, and orientation, and also to specify topologic relations with other objects. The internal organization itself may be elaborated in later stages of the design process. Hierarchical relations in a model are specified by grouping objects into more complex objects, or alternatively, by specifying new objects as modifications (subclasses) of other objects.

Ideally, an object-oriented approach is combined with a direct manipulation modelling environment. With direct manipulation [Shneiderman, 1983], the user can modify the internal state of an object by interaction with a graphical representation. Successful implementations of direct manipulation include interactive two-dimensional drawing applications such as MacDraw [Cutter et al., 1987]: all objects are presented graphically and the user can modify position, orientation and size of objects by direct manipulation on control points. Objects can also be grouped into more complex objects, and properties or operations assigned to the group are automatically inherited by its members. In this chapter we will present a similar direct manipulation technique for the specification of position, orientation and scaling of three-dimensional objects.

Apart from the general paradigms of object-oriented design and direct manipulation, the system should support a mechanism for specifying the geometric and topologic organization of objects in the part-whole hierarchy. A suitable way to specify the geometric and topologic organization is via geometric constraints. A constraint specifies a relation that should be maintained. For instance, a constraint that an object should be on top of another object. Applications of constraint-based modelling for two-dimensional drawing and picture editing are presented in SKETCHPAD [Sutherland, 1963] and the Juno [Nelson, 1985] graphics system. Borning and Duisberg [Borning and Duisberg, 1986] use constraints in combination with object-oriented techniques to describe various relations in interactive graphical user interfaces. Applications of constraints in three-dimensional modelling include human figure animation [Badler et al., 1987], kinematic analysis of assemblies [Kim and Lee, 1989], and product modelling [Kimura et al., 1986]. In this chapter constraints between objects are specified via relations between their local coordinate systems. Several objects may share a common coordinate system, and hence, their position, orientation and dimension are implicitly related.

This contribution towards the design of three-dimensional objects by direct manipulation can be summarized as follows. Section 2 presents a new direct manipulation technique for specifying three-dimensional object transformations (translation, rotation and scaling) using a two-dimensional input device (a mouse). Sections 3 and 4 present an interactive graphical technique for specifying geometric and topologic relations between various kinds of geometric primitives. Section 5 explains how new object types can be defined by the end-user. The techniques presented are based on visual programming and allow the graphical parameterization and instantiation of objects. Section 6 discusses how the various techniques can be applied to the top-down design of part hierarchies. Finally, the chapter demonstrates the application of the object-oriented paradigm in both the system implementation and the user interface.

2. Local Coordinate Systems

The position, orientation and scaling of an object in three-dimensional space can be specified as a local coordinate system relative to a global world coordinate system. The transformation of a local coordinate system is specified as a transformation matrix, involving nine different transformation parameters: three translation parameters (*tx, ty, tz*), three rotation parameters (*rx, ry, rz*) and three scaling parameters (*sx, sy, sz*). So, if one could manipulate these parameters, one would be able to control the position, orientation and dimensions of objects.

Specification of transformation parameters can be made interactive by taking their input parameters from three-dimensional input devices such as a dialbox or a bat (three-dimensional mouse). However, since these input devices are generally not in common use with current workstations and PC's, an alternative input technique using a conventional two-dimensional mouse is preferred. The problem of specifying three-dimensional transformations with a two-dimensional input device has been addressed earlier. Chen et al. [Chen et al., 1988] evaluated four virtual controllers for rotating three-dimensional objects with a mouse. Bier presented an interactive three-dimensional positioning tool for moving coordinate systems (Jacks) a three-dimensional cursor (Skitter) [Bier, 1986]. Nielson and Olsen [Nielson and Olsen, 1986] presented a method that also includes scaling and rotation. However, a disadvantage of their method is that an extra step is involved: the user has to select the required transformation (translation, rotation or scaling) prior to the direct manipulation. Both the methods presented by Bier and Nielson also require surface information in the model, and will therefore not work with other representations such as wireframe, or analytically described solids.

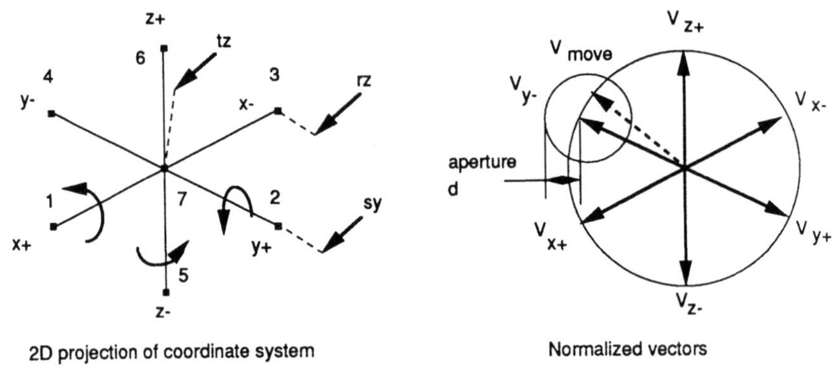

Figure 2: A coordinate system has nine degrees of freedom. The three-dimensional transformations of a coordinate system are specified graphically by dragging control points parallel or orthogonal to one of its axes.

The method described in this chapter enables a one-step direct manipulation method for the specification of position, orientation and scaling of local coordinate systems [Emmerik, 1990a] using a gestural interface technique [Rhyne, 1987]. With a gestural interface, the syntactic interpretation of graphical interaction is derived from spatial relations between mouse gestures and the graphical context in the neighbourhood of the gesture. In the system presented here, the effect of graphical interaction on a displayed coordinate system depends on the position of the cursor in the coordinate system and the direction of the two-dimensional cursor movement.

Each coordinate system is provided with seven control points which can be selected by the mouse (Figure 2). After a control point is selected, the user can drag the mouse in different directions. The selected control point and the direction of movement determine the effect of the drag operation. For instance, if the user drags control point 3 parallel to the y-axis, the coordinate system is rotated along the z-axis. If the user drags control point 2 in the same direction, the coordinate system is scaled in the y-direction. A translation of the coordinate system in the z-direction is specified by dragging the centre control point along the z-axis. Thus the effect of a direct manipulation action depends (1) on where the user selects the coordinate system, (2) on the direction of the two-dimensional mouse movements, and (3) on the two-dimensional orientation of the projected axis. An overview of all combinations of control points and dragging directions is given in Table 1. The reason for using seven control points instead of four is the fact that the control points are not visible to the user and the user should therefore be able to manipulate both ends of an axis.

controlpoint	2-D mouse movement relative to projected axes					
	x+	x-	y+	y-	z+	z-
1	sca x+	sca x-	rot z+	rot z-	rot y-	rot y+
2	rot z-	rot z+	sca y+	sca y-	rot x+	rot x-
3	sca x-	sca x+	rot z-	rot z+	rot y+	rot y-
4	rot z+	rot z-	sca y-	sca y+	rot x-	rot x+
5	rot y-	rot y+	rot x+	rot x-	sca z-	sca z+
6	rot y+	rot y-	rot x-	rot x+	sca z+	sca z-
7	tra x+	tra x-	tra y+	tra y-	tra z+	tra z-

Table 1: Manipulation of control points.

An example of three-dimensional direct manipulation is presented in Figure 3. In the first picture, a block and its local coordinate system are displayed. The user can scale the block in the *x*-direction by dragging the end-point of the coordinate system along the *x*-axis. Subsequently, the block is moved in the *z*-direction by dragging the centre of the coordinate system along the *z*-axis. Finally, the block is rotated along the *z*-axis by dragging the end-point of the *x*-axis parallel to the *y*-axis of the coordinate system. Exact specification of three-dimensional transformations is enabled by a grid-snap option [Bier and Stone, 1986] and alphanumerical feedback of transformation values during direct manipulation.

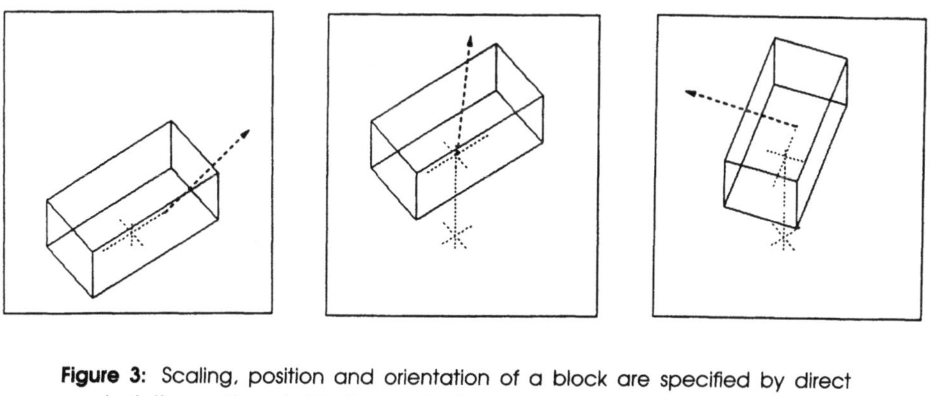

Figure 3: Scaling, position and orientation of a block are specified by direct manipulation on the primitive's coordinate system.

The method described has four advantages. First, it provides an integrated direct manipulation technique for all nine transformation parameters. Second, the technique is modeless: it does not require any special cursors or mode selection prior to the direct manipulation operation. Third, the input technique is compatible with the user's mental model for interaction of a physical (flexible) cross. Fourth, the input technique is independent of a particular geometric representation. Local coordinate systems are key entities in three-dimensional modelling, and the interaction technique can therefore be applied for specifying object transformations regardless of their internal geometric representation.

The implementation of the interaction technique is rather simple. The control points are defined as three-dimensional positions in a local coordinate system. Positions of the control points in world coordinates are obtained by transformation with the transformation matrix of the coordinate system. After the viewing transformation and the two-dimensional projection, the (x, y) positions of the control points are defined in screen coordinates. Once the user has pressed a mouse button, the current location is compared with the position of all control points. The direction of two-dimensional mouse movement $\mathbf{v}_{move}$ (Figure 2) is obtained by sampling a number of mouse events. This vector is normalized and matched with the the normalized direction vectors of the projected coordinate system. If the vector vmove matches one of the direction vectors, the coordinate system is transformed in real-time in three dimensions according to Table 1.

3. Geometric Tree

A second major entity in the modelling system is the geometric tree [Emmerik, 1989b]. The geometric tree is a hierarchical organization of local coordinate systems. Initially, one root coordinate system is presented to the user. New coordinate systems can be defined relative to the root coordinate system, or in a later stage, relative to other coordinate systems. The geometric tree is not only used as an internal data structure but is also presented to the user for graphical interaction. An example of a geometric tree is presented in Figure 4.

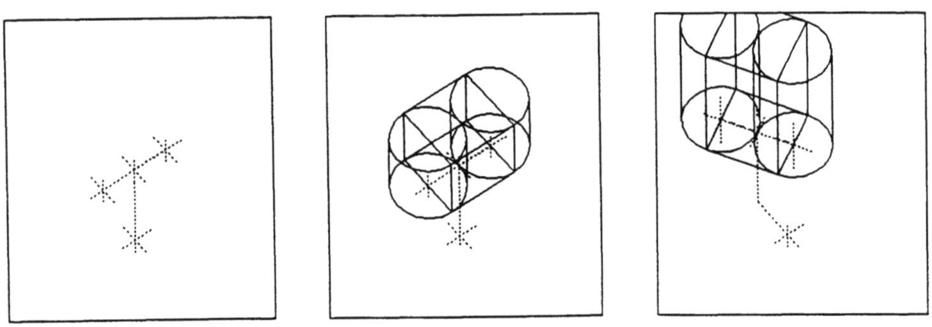

Figure 4: The geometric tree is specified graphically and the user can transform the nodes in the tree by direct manipulation. Direct manipulation on a node affects all child nodes, so that a whole branch can be transformed simultaneously.

The user can append new nodes to the tree by selecting the option 'create_axis' from a menu and pointing at the desired parent node. Nodes in the geometric tree can be translated, rotated and scaled with the direct manipulation technique discussed above.

The three-dimensional transformation of a particular node is obtained by concatenation of all intermediate transformations of parent nodes down to the root. After the geometric tree is defined, the user can append objects to the nodes in the tree by menu selection. The geometric transformation of an object is specified by the transformation of the node to which the object is appended. Since the transformation of a particular node affects all nodes lower in the tree, it is possible to transform a group of objects simultaneously.

3.1. The Class Node

Each node in the geometric tree has a pointer to its parent node and contains a record of the transformations relative to its parent. The transformation of the coordinate system in world coordinates and the two-dimensional screen positions of the control points after drawing the coordinate system are also stored. A definition of the class 'node' in C++ [Stroustrup, 1986] is as follows:

```
class node {
        class node *parent;
        class node **child;          /* list of child nodes */
        float val(9);                /* tx,ty,tx,rx,ry,rz,sx,sy,sz */
        int  2-Ddata(7);             /* 2-D positions of control points */
        matrix tm;                   /* transformation in world coordinates */
        char *id;                    /* node identifier    */
        ...
public:
        void evaluate();
        void draw();
        char *select(int x, int y);  /* hit detection */
        int *controlpoints();
        void transform(int field, float val);
        ...
};
```

Interaction with a node is controlled by a number of built-in functions. If the user has pushed a mouse button at screen position (x, y), a message 'select' is send to all nodes. If one of the control points is selected, the message returns the name of the object and a list of two-dimensional positions of control points. A member function 'evaluate' calculates the three-dimensional transformation of a coordinate system, given the transformations relative to its parent node and the three-dimensional transformation matrix of its parent. After calculation is completed, the node can be drawn on the screen and the list of two-dimensional control point positions is updated.

3.2. The Class Tree

The class 'tree' represents the hierarchy of nodes as a single object. The semantic difference between a geometric tree and a node is analogous to the difference between a list and a list item. Member functions control the appending and deleting of nodes, and the updating and drawing of the geometric tree. Functions for modifying the topology of the geometric tree by the cutting and pasting of branches in the tree are defined at this level. Although the same member functions of the geometric tree have the same interface as the member functions of nodes, they have a different implementation. For instance, the function 'evaluate' of the geometric tree does not perform any geometric calculations but only controls the sequencing of the message 'evaluate' which is sent to the nodes (e.g., breadth-first). The class geometric tree is defined as:

```
class tree {
        class node *root;    /* pointer to first node */
        ...
public:
        void evaluate();
        void draw();
        char *select(int x, int y);
        int *controlpoints();
        void append(node *parent);
        void relink(node *old, node *new);
        ...
};
```

4. Primitives

In this section we shall discuss how various kinds of geometric primitives, such as points, lines, polygons and halfspaces can be dimensioned, positioned and oriented by the nodes in the geometric tree. To create a primitive, the user selects the required type of primitive from a menu and picks one or more nodes in the geometric tree. The selected nodes are interpreted as constraints for positioning, orienting and dimensioning the primitive. For example, to specify a line, the user can pick two nodes as the begin- and end-points of the line. A user defined number of nodes can be selected as control points for a curve or a trajectory of a swept profile.

Primitives are implemented as subclasses of the superclass 'object' (Table 2). The class object describes the interface between the modelling system and the specific geometric representation of primitives:

```
class object {
        class node **par;           /* parameter list */
        struct properties *prop;    /* properties */
        char *id;                   /* object name     */
        ...
public:
        virtual int evaluate();
        virtual void draw();
        virtual char *select(int x, int y); /* hit detection */
        ...
};
```

An 'object' contains a list of nodes that specify position, orientation and dimension of the primitive and can be provided with attributes, such as line width, colour and surface finish. The class definition also comprises three functions that have to be provided with each object, regardless of their specific geometric representation. The function 'evaluate'

superclass	class	subclass
object	point	point
	curve	polyline arc Bézier B-spline
	surface	polygon
	solid	block cylinder cone sphere torus rotation sweep translation sweep sphere sweep
	halfspace	planar cylindrical conical

Table 2: Primitives.

specifies how the constraints, imposed by the selected nodes, should be evaluated to obtain the position, orientation and dimension of the primitive. The function 'draw' handles the representation of an object in a graphical environment (wireframe modeller, CSG modeller, colour or monochrome display). Finally, the function 'select' analyses whether an object is selected by a graphics pick. All basic functions are implemented as "virtual" functions. This implies that the application can address all primitives in the same way. The implementation of the virtual functions for the different object classes will be discussed below.

4.1. Points and Two-dimensional Curves

A point is provided with one node: the local coordinate system that specifies the position of the point. With a polyline, Bézier curve and B-spline curve, a user defined number of nodes can be selected as three-dimensional control points for the curve. Note that only the position of the coordinate systems is relevant for the path of the curve. An arc is a quarter of an ellipse, parameterized by two coordinate systems. The shape of the arc is defined by two constraints: the arc is tangential to the z-axis of the first node and ends at the position of the second node. Figure 5 shows a geometric tree with a point, five arcs, and three polylines and a point appended to the nodes of the tree.

Once the primitives are appended to the nodes of the tree, their position, orientation and dimensions can be modified by direct manipulation of the nodes of the tree. The geometric organization of the model is specified by the structure of the geometric tree

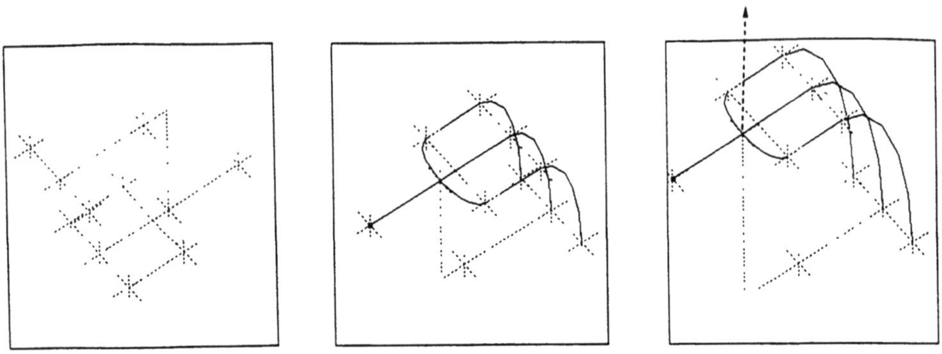

Figure 5: A point, three polylines and five arcs appended to a geometric tree.

and by the manner in which the primitives are appended to the nodes. The member function 'evaluate' calculates the position, orientation, and dimension of a primitive from the geometric transformation of the nodes that are supplied with the primitive. The hit detection function 'select' provided with each primitive is a rather straightforward check of whether the cursor position is close enough to one of the projected wire frame segments of a curve.

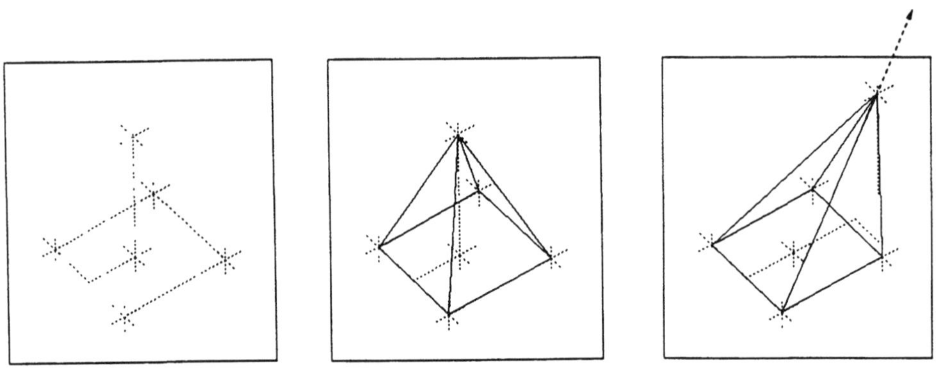

Figure 6: Polygons.

4.2. Surfaces

The only surface primitive that is currently implemented is the polygon. With a polygon, the nodes are interpreted as vertices (Figure 6). The member function 'evaluate' checks whether the nodes are all in the same plane. If not, the functions returns an error value and a message is displayed to the user. It would be possible to allow the specification of three-dimensional polygons (i.e., vertices not in the same plane) if an automatic triangulation algorithm is implemented. Hit detection is based on a scan-line intersection of the two-dimensional projection of the polygon and the y-position of the cursor, the point-in-polygon test [Rogers, 1985]. An advantage of the scan-line hit detection is that the user can pick anywhere in the enclosed region of the projected polygon. Other types of surfaces which could be implemented in future versions of the systems are Bézier and B-spline surfaces. With complex surfaces, the nodes are interpreted as control points, and the geometric tree enables the specification of a geometric organization between control points.

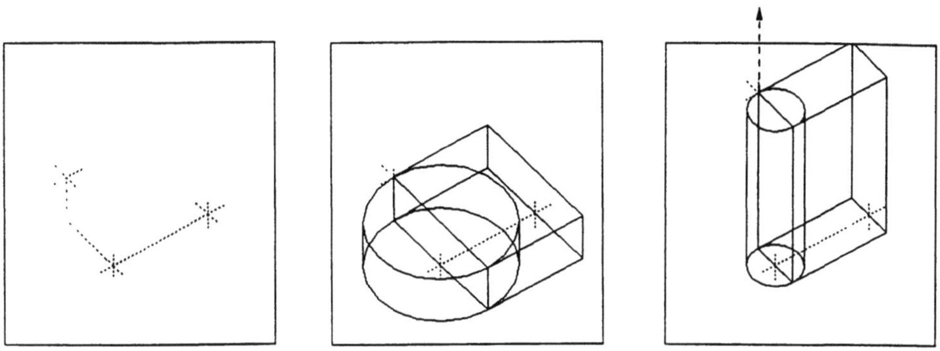

Figure 7: Volume primitives.

4.3. Volumes

The shape domain of volume primitives is split up into a set of elementary volumes and swept profiles. Position, orientation, and scaling of an elementary volume can be specified by a single node. This node is regarded as the primitive's coordinate system that can be controlled by direct manipulation (Figure 3). However, for many purposes it is convenient to use two nodes instead of one: a node that specifies the position and orientation of the primitive and a separate node that controls its dimension. The position of the second node is a constraint that specifies the edge-point of a volume (Figure 7). This enables the specification of geometric relations between position, orientation and dimension of volumes by the geometric tree. For example, the dimension of the cylinder and the block in Figure 7 are controlled by a common node and manipulation of this node would therefore control both dimensions at the same time. Also, manipulation of the node in the centre of the cylinder will affect both the position of the cylinder and the length of the block simultaneously. The modelling system supports Constructive Solid Geometry (CSG) for combining the volumes by Boolean operations (union, intersection, difference).

With swept profiles, the position of nodes are interpreted as control points for contours (e.g., rotation sweep in Figure 8) or three-dimensional trajectories (sphere sweep). The first node that is selected is interpreted as the primitive's coordinate system, analogously to an elementary volume primitive. The user can select a number of other nodes as control points for a contour or a trajectory. Each swept profile is provided with a parameter that specifies the degree of the B-spline contour or trajectory (line, quadric or cubic).

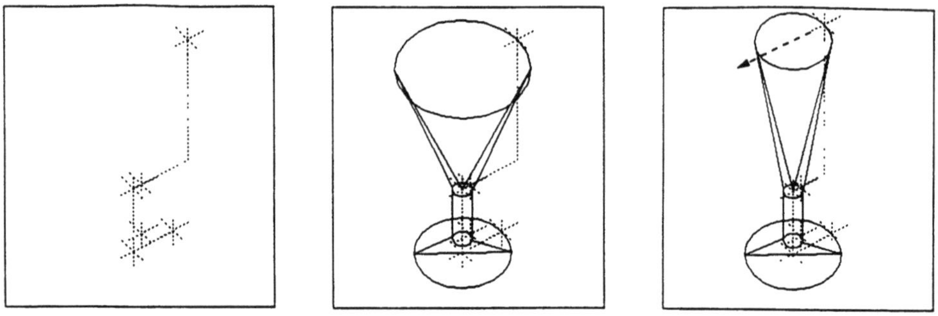

Figure 8: Rotation sweep.

The member function 'evaluate' calculates the position, orientation and dimension of a volume from the three-dimensional transformations of the nodes that are selected as parameters. Implementation of the hit detection function 'select' is based on ray-cursor intersection. After the user has picked at a location on the screen, a ray from the viewpoint of the user through the *x,y*-coordinates at the screen is constructed. The equation for the ray in the viewing coordinate system is transformed to an equation in world coordinates by multiplication with the inverse viewing matrix. The ray is subsequently intersected with all the volumes to check whether the ray hits the primitive [Hanrahan, 1988]. If more than one primitive is intersected by the same ray, the user can traverse the list of primitives by clicking at the same location. The advantage of ray-cursor intersection is that the user can activate a primitive by picking anywhere in the solid, rather than at the segments of the projected wireframe.

4.4. Halfspaces

Halfspaces are low-level CSG primitives that divide space into two regions: a solid region and an empty region. The border between the two regions is described by a surface equation, for instance a plane, a cone, or a cylinder. Halfspaces can be combined by Boolean operations to obtain a three-dimensional solid; in fact, all CSG primitives described above can be regarded as a Boolean combination of halfspaces. The reason for offering halfspaces is to allow the user to create an additional set of new CSG primitives with specific geometric properties. The user can specify a Boolean combination of halfspaces, store it in a database and use the object as a normal CSG primitive. The position, orientation and dimension (e.g., radius) of halfspaces are specified in the same manner as CSG volumes (Figure 9). Member functions for the calculation of the geometric transformation and hit detection are also identical to those described for the volume primitives.

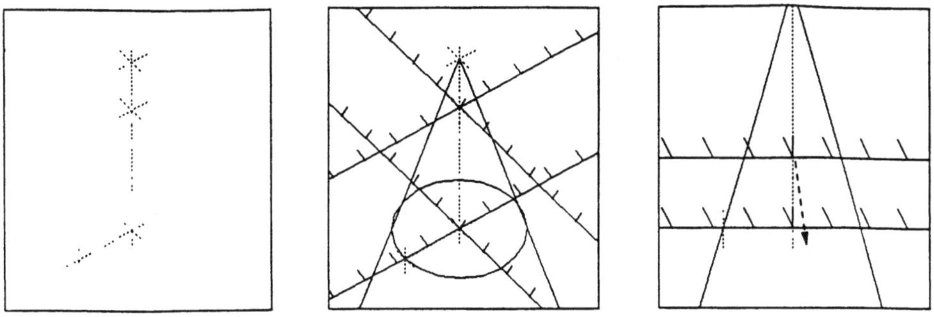

Figure 9: New CSG primitives can be specified as a Boolean combination of halfspaces.

5. Generic Objects

So far we have discussed three classes of entities for modelling: the coordinate systems, the geometric tree, and primitives. The geometric tree provides a uniform method for dimensioning, positioning and orienting various kinds of geometric primitives. It enables the interactive graphical specification of geometric relations between components. All primitives are implemented as subclasses of the superclass 'object' and their interface with the modelling system is specified via the member functions: 'evaluate', 'draw' and 'select'. Although the concepts discussed so far are adequate for modelling simple objects, they do not address the topic of assembly hierarchies. We show how compositions of primitives can be stored as re-usable objects and how simple objects can be grouped into complex objects.

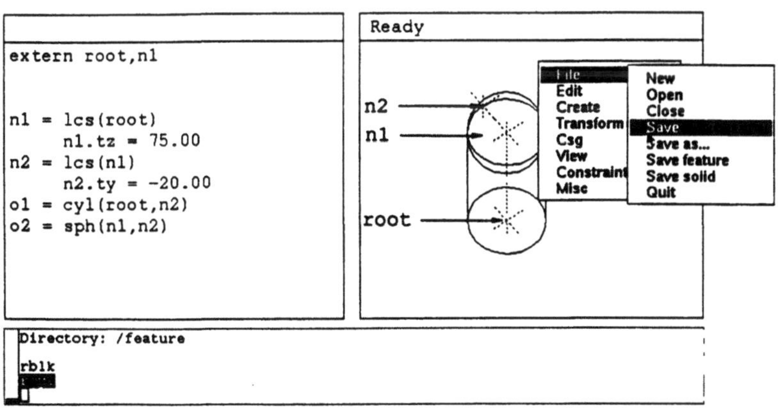

Figure 10: The direct manipulation actions are translated to textual commands that form a procedural object representation. The procedural representation is stored in a library and can be re-executed in other designs.

Objects are internally described by a procedural (textual) representation that is automatically generated by the graphical user interface. Figure 10 shows two representations of a simple object: a procedural representation and a graphical representation. Both representations are integrated and the user can edit the representations, by an editor and a direct manipulation interface respectively. Direct manipulation of the graphical representation will automatically update the procedural representation and vice versa. The idea of using two integrated views is applied in several systems, for example Juno [Nelson, 1985] and Peridot [Myers, 1988]. Automatic generation of a procedural representation by graphical interaction is generally referred to as *visual programming*.

The two-view approach has several advantages. It combines the features of a command line interface and a graphical interface, since the user can select the interface style that is most suitable for a specific task. Several text-based utilities such as 'learn', 'undo', 'redo' and 'macro substitution' can be integrated easily. Integration of the modelling system with other text-based applications, such as editors and filters is facilitated for the same reason. However, the primary reason for the two view approach is the combination of a user friendly graphical interface with the powerful functionality of a modelling language [Emmerik, 1989b]. A modelling language, such as SML [Wijk, 1986], enables a high-level model specification by using variables (parameterization), repetition constructs (iteration), conditional statements (design rules), and functions (hierarchy). Integration of direct manipulation with a procedural model representation will therefore provide a user friendly environment for modelling complex objects.

Procedural modelling commands are generated from template command statements. Template commands comprise a number of variables that are filled out by graphical actions such as picking and dragging. For instance, the template commands for creating a new node [5.1] and specifying a node transformation [5.2] are as follows:

```
N = lcs(P)        (e.g. n1 = lcs(root))        (5.1)
N.T = V           (e.g. n1.tz = 80 )           (5.2)
```

with

```
N = node identifier
P = parent node
T = transformation
V = real value
```

Template [5.1] creates a new coordinate system relative to another coordinate system. After the user has selected the option 'create-axis' from a menu, a default node identifier is generated (e.g., 'n1') and the system requests the user to pick a parent node 'P'. The second template is activated by a mouse down event, followed by a mouse drag event. The variable 'N', the name of the selected node, is obtained by sending a hit detection request to the geometric tree. As discussed earlier, the intended transformation 'T' can be derived by comparing the direction of the two-dimensional mouse movements with the orientation of the projected coordinate system. Subsequently, the value 'V' is set to the current transformation value, and is incremented or decremented during the drag operation. After a template statement is filled out, it can be appended to the procedural representation. In this case there are two possibilities: the statement is either added to the description, or it replaces an earlier defined statement (e.g., an old statement 'n1.tx = 40' should be replaced by the new statement 'n1.tx = 80').

After the user has finished the specification of an object, the procedural description is saved as a new generic object ('/feature/rcyl') in a library. Several instances of the new generic object can be appended to the nodes of a geometric tree, analogously to an elementary primitive (Figure 11). To enable variable positioning, orienting and dimensioning of an instance, the user can pick one or more nodes in the generic object description and declare them as 'extern'. For example, the nodes 'root' and 'n1' in the generic description are defined as 'extern'. This implies that the user can select a local 'root' and a local 'n1' for each instance, so that position, orientation and length of the instance can be specified separately for each instance. External nodes are the variables in the geometric tree which can be compared with the arguments supplied to a function call in a programming language.

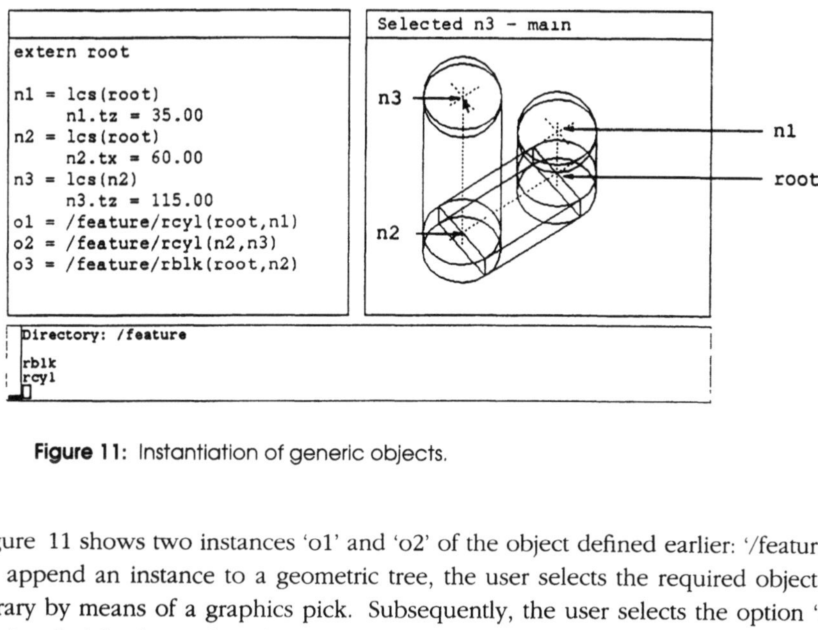

Figure 11: Instantiation of generic objects.

Figure 11 shows two instances 'o1' and 'o2' of the object defined earlier: '/feature/rcyl'. To append an instance to a geometric tree, the user selects the required object in the library by means of a graphics pick. Subsequently, the user selects the option 'create-part' and picks the nodes which should be supplied as parameters to the instance. The nodes that are supplied as parameters replace the external nodes in the generic description of the object. Note that the mechanism of external nodes enables the specification of position, orientation and dimensions of separate instances by direct manipulation. The composition of the tree instances 'o1', 'o2' and 'o3' in Figure 11 can be saved as a new generic object in the library. The user can group a set of primitives into a generic object, and instances of generic objects into complex objects.

Instances of generic objects share all the characteristics of the class 'object', but have an additional function 'open'. The function 'open' allows the user to edit the generic description of the instance. Modifications of the generic description of an object are

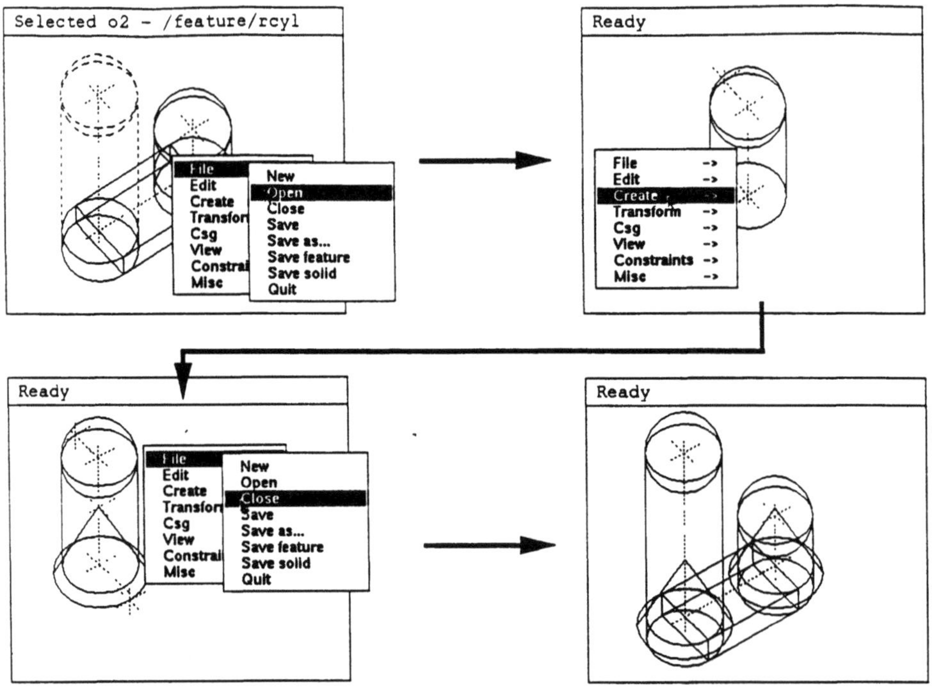

Figure 12: The assembly hierarchy can be traversed graphically by a *select-open-close* mechanism.

automatically propagated in all instances of the object after re-interpretation of the model, since instances are internally defined as function calls. The generic description is the body of the procedure, the external nodes are the parameters, and the nodes which are selected with each instance are the arguments. This approach differs fundamentally from the application of macro's, where a particular sequence of commands is merged into the object description. With macros, the original description is "forgotten" after the macro is executed. Figure 12 shows an example of editing the generic description of the object '/feature/rcyl'. The user can pick an instance of the generic object and select the option 'open' from the menu. Subsequently, the generic description of the object is recalled from the library and presented to the user. After editing the generic description of an object, the user can 'close' the generic description, and all instances of the object are automatically modified after re-interpretation of the model.

Another example of hierarchy, besides grouping objects into a compound object, is the specification of new objects as modifications, or special cases, of other objects. For example, a square hole can be regarded as a special case, or subclass, of a rectangular hole. There are a number of reasons why it is more convenient to specify objects as subclasses of other objects. First, the specification process itself is more efficient since the user only has to define the particular differences, rather than rebuilding a new model. The storage of an object is less space consuming for the same reason. However, the most important advantage is that there is a functional relation to the superclass from which the object is derived. Modifications in the superclass are automatically propagated to all objects that are defined as subclasses.

Figure 13 shows how a new object can be defined as a subclass of the object '/feature/rcyl'. The generic description of the new object comprises an instance of the superclass '/feature/cyl' plus some additional modifications, in this case a small hole at the bottom. The object can be saved as a new generic object '/feature/rhcyl': a cylinder with a rounded top ('/feature/rcyl') and a small hole at the bottom. If the generic description of the superclass '/feature/rcyl' is modified into a rectangular block, the subclass '/feature/rhcyl' is automatically modified into a rectangular block with a small hole at the bottom.

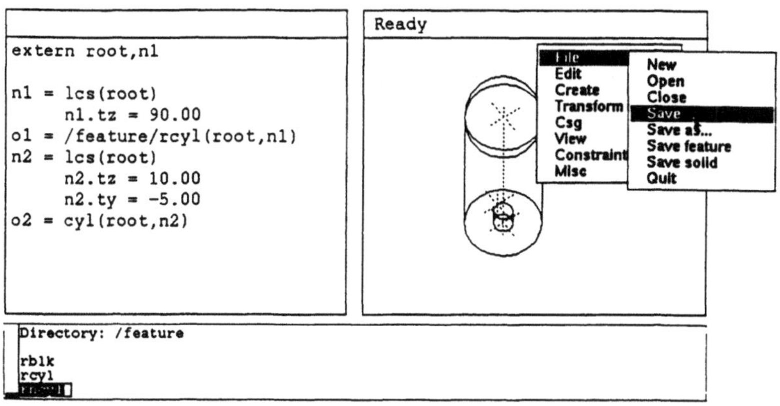

Figure 13: Specification of a new generic object as a modification of an other object.

6. Top-Down Design

The examples that are discussed in the previous sections are cases of bottom-up design: an object is defined by grouping primitives or predefined objects into more complex objects, or alternatively, by modification of earlier defined objects. A bottom-up design approach is suitable when the design problem is already decomposed into assemblies, sub-assemblies and parts. However, the design process generally starts which a schematic concept that is refined into a more detailed result. If a computer-aided design system is used as a tool during the design process itself, it should provide facilities for top-down refinement.

Figure 14 shows how the top-down refinement of a model can be implemented in the system. Initially, the user has defined an assembly, comprising a geometric tree with four nodes ('n1', 'n2', 'n3', 'n4') and three sub-assemblies 'A', 'B' and 'C'. Each sub-assembly can be visualized by a simple geometric representation, such as a line, a

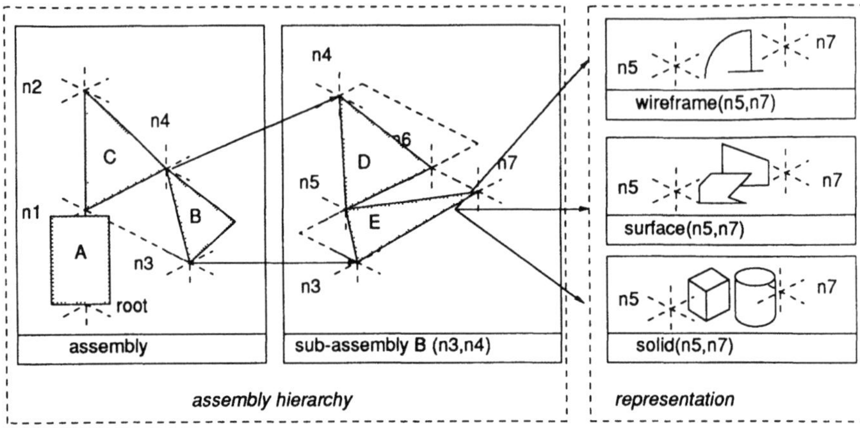

Figure 14: Sub-assemblies are implemented as generic objects that can be decomposed into other sub-assemblies during the design process.

polygon or a block. The structure of the geometric tree specifies the global geometric organization of the sub-assemblies in the conceptual design. For example, sub-assembly 'B' is connected to sub-assembly 'C' since they share a common coordinate system. Global dimensions are specified by the position of the nodes that are supplied as parameters ('n3' and 'n4'). Subsequently, the designer can click on instance 'B', select the option 'open' from a menu, and edit the generic description; in this case the generic description is decomposed into two sub-assemblies 'D' and 'E'. After the designer is satisfied with the global decomposition of the product, he or she can materialize the sub-assemblies at the leaves of the hierarchy. The simple geometric representation is worked out into a detailed three-dimensional component, either by selecting a predefined component from a library, or alternatively by building a new component from primitives and generic objects.

6.1. Conceptual Design

An example of an assembly hierarchy is presented in Figure 15. The model represents a conceptual scheme of a cart, composed by six instances ('o1..o6') of three generic objects ('/cart/board', '/cart/axle' and '/cart/wheel'). The topologic and geometric organization of the instances is specified by a common geometric tree. For example, the two front wheels are connected to the axle and the axle is connected to the board. The length of the axle is specified by the distance between the nodes that are supplied as parameters ('n7' and 'n8'). Internally, the generic descriptions are represented by simple geometric objects: the wheels are represented as a cylinder, the board is represented as a polygon and the axle is represented as a line.

Once the object is assembled, the user can generate alternatives by direct manipulation on the nodes (Figure 16). In this stage it is a major advantage that the topologic relations between the functional units are implicitly defined by the geometric tree. If the

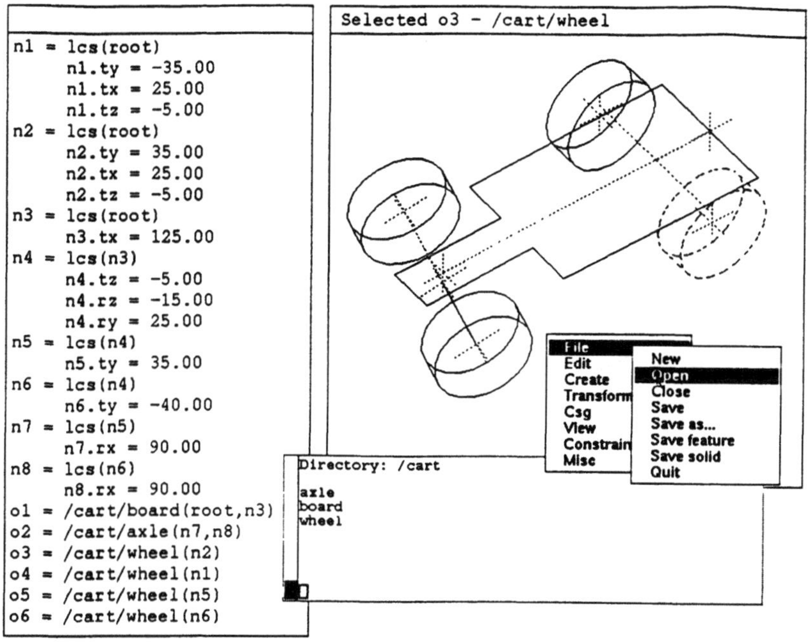

Figure 15: Conceptual design of a cart.

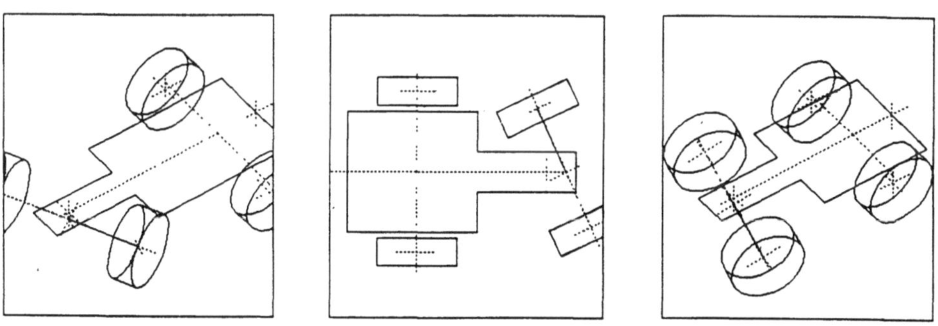

Figure 16: Alternative configurations are generated by direct manipulation.

user translates the node that specifies the length of the board, the sub-tree with the axle and the two wheels will also be automatically translated. The sub-tree with the axle and the two wheels can be rotated as a whole by manipulation of a single node. Figure 16 shows some alternative configurations of the cart that are generated by direct manipulation on the nodes. Note that direct manipulation on coordinate systems also works if the user has selected an orthogonal view.

6.2. Refinement of the Assembly Hierarchy

In the next design stage, the assembly hierarchy can be refined in further detail. For instance, the assembly '/cart/wheel' can be decomposed into two sub-assemblies, '/cart/tire' and '/cart/rim'. First, the designer creates two new generic objects, '/cart/tire' and '/cart/rim', and stores the new objects in the library. Subsequently, the user can select one of the wheels in the cart by graphics pick. The system displays the name of the instance and the name of the generic description (Figure 15). After selecting the option 'open' from the menu, the generic description of the wheel is recalled from the library and presented to the user. The current internal description of the wheel can be replaced by two instances of the generic object '/cart/tire' and '/cart/rim' (Figure 17). As a result, the assembly hierarchy now comprises three levels: the cart, the wheel and the tyre. The assembly hierarchy can be traversed one level at the time. To go down from the main level to the level of the wheel, the user can either pick at the tyre or at the rim, since both objects are sub-assemblies of the wheel. After opening the description of the wheel, the user can go down one more level by selecting the tyre or the rim.

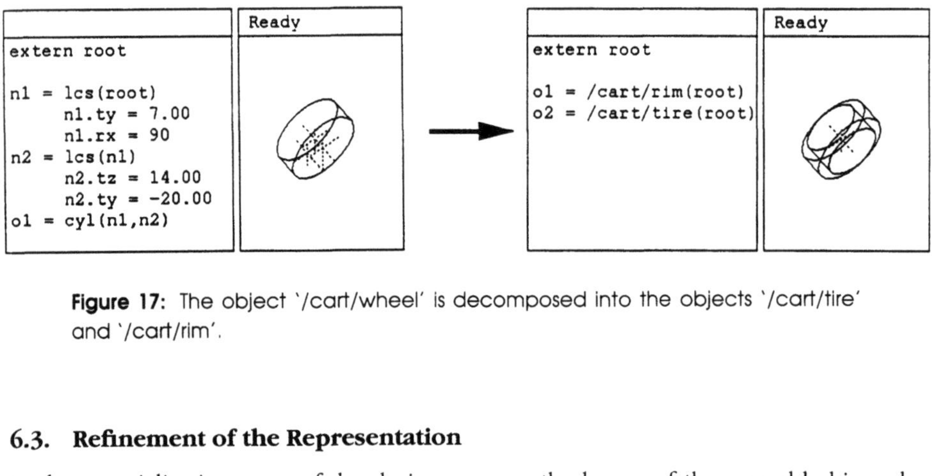

Figure 17: The object '/cart/wheel' is decomposed into the objects '/cart/tire' and '/cart/rim'.

6.3. Refinement of the Representation

In the materialization stage of the design process, the leaves of the assembly hierarchy are supplied with detailed three-dimensional components. The components can either be selected as predefined objects from a library, or alternatively, can be created bottom-up from primitives and other generic objects. For instance, to materialize the sub-assembly '/cart/tire', the user can open the directory '/tire' and select one of the available tyres (e.g., '/tire/dunlop', '/tire/goodyear' or '/tire/michelin'). Several alternative new designs for a particular component can be created and stored in the database under different names (e.g., '/board/design_A', '/board/design_B', etc).

The design of a component can be done separately from the design of the cart itself. To replace the simple geometric representation by a detailed component, the designer loads the conceptual design of the cart from the library, and picks the sub-assembly that should be materialized. After the generic description of the sub-assembly is opened, the user can pick one of the alternative materialization options (components) in the library, and select the item 'load' from the menu. As a result, the simple geometric

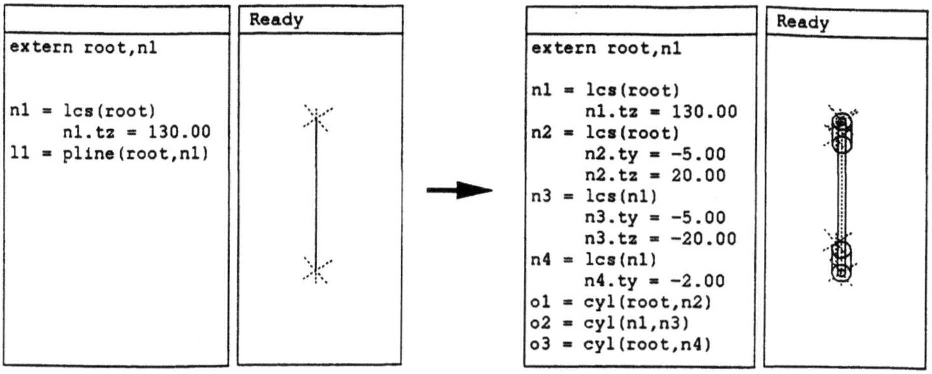

Figure 18: Materialization of the axle.

representation is replaced by a detailed three-dimensional model of the component. Note that the parameters (the external nodes) of a sub-assembly can be regarded as constraints for the design of a component. For example, the axle in Figure 18 is an object, constrained by two external nodes, root and n1. The design of the component axle can be regarded as the design of a "cylinder shaped object" that fits between the two nodes.

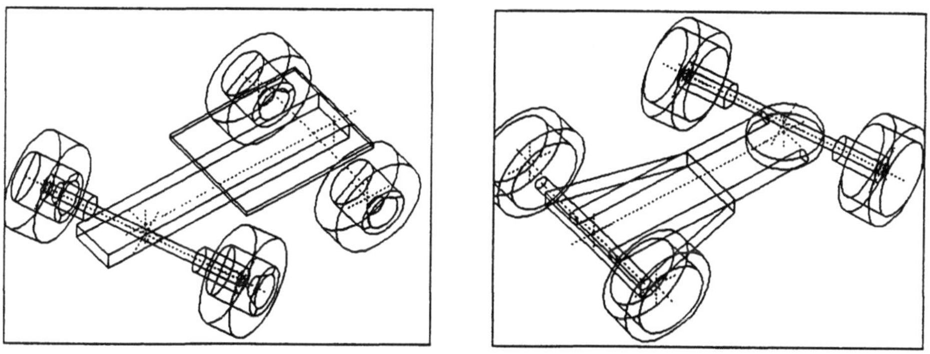

Figure 19: Several alternative configurations can be generated by substitution of components.

Alternative materialization options can easily be generated by opening the generic description of a sub-assembly and loading another predefined component. For example, Figure 19 shows two configurations of the cart with different solutions for the board and the rim.

6.4. Member Functions and Properties

Generic objects (assemblies) are provided with the member functions as described in the class object: 'draw', 'evaluate' and 'select' (see Section 4). If a 'draw' request is sent to an instance, the request is passed to the individual primitives in the representation which invoke their own drawing routines. A hit detection request is sent to the instance as a whole. The request is passed to the primitives which execute their own hit detection routines. If one of the primitives in the representation is selected, the whole instance is high-lighted and the system returns the name of the instance and the name of the generic object to which it belongs.

Properties can be assigned to instances by menu selection and are appended to the procedural object description with the template mechanism described earlier, for instance:

```
o1 = /cart/board(root,n3)
        o1.line_width = 1
        o1.line_style = dotted
        o1.colour = yellow
        o1.surface = 0.7
        o1.material = ABS
```

Properties can be assigned to separate primitives or to generic objects. If a property is assigned to a generic object, it is passed to all the primitives in the generic description. Some properties assigned to instances may be disregarded with a specific geometric representation. For instance, a line_width property is disregarded if the instance is internally represented as a solid model. However, *if* the instance is represented as a wireframe, *then* the line width is '1' *and* the line style is dotted. The manner in which the properties are visualized is also device dependent. A yellow object is represented by a black and white dither pattern on a monochrome display and in full colour on a colour display (Figure 20).

Figure 20: Shaded image of the cart.

7. Implementation

The ideas presented in this chapter are implemented in a modelling system called GeoNode. The system is implemented as a set of independent modules: a user interface, a linker, a database manager, an interpreter, a geometric module and a display module (wireframe and raytracer). The modules are separate applications that are connected via Unix pipes [Kernighan and Pike, 1984].

The user interface implements the event handling and graphical display of the model. Basic functionality for window management and graphics display are implemented with the X11 window system. Special user interface features such as pop-up menu's, scrollbars and editor windows are implemented with the Xr11 user interface toolkit. If a new command is generated, the system checks whether the new command is a built-in function (e.g., a node or a primitive) or a reference to a generic object in the library. In the latter case, the generic description is recalled from the library and linked with the rest of the object description. Subsequently, the procedural description is processed by the interpreter, and converted into an internal structure of nodes and primitives. The interpreter is implemented as a virtual stack machine. Lexical analysis and syntax parsing are implemented with Lex and Yacc [Kernighan and Pike, 1984]. Geometric processing of the model is performed in two stages. First, the three-dimensional transformation of the nodes in the geometric tree are calculated by concatenation of parent node transformations. Next, all constraint evaluation functions of the primitives are invoked. All primitives are now provided with a three-dimensional transformation and are processed by a modeller, resulting in a parallel or a perspective projection that is visualized by the user interface.

A central program starts up all applications and controls the data flow. This control is essential for efficiency considerations: the system would be to slow if the whole modelling pipeline has to be traversed for each incremental modification. Instead, each user action is analysed to determine the most efficient way to re-process the model. For example, if a new primitive is appended to the model, it is not necessary to re-evaluate the geometric tree and the other primitives. If a particular node is transformed, a local update of the branch connected to the node will suffice. The current implementation, on a Sun 3/60 workstation with floating point processor, enables real-time perspective transformation of the nodes. In the worse case, if the user has modified a generic description in the library so that the whole model has to be re-linked, the response time is still in the order of seconds.

8. Discussion

GeoNode offers a direct manipulation environment for modelling hierarchically structured objects. The concept of the geometric tree provides a uniform scheme for dimensioning, orienting and positioning various kinds of geometric primitives in three-dimensional space. Geometric relations between primitives are implicitly specified by the structure of the geometric tree and the manner in which the objects are appended to the nodes of the tree. Parameterization and part-hierarchies are implemented via an underlying procedural modelling language. The mechanism of the external nodes enables the designer to manipulate generic objects graphically while their internal representation remains hidden. The internal representation itself can be elaborated in later stages of the design process. This chapter demonstrates how the paradigm of direct manipulation can be applied for three-dimensional modelling and that the use of direct manipulation goes beyond the level of moving objects on the screen. All examples presented in this chapter are specified by graphical interaction only (except for entering a name with a new generic object).

Object-oriented techniques have been incorporated on two levels: in the interface to the user and in the technical implementation. From a user point of view, all entities, such as nodes, primitives and assemblies, are graphical objects that can be controlled by direct manipulation. Objects are grouped into more complex objects and properties assigned to groups are inherited by their members. The technical implementation has also benefited from the object-oriented principles incorporated in the C++ programming language. The object-oriented approach forces a thoroughgoing specification of the hierarchical organization in the modelling system and the operations that should be provided with each object. Once the classes and operations are defined, it is easy to expand the system by adding new objects. Implementation of a new object or class of primitive only requires the specification of three basic member functions: 'evaluate', 'draw', and 'select'.

A current restriction of the modelling system is that only one geometric representation can be assigned to a component in an assembly hierarchy. It would be convenient if more than one representation could be assigned simultaneously. The actual representation of components would depend on the "view" that is selected by the user. In a "functional view", the model can be represented as a two-dimensional graph with the names of the functional units represented as icons in the nodes of the graph. For the generation of alternatives the user would select a "simplified three-dimensional view" (lines, arcs) that hides details and offers real-time visualization, while the "detailed three-dimensional view" is required in the last stages of the design process. A method to implement a multiple view approach is the application of layers. The generic description of an object comprises several instances of alternative representations that are provided with a layer identifier, for example:

```
generic /cart/board() {
        o1 = /cart/board_simple_rep()
                o1.layer = 1
        o2 = /cart/board_complex_rep()
                o2.layer = 2
        o3 = /cart/board_detailed_rep()
                o3.layer = 3
```

The user can switch between the alternative representations by activating one of the layers.

The version of the system presented in this chapter uses constraints to position, orient and dimension geometric primitives by nodes in the geometric tree. Each primitive is supplied with an evaluation function that specifies how the constraint, imposed by the selected nodes, should be interpreted in order to obtain the three-dimensional transformation. Currently, the use of constraints to specify flexible geometric relations (e.g., radial distance, parallelism) between local coordinate systems is under development [Emmerik, 1990b].

Acknowledgements

I gratefully acknowledge the support of TNO-Bouwinformatica, especially in the person of Peter Kuiper. I would also like to thank Erik Jansen and Wim Bronsvoort for valuable suggestions and ideas that have been incorporated in the system and for reviewing an earlier version of this chapter.

References

Badler, N.I , Manoochehrik, H., and Walters, G (1987) "Articulated figure positioning by multiple constraints," *IEEE CG&A*, vol 7, no 6, 28-38.

Bier, E A (1986) "Skitters and Jacks. Interactive 3D positoning tools," *Proceedings ACM Workshop on interactive 3D graphics*, University of North Carolina, 183-196

Bier, E.A and Stone, M C (1986) "Snap-Dragging," *Computer Graphics (Proceedings Siggraph '86)*, vol 20, no 3, 28-38

Borning, A and Duisberg, R. (1986) "Constraint-based tools for building user interfaces," *ACM Transactions on Graphics*, vol 5, no 4, 345-374

Chen, M., Mountfort, S J., and Sellen, A (1988) "A study in interactive 3-D rotation using 2D control devices," *Computer graphics (Proceedings Siggraph '88)*, vol 22, no 4, 121-129

Cutter, M , Halpern, B , and Spiegel, J (1987) *McDraw*, Apple Computer Inc..

Emmerik, M.J G.M. van (1989b) "Graphical interaction on procedural object descriptions," *Theory and practice of Geometric Modelling*, Springer Verlag, 469-482

Emmerik, M J G.M van (1990a) "Direct Manipulation of 3D objects with a 2D input device," *Automatika*, vol. 31, no 1-2, 95-99 Proceedings Yugraph '90

Emmerik, M J G.M. van (1990b) "A system for interactive graphical modeling with 3D constraints," *Proceedings Computer Graphics International '90*, Springer Verlag, 361-376

Hanrahan, P (1988) "A survey of ray-surface intersection algorithms," *Siggraph course notes*

Kernighan, B.W and Pike, R (1984) *The UNIX programming environment*, Prentice-Hall Inc, New Jersey.

Kim, S H. and Lee, K (1989) "An assembly modelling system for dynamic and kinematic analysis," *Computer-Aided Design*, vol 21, no 1, 2-12

Kimura, F., Suzuki, H., and Wingard, L (1986) "A uniform approach to dimensioning and tolerancing in product modelling," In· *Proceedings CAPE'86*, Elsevier Science Publishers, pp 165-178

Myers, B A (1988) "Creating user interfaces by demonstration," *Perspectives in computing*, Academic Press Inc., vol. 22

Nelson, G. (1985) "Juno, a constraint-based graphics system," *Computer Graphics (Proceedings Siggraph '85)*, vol 19, no 3, 235-243

Nielson, M N. and Olsen, D R. (1986) "Direct manipulation techniques for 3D objects using 2D locator devices," In· *ACM Workshop on interactive 3D graphics*, University of North Carolina, pp 175-182

Rhyne, J (1987) "Dialogue Management for gestural interfaces," *Computer Graphics*, vol 21, no 2, 137-142.

Rogers, D.F (1985) *Procedural elements for computer graphics*, MacGraw-Hill Book Company.

Shneiderman, B (1983) "Direct manipulation. a step beyond programming languages," *IEEE Computer*, vol. 16, no 8, 57-69.

Stroustrup, B. (1986) *The C++ programming language*, Addison-Wesley publishing company

Sutherland, I.E. (1963) "SKETCHPAD. a man-machine graphical communication system," *Proceedings Spring Joint Computer Conference*, 329-346.

Wijk, J.J van (1986) "SML: a solid modelling language," *Computer-Aided Design*, vol. 18, no 8, 443-449

Part III

Graphics Systems

10

The Design of the Doré Graphics System

Michael R. Kaplan

Doré is an application interface for three-dimensional graphics designed to provide a highly abstract core environment for applications involving both interactive display and high quality image generation. Capable of spanning multiple platforms, technologies, and interface models, its goal is to provide an extensible framework for three-dimensional graphics that can grow with rapid advances in both dynamic and photorealistic image generation.

1. Introduction — The Need for 3-D Graphics Interfaces

Why do we need three-dimensional graphics interfaces? One answer is that a graphics interface can encapsulate algorithmic and systems knowledge. For example, a great deal of thought must go into the design and implementation of algorithms for adaptively tessellating a surface patch into polygons for display. Adaptive patch subdivision might need to take into account curvature, environmental attributes, the projection of the patch into screen space, and other factors. If each user had to write this code, the impact on development would be substantial. Thus, one way in which a graphics system can aid the user is by providing prepackaged expertise.

Graphics interfaces can also help to ensure a long lifetime for the applications that use them. If the platforms on which the interface is supported change, it is the expectation of the application's developer that these platforms will continue to support the interface. Furthermore, such an interface can help to make applications portable across a variety of platforms, spanning a wide range of price and performance. It is usually much easier for the developer of a new graphics system to port a few high-level interfaces, than for each application developer to port his graphics code to "yet another low-level interface".

A developer must climb a "learning curve" for each interface that he uses. If a given interface is elegant and orthogonal, then the system will be easier to learn, and new features will be easier to understand when they are added. Furthermore, the wider the application of the graphics interface, the fewer learning curves the programmer will have to climb in order to implement a fully featured system.

Figure 1: Visualization for Architecture and Interior Computer Aided Design. Image courtesy of Nissei Sangyo Co., Ltd. Created using Doré with the Media Logic Renderer through R-system which was developed by Kubota Computer for Nissei Sangyou Co., Ltd in Japan. Copyright 1990 Kubota Computer Inc.

Doré is an application interface for three-dimensional graphics, and the need for such a system is shown by the large number of applications that have been implemented on the interface since it became available. These applications include many in the areas of scientific visualization (Stardent Computer's AVS scientific visualization system uses Doré as its portable graphics base), molecular modelling, mechanical computer aided design, medical computing, and architecture and interior design. Some of these applications are represented by the colour Figures 1 and 2.

In Section 2 the design issues for graphics software in general are discussed. In Section 3 the design goals of Doré are outlined and then follows the overview of the Doré architecture (Section 4). The way in which the design goals are met is treated in Section 5. Finally the past, present and future of Doré serves as the concluding discussion. In this last section further attention is given to the uses to which Doré has been put.

2. Graphics Packages: Design Issues

There are a number of areas in which graphics systems, through their architectural design, can force the user to make fundamental choices early in the software development process. These choices can result in severe constraints later in this process. A number of these areas are addressed below. Taken together, they generate a multidimensional space of design goals in which the Doré system lives.

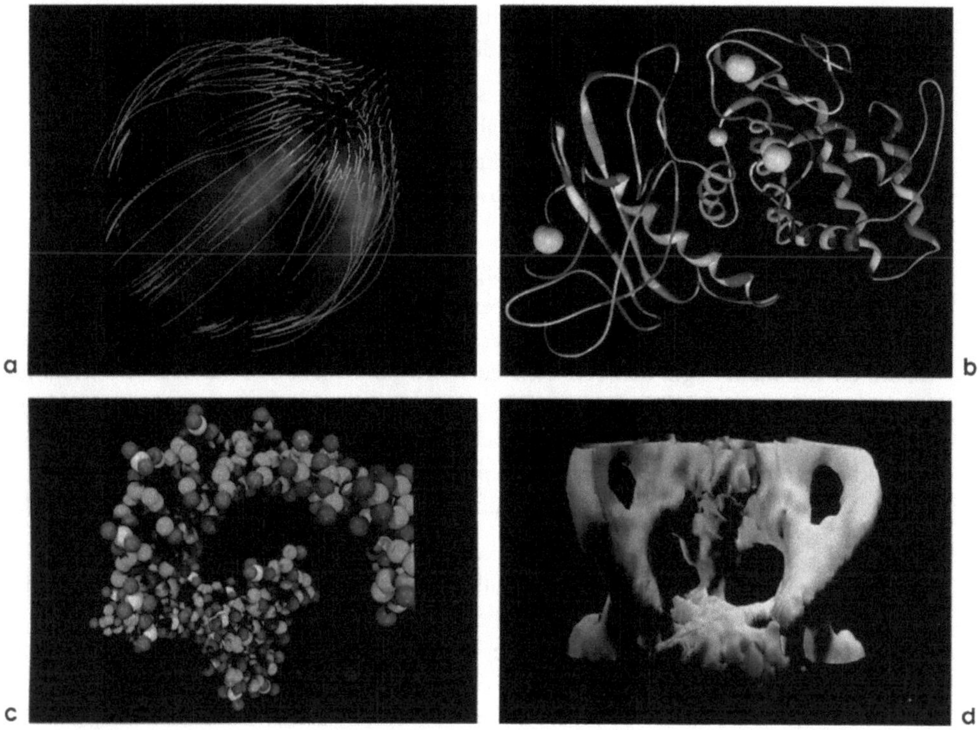

Figure 2 (a-d): (a) Scientific Visualization. Computational fluid dynamics of a simulated flow field over a sphere.
(b) Molecular Modelling. A thermolysin molecule. The complex structure of this protein is represented by a ribbon with vertex colours depicting the different amino acid types that make up the molecule. This ribbon approximates the position of the backbone atoms of the protein. The spheres represent metals bound to the enzyme.
Both (a) and (b) were rendered using one of Doré's dynamic renderers.
(c) Another molecular modelling example, but this picture was rendered with Doré's raytracing production renderer.
(d) Medical Visualization. A human torso, rendered using one of Doré's dynamic renderers.

2.1. Database Issues

2.1.1. Combining Immediate Mode and Display List Models

Graphics interfaces usually present either an *immediate mode* or a *display list* model to the user. The immediate mode model requires the application to describe the scene to the rendering system completely each time it is to be displayed. The scene may contain primitives, their attributes, and a description of the viewpoint and light sources. Whenever an object in the scene is moved or rotated, or the viewpoint is changed, it is the responsibility of the application to retransmit all of the scene data, not just the data that changed, for each individual frame in the display sequence.

The immediate mode model can be the source of great flexibility to the application. Since there is no permanent graphics database maintained outside of the application, it can quickly and efficiently modify the primitives, their attributes, and other characteristics of the scene. The display can thus closely track the state of the application's internal database.

On the other hand, there are a number of disadvantages to this scheme. Each application must include the code to generate scene data in a manner acceptable to the graphics system, and keep track of and update information about the viewpoint and overall scene environment (light sources, etc.) each time the scene is rendered. If rendering requires multiple, specialized, passes over the database, or special initialization of the environment, these functions must also be explicitly provided by the application. Also, offloading rendering to a special purpose processor, or over a network, may be impossible or inefficient when the overall organization of the database is known only to the application.

The display list model works by allowing the application to build a database maintained within the graphics system itself. Once the display list has been constructed, the graphics system can produce frames with little work on the part of the application. If intermediate data needs to be generated or cached to improve performance or deal with graphics hardware limitations, the renderer can take advantage of full knowledge of the scene to be rendered. To make a small change in the database, like the position of the viewpoint or of an individual primitive in the scene, the application can make use of *editing* calls. Having modified the graphics database in this manner, a new frame can be generated by making a single request to the graphics system. Large portions of the database can also be automatically maintained by the graphics system at the end of a network connection.

Of course, there are disadvantages to this scheme as well. If the application needs to rapidly modify large portions of the scene database on the rendering of each frame, or the application is highly interactive, editing of the display list may be very inefficient. If a network is involved, this problem can become especially difficult. It may also be difficult for the user to write code which allows the display to track the status of his internal data representations closely. Finally, integration of user interaction with display processing can be difficult to achieve.

2.1.2. Primitive Abstraction Issues

We can define a *primitive* as a displayable entity in a scene to be rendered. Examples of surface primitives are polygons and mathematical surface patches. Primitives can also represent solids (sphere, cone, box, etc.), or other non-surface entities like points, lines, and text. *Procedural* primitives can represent the properties of a field to be displayed, like fog in a visual simulation, or a vector field in a scientific visualization.

Some graphics systems allow only low-level primitives to be defined. These primitives are closely matched to the hardware or software that renders them. Primary examples of such systems can be found in graphics libraries whose only three-dimensional surface primitives are polygonal. Other graphics systems allow more abstract primitives, like surface patches, to be specified as part of the scene.

If an application is written using a graphics interface that provides only low-level primitives, then it is the responsibility of that application to convert any abstract representations that it may use into collections of these primitives. The algorithms to perform this conversion may be difficult to implement, either from the point of view of accuracy, storage requirements, or speed of conversion. Each user must reimplement these algorithms in his application. Further problems occur when such an application is ported to a graphics system which provides abstract primitives. In this case, a simple port will not take advantage of the advanced capabilities of the new graphics system, and a port which does deal with abstract primitives will probably be difficult to write.

A number of other issues appear in this category. Very often, an application will wish to display different representations of the same basic primitives. For example, the user might want to display a surface patch as a wireframe at one time and as a shaded surface at another. When a mathematically defined patch is displayed on a certain graphics device, its overall appearance may be determined by the number of polygons into which it is tessellated. The user may want this value to be interactively adjustable, so that the accuracy of rendering of the patch can be increased simply by turning a knob. In both of these cases, the set of low-level primitives which approximates the abstract primitive will vary under the control of the user. It would thus be beneficial for the graphics system to deal directly with abstract primitives.

Another issue involves the relationship between the primitives in the application database and the primitives that can be handled directly by the graphics system. If these categories are far from each other, then the user will have a difficult time maintaining a mapping between his internal database and the scene as it is described to the graphics system. The closer the primitives in the graphics system to those directly manipulated by the application, the cleaner and more elegant will be the interface between these systems.

2.1.3. Primitives in User Space

Applications which emphasize three-dimensional graphics frequently maintain one or more large databases of their own. These databases might contain the complete geometric description of complex objects, or large datasets of engineering and scientific analysis information. If the application cannot share its internal database with the graphics system, then it must copy all of the relevant data from its internal database to the graphics system in order to define each displayable primitive. Whenever this data changes, the corresponding primitives must be either updated or, in the worst case, completely redefined. This can require the transfer and replication of a very large amount of data. If, however, sharing is allowed, improvements in memory utilization and display performance can result.

2.2. Interface Issues

2.2.1. Modularity

A graphics system presents one or more interfaces to the user. Most systems include all of their functionality in a single, fixed, interface. The functions needed by a particular class of user cannot be isolated into a subset interface. Thus, all of the complexity of the system is visible to each user, regardless of his particular needs. This can make the system difficult to learn and use, as each user must determine which parts of the system apply to his application, and which can be safely ignored.

A *modular* system, however, can have a more flexible approach to the application interface question. If capabilities can be modularized into distinct and independent subset packages, the user need only become familiar with the subpackage that most closely suits his needs. So, for example, the interface most useful to the developer of a mechanical CAD package might not include all of the attributes needed for realistic rendering, although it might be possible to add these capabilities at a later time. In another example, the interface presented to the developer of high-level scientific visualization software might not include any primitives involved in the display of realistic objects. In both cases, however, the core technology would be the same. One could further imagine a highly modular package which allowed users to create their own custom interface subsets. Programmers responsible for supporting other developers in their work group might find this feature extremely useful. Developers could even exchange and distribute interface packages.

2.2.2. Single/Layered Interface

If the application's developer wants to provide packages of functions built to work with certain graphics interfaces, he must do so in a strictly layered fashion. This means that all code written to interact with the graphics interface must be layered above it. The developer does not have access to any of the interfaces which may be considered internal to the graphics package. This limits the extensibility of the graphics system.

2.3. Performance Issues

2.3.1. Interactive Performance

Low-level graphics libraries, tuned to a specific manufacturer's display system's capabilities, frequently offer high performance and fine control over display functionality. Unfortunately, these packages rarely extend over multiple platforms. High level graphics software systems can address this problem. However, for interactive graphics, these systems rarely provide the efficiency of a direct interface on any individual graphics system. So, the user is forced to make a decision. If he chooses a low-level interface, he will be forced to recode significant parts of his application in order to run efficiently on different platforms. On the other hand, if he chooses a high-level software package, he may have to sacrifice efficiency on one or more platforms, and an interactive graphical application which does not perform smoothly is hardly usable.

2.3.2. Portability

In order to prove useful as a device-independent graphics software system for interactive display, the system must maintain a high-level of interactive performance across multiple platforms. Thus, issues of portability are intimately connected to those of performance. Portability of graphics software is often achieved at the expense of performance on any specific platform. Even more rare is a system which achieves good performance on multiple platforms, especially when they have differing display architectures.

2.4. Rendering Issues

2.4.1. Combining Interactive Display and Realistic Rendering

Research and development in three-dimensional graphics has long consisted of a number of parallel streams. Even in the area of rendering, development has proceeded along widely divergent paths. For example, much research has focused on hardware and software systems for rendering images in "real-time". These *interactive* systems are capable of displaying moving images of three-dimensional objects, either in wireframe or solid shaded form. The most powerful interactive systems have the ability to smoothly shade and apply texture to surfaces as they move through a simulated environment.

In another area, development has concentrated on the problems involved in rendering photorealistic images. Here the focus is not on interactivity, but on the quality of the final image. In most cases, images are recorded one after another to produce smooth animation. Here, recent advances have been made in incorporating elaborate lighting models, the simulation of reflection and refraction, and diffuse reflected light (radiosity) into the rendering process. The images that result can truly be called "photorealistic".

These two streams of development have rarely intertwined. As a result, there tends to be a dichotomy between application interfaces designed for interactive graphics and those intended for photorealistic image generation. Users who want to write software for interactive modelling, for example, must usually use a different interface to describe the scene and control the display device than they would use to interface to a high-quality renderer.

The requirement to interface with different packages in order to obtain different types of rendering places an increased burden on the user. First, he must learn and write code to interface to each package. This may involve describing the scene differently, depending on the type of rendering to be performed. This may in turn force him to maintain multiple internal representations of his data. In addition, he must keep these multiple representations synchronized not only with his application, but possibly also with each other.

When a single, consistent, interface to interactive display and realistic rendering is available, the user incurs a number of advantages. Obviously, he need only learn and code to the one interface. In addition, the combined system makes it possible for him to work with a high-level scene description, regardless of rendering style, and makes it easier for him to synchronize the graphics system with the internal state of his application. Since the graphics system maintains an implicit link between the scene description for both interactive and high-quality rendering, the same software that is used for interactive modelling and preview can drive the production of stop-frame animation sequences.

2.4.2. The Tradeoff Between Realism and Rendering Time

Another issue in the rendering area concerns the ability to balance realism and rendering time within a specific renderer. High-quality, software based renderers tend to offer a fair amount of flexibility in this regards. Very often, they allow the user to speed up the rendering process by choosing shaders which do not take into account global lighting effects (reflection, refraction, radiosity, etc.), or by decreasing the resolution of the final image or the use of anti-aliasing. Interactive systems, on the other hand, generally offer little capability in this area, rendering time being directly dependent on the number of primitives being rendered.

2.4.3. Rendering Abstraction

Many graphics interfaces, especially interactive ones, have rendering styles determined almost completely by the contents of their databases. The primitives in these databases directly map to a particular rendering style (polygonal, Gouraud shaded, etc.). There are a number of problems with systems of this type. First, it is difficult to port such a system to a wide variety of platforms having differing display architectures, since the manner in which rendering is performed cannot be changed without invalidating the assumptions of the package. Second, the graphics interface cannot easily track advances in display hardware and rendering algorithms, since the algorithms that it uses are "built in" to its database description. Finally, it is difficult for the user to adjust realism either up or down, for the same reason.

The distinction between interactive and realistic rendering is blurring rapidly with new developments in display hardware and rendering algorithms. Some of these developments are:

a. New display hardware allows interactive processing of effects such as lights in the scene, true transparency, and texture mapping.

b. New algorithms for realistic rendering make use of display hardware in a multiple pass mode to achieve advanced realistic rendering effects. These effects include subpixel anti-aliasing and environmental texture mapping.

c. New algorithms allow interactive processing to be merged with preprocessing, in order to achieve very sophisticated rendering effects. The best example of this is found in a two-step approach to the implementation of radiosity. The radiosity of a scene is first computed during a preprocessing step. The radiosity values are then assigned to polygon vertices in the scene database. Interactive rendering of this scene allows the user to move through it, with the radiosity effect being maintained throughout the interactive display process.

In order to take advantage of these advances, it is crucial that a graphics software system abstract rendering style away from its database.

3. Doré: Design Goals

As we have seen in the discussion above, graphics software exists in a very large multidimensional design space. There are many issues which must be considered. Trade-offs can be made in a number of areas, and the types of features that would make a system applicable to a wide audience of users often seem to be contradictory. During the design phase of the Doré project, these issues were investigated. As a result, a small number of design goals were chosen in each category. These goals, which are described below, were the driving force behind many of the individual architectural choices made during the design of the system. By looking at these goals together, a secondary list of more general design criteria was generated. It is these criteria which drove the fundamental architecture of the system.

3.1. Database Goals

- The graphics system should provide a flexible approach to the graphics database question. The application should be able to intelligently trade off the use of immediate and display list modes.
- The system should allow primitives to share application data directly.
- The system should provide a range of primitive abstraction, and the flexibility to create user defined primitives, more closely matched to the application database.

3.2. Interface Goals

- The system should be modular with respect to functionality and the interface that it presents to the user. This means that capabilities should be divisible into packages which are designed to meet the needs of users in specific categories.
- The system should present a multiple layer interface architecture. That is, the user should be able to interface to the system at different levels, depending on his needs and level of sophistication.

3.3. Performance Goals

- The system should approach the maximum performance on any interactive display system to which it is ported.
- While presenting a highly abstract and consistent application interface, the design should allow efficient ports to a wide variety of interactive graphics systems. It should be able to efficiently make use of any special rendering hardware or other features of the platform, without changing the interface to the user.

3.4. Rendering Goals

- Ideally, the graphics system should provide the user with a single, consistent, application interface to both interactive and photorealistic display capabilities.
- The system should allow the user to smoothly trade realism against rendering time within a specific renderer, no matter what type of rendering is being performed. This should apply to interactive as well as to high-quality rendering.
- Rendering style should be abstract with respect to the graphics database. The database should described the contents of the scene to be displayed in an abstract manner, but should not determine the overall rendering style.

3.5. General Design Goals

Upon consideration of the goals described above, it became apparent that the keys to the Doré architecture could be found in a very small set of abstractions: *ease of use*, *flexibility*, *modularity*, and *extensibility*. The overall design goal adopted by the Doré development group, therefore, was to provide a modular and extensible framework, along with a rich set of components. The framework would provide the benefits of high-level graphics software systems, but would also overcome many of their traditional liabilities. The resulting system would have a long lifetime, be portable to a wide variety of platforms, and have a wide area of applicability. By providing a pluggable component model, the system would also allow for a great deal of extensibility. This, in turn, would enhance its lifetime. Furthermore, by allowing more than one interface to be exposed to the developer, the system would also benefit from extensibility at multiple layers.

4. Doré: Architectural Overview

4.1. An Object-Oriented Methodology

Doré is fundamentally *object-oriented*, both in architecture and in implementation. The advantages of object-oriented design are frequently enumerated as: ease of use, flexibility, modularity, and extensibility, exactly those required for our system.

The overall architecture of the Doré graphics system takes the form of a collection of intercommunicating *objects*. Each object is an *instance* of an *object type*, and consists of an encapsulation of local instance data and a reference to the functions which implement its *methods*. An object type is an abstract concept, encompassing the collection of methods necessary for an object instance of that type, along with a *creation* method for creating a new object instance of the type.

When the user creates an object, a *handle* or *reference* to the object is returned to him. In all future Doré operations, the handle is the equivalent of the object itself, and all Doré functions which operate on an object take an object handle as a parameter. A handle is guaranteed to be unique during a single Doré session, and can be stored and used by the application like any other integer or memory pointer value.

When an application wishes have an object perform some function, it tells the object to *execute* the appropriate *method*. Most top-level method execution is actually requested by Doré's high-level interface routines, or as the result of the execution of the top-level methods. For example, during the process of rendering, each object in the scene will be asked to execute its *rendering method*, or simply to *execute* itself. We will use this terminology interchangeably. So, when we mention *object execution*, it refers to an object executing the appropriate method for whatever type of processing is under discussion.

4.2. The Doré Layer Mandala

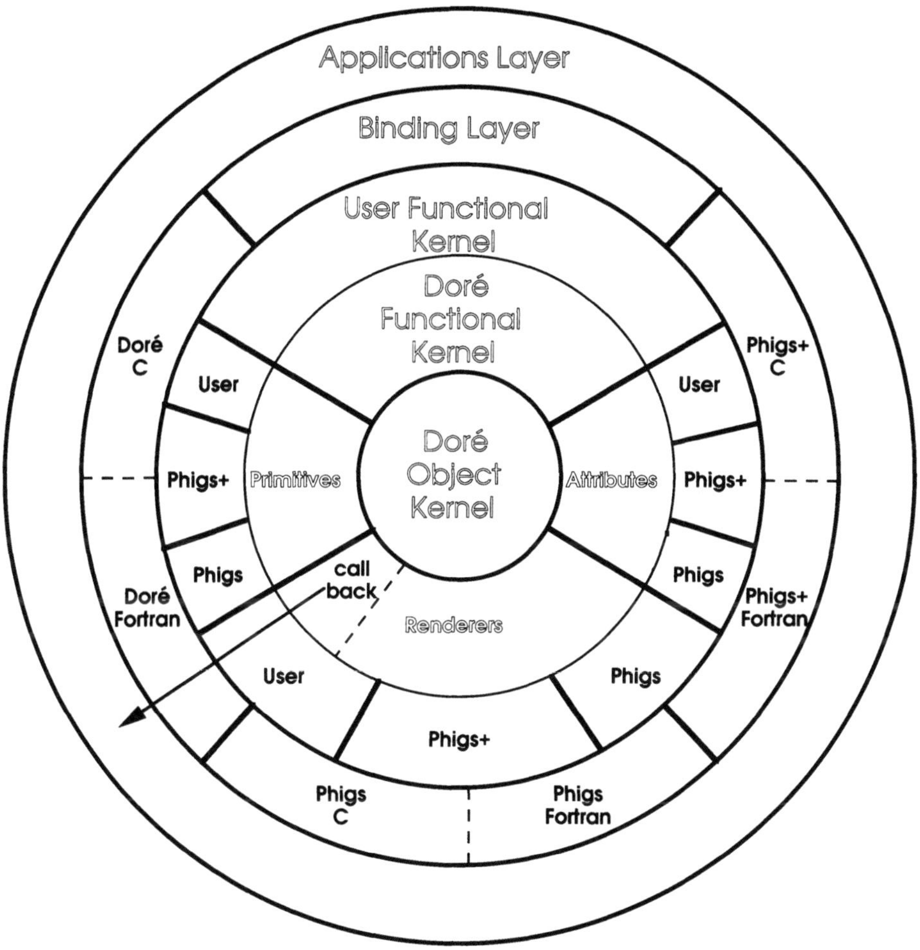

Figure 3: Doré Architecture Mandala. A layer diagram of the architecture of the Doré system.

Figure 3 illustrates the internal structure of the Doré system. It consists of three layers: from innermost to outermost the *object kernel*, the *functional kernel*, and the *binding layer*.

Underlying the architecture of Doré is the *object kernel.* The kernel is responsible for the allocation, execution, and destruction of objects. It is structured so that new object types can be defined by the user and installed at run-time. This can be done without the necessity of access to Doré source code. In fact, all object types are installed at run-time. Doré thus views all object types, whether distributed as part of the standard system, or user supplied, as equal citizens.

The primary design goals for the kernel were related to performance and consistency of execution. Since interactive display, the most time-critical type of rendering, can require extensive method execution, one goal was to keep method execution overhead to a minimum. As a result, a procedure call mechanism was used to implement method execution, rather than a more traditional message passing mechanism. In addition, method types are installed and referenced with integer names, rather than arbitrary string names. This allows the method lookup function to be implemented through a simple table lookup, further speeding method execution. Finally, the object kernel performs no garbage collection, objects must explicitly allocate and deallocate all of their dynamic memory, although Doré provides support mechanisms and defines methods to make this task easier for the programmer of new object types.

The *functional kernel* contains all of the utility code and all of the object types that are installed in the system, and hence known to the object kernel. Utility code includes code which is used by object methods. Utility code is just straight line code, without the encapsulation provided to the object methods. The functional kernel can be thought of as being further subdivided into two concentric rings, the *Doré functional kernel* and the *user functional kernel.* In actuality, there is no difference between objects in one ring and objects in the other. The only conceptual difference is that objects in the inner ring are distributed with the standard Doré system. These include *groups*, *views*, and other object types which are essential to the functionality of the system, as well as a rich assortment of primitive and attribute objects.

The *binding layer* surrounds the functional kernel, allowing multiple interfaces to be defined for the system. Interfaces may differ only in their language binding, or they may substantially divide functionality into independently distributable functional subsets.

4.3. The Scene Metaphor

The primary metaphor in Doré is that of a scene to be photographed. In this simulated scene are placed the objects to be displayed, the camera which will produce the picture, and lights to illuminate the objects. Of course, since this is a simulation, the scene can be as large as needed, object's can have various non-physical attributes, and the user can place as many lights in the scene as desired. In Doré the collection of information that completely specifies the scene is called the *scene database.* To the user, then, the architecture of Doré is mainly visible in the manner in which the scene database is specified and manipulated.

4.3.1. Building the Scene

Doré's object-oriented architecture is revealed at the user level by the way in which the scene database is defined. The scene database is simply a collection of Doré objects. These objects fall into a number of general categories. The categories, along with examples of component types, are described in more detail below. It is important to remember, however, that the specific object types described represent only a cross-section of those available to the user, and that the repertoire of types can be extended at any time.

Primitive objects, or simply *primitives*, include all of the object types which are directly displayable in a scene. Primitives can be thought of as being fully defined by a collection of *attributes*. These attributes, when processed by a given renderer, completely determine the appearance of the primitive when it is displayed, Attributes which determine geometry (spatial location and curvature) and topology (spatial connectivity) fall into the category of *geometric* attributes. *Appearance* attributes are usually concerned with the way primitives interact with light in the environment. Diffuse colour, specularity, reflectivity, transparency, and surface texture all fall into this category. In addition to their traditional use to describe physical appearance, these attributes may be used to represent the results of engineering or scientific analysis. In this case, colour might be used to represent the scalar or vector properties normally associated with solids or fields (see Figure 2a).

When an primitive is asked to display itself as part of a scene, it can use attributes from a number of sources. First, it can reference attributes stored as local *instance data*. These attributes, called *local attributes*, are part of the primitive itself, and are carried along with it, no matter where or when it is displayed. Generally, these attributes are specified at the time of object creation. A simple example of this is the specification of vertex locations during the creation of a polygonal primitive. Local attributes may also be manipulated through the execution of methods on an already existing object. For example, a polygonal object could be asked to add a constant to the x coordinate of all of its vertex locations. The resulting data would still remain local to the object.

A primitive object can also obtain attributes from the environment at rendering time. Attributes obtained in this manner are called *inherited attributes*. Unlike local attributes, inherited attributes are not carried along with the primitive object, they depend on the state of the rendering environment at display time. The mechanisms which Doré provides for inheriting attributes are discussed in more detail below. It suffices to say at this point that inheritance can play a big role in the specification of primitive attributes.

Attribute objects, or simply *attributes*, are the primary mechanism by which inherited attributes are specified by the user. When an attribute object is executed before an primitive object, it may apply, or be bound, to that primitive. Conceptually, the global attribute information specified or modified by the attribute object is available for inheritance by all subsequent primitives in the scene.

Doré maintains a number of *global objects*, or simply *globals*, during rendering. At the beginning of the rendering process for each frame, these globals are assigned default values. There is a global object for each *global attribute* in the system. When a primitive executes its rendering method, it can access the state of any of these global attributes, and thereby inherit, or bind, their values. For example, there is a global attribute defining the diffuse colour of an primitive. When a primitive which does not have its diffuse colour defined locally is asked to render itself, it can use the current value of the diffuse colour global attribute. So, if the diffuse colour global has the value of red when a sphere primitive is asked to render itself, the primitive will appear as a red sphere in the rendered image.

Attribute objects either set or modify the value of one or more of these globals. For example, a diffuse colour attribute can set the value of the diffuse colour global, while a tint attribute can modify the luminance of the diffuse colour global without changing its hue or saturation. In this manner, attributes can be defined that operate on the environment in subtle ways. In another example, a number of attributes could be used in combination to specify texture mapping, or surface patch subdivision.

Organizational objects are used to form structured collections of other Doré objects, and to control execution of the database. The primary example of an object type in this category is the group. A group contains an ordered list of object handles, or *references.* A group might be used to represent an automobile in a mechanical CAD system, or a house in an architectural application. A group can contain references to objects of any type, including other groups. In this manner, a hierarchy of parts can be represented.

The primary function of a group is to apply methods to each of its component objects. When a group is asked to render itself, it simply asks each of the objects in its reference list to execute the same method. During this process, the group is also partly responsible for the maintenance of the global objects in the environment. Pushing and popping of attributes is performed by groups. Groups also have *editing* methods, unique to their object type, which allow the contents of a group to be manipulated after it has been created. Examples of editing methods are "add object reference at beginning of group" and "delete object reference after label object".

A single object can be referenced in any number of groups, allowing it to be *instanced* in the database. Of course, if an object is instanced multiple times in the scene database, it is useful if they can differ in some of their attributes. This is achieved through the attribute inheritance mechanisms.

5. Doré: Addressing the Design Goals

5.1. Database Goals

We wanted Doré to allow immediate and display list models of database specification to be intermixed cleanly in a single scene. We have already described how groups are used to build hierarchical display list structures. As we have seen, all of the features of a standard display list architecture are present, including object instancing, attribute inheritance, and display list editing. At this point, we will show how immediate mode features can also be obtained in Doré, and how they can be intermixed with the display list model.

A number of design elements in Doré cooperate to produce this functionality, the most important being the *callback object*, or simply *callback*. A callback is an organizational object which has special properties with respect to method execution. When execution reaches a callback, its function is to cause execution of a user specified subroutine. In essence, callbacks implement coroutine calls back into the application. The application is then free to perform any normal processing, with one additional characteristic: *it can also cause any Doré object to be immediately executed*. This is done through a call to Doré's "execute object" system function. This function is passed the handle of the object to be executed, with the result being that the object is asked to execute the "current" method. The "current" method is, of course, the same as the method executed by the callback object. During callback execution, Doré continues to maintain its execution environment exactly as during group traversal, so object execution has the expected results.

We have mentioned two of the design elements crucial to immediate mode functioning in Doré. These were the callback object, and the "execute object" system function. A third design element is so implicit to Doré, that it may easily be overlooked. It is simply the fact that the user is always given a handle to any Doré object that he has created. This handle is all that is needed to execute the object during callback execution. The user can be extremely creative in the use of these mechanisms. For example, he could achieve a "flip-book" animation effect by creating a large number of objects, and executing a different one for each frame that is rendered.

Another database goal was that the system should allow primitives to share data in the application database. By allowing for the extensibility of the system with respect to user written primitives, this capability was embedded in the system. A good example of this is the *variable polygon mesh primitive*. Like the *polygon mesh* primitive that is part of the standard system, this primitive contains a collection of vertices, each of which has a three-dimensional location, and possibly also colour and normal information. The primitive also has a vertex connectivity list, which determines the topology of the mesh. The variable object differs from the standard object in that its vertex data is referenced directly out of the application's data space. When the object is created, pointers to the vertex data are passed as parameters to the creation method. The primitive's methods reference this data exactly as if it was instance data local to the object. Additional methods, unique to the object type, allow the application to notify the object when it needs to synchronize internally computed data with changes in application data structures. In all other respects, including attribute inheritance and rendering execution, the primitive behaves to the user just like the standard polygon mesh.

Finally, we wanted the system to offer a wide range of primitives, from the primitive to the abstract, and for this set of primitives to be extensible. We have already described the mechanisms by which new primitives can be added to the system. Here we will go into more detail on the architectural features in Doré which help to achieve abstraction.

First, and most important, every primitive object has its own method for rendering execution. In general, primitive rendering methods operate as follows:

a. The primitive consults the state of certain global attributes in the environment to determine characteristics like representation type and shading model.

b. The object determines, based on its level of abstraction combined with the current rendering characteristics, whether it has access to local data in a form suitable for "direct" rendering.

c. If suitable local data is available, the object calls whatever utility routines are necessary to cause it to be rendered.

d. If no suitable data is available, the object creates an *alternate object* with the desired characteristics, and tells this new object to execute the current rendering method. The alternate object is then *cached* with the local instance data for the primitive, if repetitive rendering is expected to be performed.

This rendering method execution scheme is flexible, and helps Doré to achieve many of its database goals. Primitive's will generally be able to render themselves directly. For example, if a triangle list primitive is asked to interactively render itself with a representation style of wireframe, and a diffuse colour shading model, it will usually be able to pass its vertex data directly into to a lower-level of pipeline processing.

Abstract primitives, on the other hand, will most likely need to create alternate objects. Alternate object creation and execution are performed exactly in the same manner as in an application. If an primitive wishes to cache the alternate object, it merely has to retain its handle. An example of an abstract primitive which generally caches an alternate object is the surface patch. Most display hardware does not render patches directly, so a surface patch must subdivide itself into the appropriate low-level primitives before rendering. This subdivision is performed by the primitive rendering method itself, but can be modified through inherited attributes. The standard Doré system includes attributes to specify both subdivision type (fixed, adaptive, etc.) and level (fineness of subdivision). If subdivision attributes change on a later rendering execution, then the patch object may have to discard the previously created alternate object and build a new one. In any case, caching insures that repetitive display of abstract primitives will be fast after the first display of the primitive.

It is interesting to note that what may be considered an abstract primitive for a particular port of Doré may be considered a primitive primitive for a different port. For example, surface patches are abstract with respect to most interactive display platforms. However, some high-end platforms contain hardware for direct patch rendering. On these systems, the surface patch primitive executes its rendering method as if it is a primitive of the system, sending its patch description data directly to the display hardware. Because of Doré's object-oriented architecture, only the patch object methods need to be rewritten in order to allow this to happen. It is thus very easy to port Doré to a wide variety of systems, having vastly different display capabilities. The same architecture allows Doré to grow cleanly with advances in display hardware and the development of new rendering algorithms.

5.2. Interface Goals

Doré achieves a modular interface through the run-time installation of object types. All object types in Doré are equal citizens, even though they may come from different sources. A good example of this is found in the Doré user group distribution, which contains new packages of objects contributed by users and developers. The objects in this distribution can be obtained by users and installed in the system on a selective basis, depending on their needs.

In addition to providing a modular application interface, Doré also provides a number of well defined lower level interfaces to rendering. The overall rendering architecture is illustrated in Figure 4. At the top is visible the *application interface* (or the *Doré API*). This is the primary level at which applications programmers and systems developers interface to the system. It defines the interface between the applications program and the Doré functional kernel, described above.

At the next level down is found the *rendering interface*. This is the interface between the object rendering methods of the functional kernel and the pluggable Doré renderers. It is important to remember that Doré does not contain a fixed notion of rendering style. Any number of renderers, having different capabilities and performance ranges, may be plugged into the system framework, and be controlled from the functional kernel. The rendering interface defines the connection between the functional kernel and the pluggable renderers. This interface is further divided into two subsets. By providing a renderer which accepts the calls defined in the *dynamic rendering interface*, the developer "plugs in" a renderer through which Doré can interactively display the scene database. By providing a renderer which accepts the calls defined in the *production rendering interface*, the developer "plugs in" a renderer through which Doré can produce high-quality static images from the same database.

Below the rendering interface is found the *device interface*. This is the interface between renderers and the pluggable Doré devices. Again, it is important to note that Doré does not contain a fixed set of devices to which it can render. Instead, it provides a well defined interface into which developers can plug both dynamic and production devices. A *dynamic device* is an abstract entity which is capable of taking commands from a dynamic renderer, and outputting to a given type of display. For example, one of the commands in the dynamic device interface may instruct the device to output a shaded-depth buffered triangle. The *dynamic renderer output interface* for a dynamic device like a hardware display pipeline would accept this command and, with minimal processing, send it down to the hardware to be rendered. A dynamic device for displaying across a network to a simple pixel mapped display, however, might have to render the triangle in software, and send a stream of pixels to its display. In either case, the device interface seen by the dynamic renderer remains the same.

A *production device* is an abstract entity that simply knows how to display image results. It is not expected to perform a significant part of the rendering process, as may be the case for a dynamic device. Production renderers interface to production devices by sending them image data. The production device may, however, be responsible for

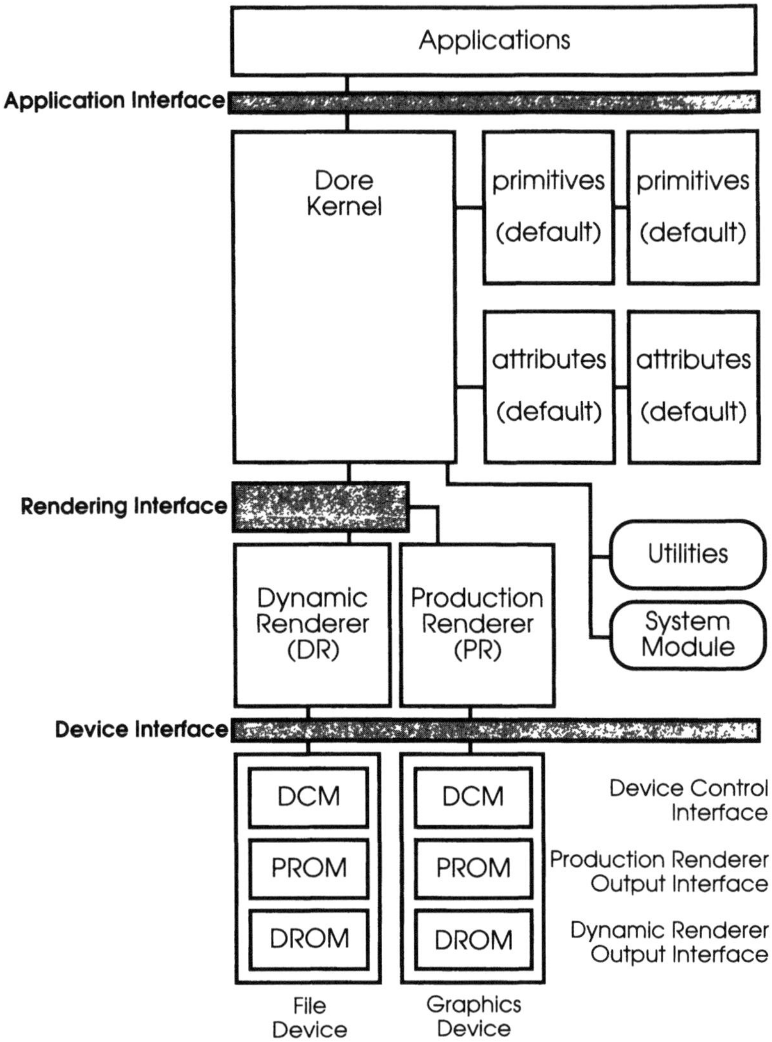

Figure 4: Doré Interface Layers. A block diagram showing the rendering architecture of the Doré system, with reference to the multiple well-defined interfaces which the system presents to the developer.

colour quantization, dithering, and other types of image processing operations on the output image data.

This architecture allows developers to interface to the system at a number of different levels. For example, a developer might choose to plug a new dynamic device into the system. In this case, the dynamic renderer would not have to be changed. Or he might choose to add a dynamic renderer designed to drive a new type of display hardware. In this case, the object methods for interactive rendering would not have to be changed.

5.3. Rendering Goals

In Doré, a large number of attributes, both local and inherited, can be *overloaded* onto a single primitive. When the primitive is rendered, it can, depending on the type of rendering being performed, use any subset of these attributes to define the way it will appear in the resulting image. Thus, the goal is to allow the primitives to be defined as completely or as abstractly as possible, regardless of the type of rendering that is to be performed. As a result, the same Doré scene database which supports efficient interactive display can also drive sophisticated photorealistic renderers.

A number of features of Doré's architecture makes this possible. First, Doré is capable of maintaining a large number of global attributes without incurring a high overhead during execution for those that do not change frequently. Second, since the processing performed by objects during rendering execution is up to the objects themselves, the architecture allows superfluous attributes to be ignored during interactive rendering and taken into account for photorealistic image production. We call this technique *intelligent backoff*. Finally, since Doré is extensible with respect to primitives and attributes, new renderers can be supported through the addition of new object types. For example, the original Doré development group recently added a full complement of texture mapping attribute objects to Doré, along with some new primitive types, in order to support a new high-quality renderer capable of displaying textures. Doré was later ported to two interactive display systems which have the ability to render texture mapped images interactively. The new ports were able to take advantage of the same attributes and primitives that had been added to support the high-quality renderer. In effect, scenes which previously rendered with texture only through the use of a non-interactive software renderer, now displayed with texture in real-time, with no changes required on the part of the user program.

Figure 4 is a block diagram of the overall rendering architecture of Doré. As can be seen, Doré is designed to drive multiple renderers, of differing types. In order to accomplish this, the rendering architecture is broken up into a number of distinct interfaces. This enables developers at varying levels of sophistication to tap into the system at different levels, in order to achieve the goals mentioned above.

5.4. Performance Goals

Doré achieve high interactive performance on a wide variety of platforms. It does this through the combination of a number of architectural features. The fundamental features which make high performance ports of the system possible are discussed below.

The multiple layered rendering architecture of Doré, discussed above, allows ports to be customized at the appropriate level, so that they can take advantage of varying display architectures. The distributed rendering model, with processing spread across the rendering methods of primitive, attribute and organizational objects is also fundamental to attaining high interactive rendering performance. We have already seen how primitives can create cached alternate objects to speed repetitive display. Since organizational objects also have their own rendering methods, they could also have the capability of "compiling" their contents into more efficient alternate forms. So, for example, the alternate form for a compiled group might be a data structure residing completely in specialized display hardware. A similar technique could be used to distribute groups across a network. This distribution would be transparent to the application, unlike in systems which always assume a network architecture.

6. Doré: Past, Present, and Future

The purpose of this chapter has been to give insight into the design issues associated with three-dimensional software interfaces, the fundamental architecture of the Doré system, and the ways in which this system addresses the design issues. Doré is a large, comprehensive system, however, and no exposition of this limited length can go far toward fully describing the capabilities that it offers or the feature sets which it includes. A short history may better illustrate the growth of the system and its future potential better than a comprehensive feature list.

From the time when the design of Doré was begun in June of 1986 to its first shipment in May of 1988, there were a number of influences on its development. GKS [ISO/SC24, 1985a] was already a well established standard for two dimensional device independent graphics. The Silicon Graphics GL language [Silicon Graphics, 1988] was used as a low-level interface by a number of applications. The SIGGRAPH Core [GSPC, 1979], GKS-3D [ISO/SC24, 1985b], PHI-GKS, and Phigs [ISO/SC21, 1989] standards were the primary representatives in the area of structured (display list) interactive three dimensional graphics. High quality (photorealistic) rendering was available to users, although not to programmers, mainly through turnkey packages from companies such as Wavefront and Alias. By the time Doré development was begun, attention from the standards community (at least in the United States) had shifted primarily towards expanding the Phigs standard to include obscuring surfaces and light source shading. These efforts culminated in the Phigs+ standard definition [van Dam, 1988; ISO/SC24, 1989], and the subsequent PEX (Phigs in X) [Clifford et al., 1988] specification, which continue to gain support as defacto industry standards for a certain class of applications and systems.

Although many of these packages had and have important roles in meeting the needs of graphics programmers, it was felt that none of these interfaces, taken singly, would cleanly address all of the design goals set forward above. In particular, a solution based on an existing package which could combine both interactive graphics and high-quality rendering was not evident. It was also evident to the design team that no fixed three-dimensional graphics interface could encompass the rapid advances in rendering algorithms and display and computational hardware that were to occur in the immediate future. Thus, the decision was made to focus on an extensible framework for both interactive and high-quality rendering. It was also decided that a new model for graphics software should include the best features of both the immediate mode and display list paradigms. In some sense, these decisions grew out of the need to support and open up the capabilities of the graphics superworkstation architecture that was being developed in conjunction with Doré. This architecture featured a flexible rendering pipeline, extremely high levels of computation provided to a single user, and close integration between user processing and graphics display functionality. We assumed, rightly it seems, that these capabilities would rapidly find their way into lower cost systems.

When Doré was first shipped to customers in May of 1988, it included a completely functioning framework, along with a rich set of objects. Primitives included not only the more traditional polygonal elements, but abstract surface patches, NURBS, meshes, and cubic solids. Attributes included those related to the interactive display of Gouraud and Phong shaded surfaces, along with those related to high-quality image generation, including shadows, transparency and global reflection. The system shipped with two renderers, a Dynamic Renderer which made use of the Ardent system's real-time graphics functionality, and a Production Renderer based on a spatial- subdivision raytracing algorithm.

Doré was shipped not only to Ardent customers as a callable library, but also in source code form to both non-profit and commercial institutions. Universities and other non-profit research institutions have always been able to obtain the complete source code for Doré for a nominal distribution fee. This policy was intentionally designed to increase the scope of the system, and to encourage bright people to build on the Doré framework.

Since its first delivery, the Doré system has grown in a number of ways. The fact that it has grown, and continues to grow, is an indication that the framework concept on which the system was based is not only interesting but also practical. User's can now obtain plug-in Dynamic Renderers for multiple workstation platforms, including X-Windows, Sun Microsystems, Silicon Graphics, and Hewlett-Packard. Packages of additional primitives are available, including Beta-Spline surface patches, curves, sphere and cylinder lists (for molecular modelling applications), and volumetric objects with arbitrary slicing planes. At least two commercial firms offer plug-in high-quality renderers for Doré (Media Logic and Intelligent Light). Users have generated network protocol bindings to the Doré functional kernel (for Supercomputer and networked graphics applications). Probably the most unusual user-written object is a new organizational object which implements the combination of primitives using constructive solid geometry operations (University of Michigan).

Some of the many applications implemented on the Doré interface were mentioned in the introduction and illustrated in Figures 1 and 2. As predicted, major advances in rendering algorithms and display hardware have taken place in the intervening years. A new class of graphics workstations include the capability to interactively produce images containing such advanced effects as transparency, texture mapping, environmental reflection, multiple focused lights in the scene, and shadows. New plug in Dynamic Renderers for Doré already take advantage of these systems, producing images in a few seconds which used to require minutes or even hours of processing by a software based renderer (frontispiece). Applications which previously could expect these effects only in static imagery can now obtain them interactively, without changing their interface to the underlying graphics software.

Acknowledgements

It would be impossible to acknowledge individually the efforts of all of the people who have contributed to Doré over the years. One would have to name the members of the original Doré development group, the users who have added public domain capabilities to the system, the organizers and members of the Doré user's group, and so on. I would like to express my heartfelt gratitude to all of these people. However, one group deserves to be mentioned by name, the Advanced Graphics Group at Ardent Computer, which assumed responsibility for the system when it was just an infant, and saw it through its early childhood and adolescence. The group is headed by Kevin Weiler, and includes Dan McLachlan and Helga Thorvaldsdóttir. I would like to thank each of them for their efforts.

The author would also like to thank his employer, Apple Computers, Inc., for the freedom to devote time to writing this chapter.

References

Clifford, W.H., McConnell, J I , and Saltz, J S (1988) "The development of PEX, 3D graphics extension to X11," In· *Proc. Eurographics '88*, North-Holland, pp. 21-30

Dam, A. van (1988) "Phigs+ Functional Description, revision 3 0," *Computer Graphics*, vol. 22, no. 3 (July), 125-218.

GSPC (1979) "CORE Status report of the Graphics Standards Planning Committee," *Computer Graphics*, vol. 13, no. 2.

ISO/SC21 (1989) "Programmer's Hierarchical Interactive Graphics System (PHIGS) functional specification," ISO/IEC 9592

ISO/SC24 (1985a) "Graphical Kernel System functional specification," ISO 7942-1985

ISO/SC24 (1985b) "Graphical Kernel System for Three Dimensions (GKS-3D), functional description," ISO DIS 8805.

ISO/SC24 (1989) "PHIGS PLUS Working Draft," ISO/IEC JTC1 SC24 WG2 N37

Silicon Graphics (1988) "Graphics Library Reference Manual," Document Number 007-1203-020 C Edition, Version 2

11

The New Graphics Standard — Object-Oriented!

Peter Wisskirchen and Klaus Kansy

Work towards the second generation graphics standard NewAPI has just started. This occasion is taken to compare the needs of graphics standards and the benefits of object-oriented systems. It is argued that the open demands for graphics standards can reasonably be met only by adopting an object-oriented approach. Advantages of such an approach are summarized. Open issues are discussed.

1. Motivation

Many ambitious and trend-setting developments in the area of computer graphics are based on the paradigm of object-oriented programming. In addition, object-oriented graphics kernels are becoming more and more relevant for industrial applications and they are provided by different prominent software environments such as News, OSF-Motif, NeXT, Lisp environments, etc. Particularly in connection with graphical workstations and user interface management systems, the object-oriented approach has become more and more predominant.

These results and successes are sharply in contrast with the present results in the field of graphics standardization. Systems such as GKS [Enderle et al., 1987] or PHIGS [ISO, 1989a], which we call *traditional* systems in this chapter, are in no way affected by the object-oriented paradigm and philosophy. Currently new efforts are starting under the heading of a new application programmer's interface (NewAPI) for the definition of second generation graphics standards. This situation brings up the opportunity to define an object-oriented standard or a functional specification which is heavily influenced by object-oriented design principles. 'Functional specification' means the description of the functionality in a language independent way as the basis for specific language bindings. These language bindings can be developed for object-oriented languages or language extensions. It is an open question whether the functional specification could also be used for traditional procedural languages (Pascal, Fortran, C).

Standardization requires much more than the specification and realization of a useful kernel for a given object-oriented environment. The definition must be language independent and different aspects of portability have to be assured. In this context, questions arise concerning an object-oriented approach. These questions will be discussed in this chapter and could serve as a basis for further discussions.

2. History of Graphics Standardization

The first graphics standard, the Graphical Kernel System GKS [Enderle et al., 1987], was developed around 1980 and finished in 1985. It was aimed at the application programmer and described a programming language for the definition and manipulation of graphics. However, the hope to cover the needs of a majority of graphics programmers by one standard graphics language were not fulfilled. Since GKS, the development of more standards has continued. The need for three dimensional graphics was covered by GKS-3D [Enderle et al., 1987], an editable hierarchical graphical structure was provided by PHIGS [ISO, 1989a], and advanced surface primitives and rendering techniques are currently defined under the name of PHIGS PLUS [ISO, 1989c].

These continuing efforts do not compromise the existing standards but reflect the complexity of graphics and the vast diversity of constituencies with differing requirements which hardly can be fulfilled by one standard. For example, cartographers need specific line primitives (for highways), signatures (characterizing land use), elaborated text (along rivers), specific transformations, etc. For realistic images complex surface primitives with reflectance attributes, lighting models, etc. are needed. CAD applications need different data structures than geographical applications. In addition, the technical progress (increased capabilities and power of graphics workstations, new user communities due to price cuts) and developments in related areas (windowing, document architecture, print technology) led to new requirements.

However, it is not desirable to provide a separate standard for each constituency as this would be too expensive for developers of graphics systems, too difficult for educating graphics programmers, and it would destroy the benefit of portability of programs. Furthermore, the extension of existing standards has led to standards which are nearly unmanageable due to their complexity — one just needs to look at the size of the respective standards documents as an indicator. Therefore, a new effort has been started to generate a second generation graphics standard which comprises the capabilities of existing standards, avoids the errors and pitfalls of the first generation standards, is sufficiently flexible to be adapted to the needs of a variety of applications, and provides all these capabilities in a well structured way.

The major areas which are felt to need further development include:

- new output primitives and attributes,
- picture structuring and access,
- attribute setting and binding to primitives,

- flexible input techniques correlated with output,
- interfacing to text and document standards,
- refined data types.

This work is tackled by the standardization committee ISO/IEC JTC 1 SC 24 WG 1 under the heading of New Application Programmer's Interface (NewAPI). The first proposals submitted so far address a variety of aspects.

[Kansy and Wisskirchen, 1989] have recommended the object-oriented philosophy as the appropriate way to cover the requirements in a reasonable way.

The Input Study Group [ISO, 1989b] has developed an input model which provides an improved application control over mapping of physical to logical devices, a stronger symmetry between input and output, extensibility, and input device composition.

A new standard proposal has been developed by [Brodlie et al., 1989] which covers many other aspects in a new picture concept called NDC picture, which fully determines the geometrical picture and a picture part store.

3. Why Do We Need an Object-Oriented Standard?

The deficiencies of existing graphics standards are primarily limitations in functionality and in picture structure. These enhancements can reasonably only be done by using an object-oriented philosophy. The graphics capabilities of existing object-oriented systems are too low level and do not cover these needs.

3.1. Characteristics of Existing Graphics Standards

Graphics systems provide a language to describe a picture and the operations on pictures. Classical graphics systems have focussed on providing sufficient functionality and have missed the target of providing a language which is elegant and appropriate for the description of graphical items and their features. They either restrict functionality to a level which can appropriately be handled with the respective language, or they provide elementary graphical operations on pictures only through complicated constructs of the programming language.

For example, PHIGS does not deal directly with the interactive graphical interface but allows the definition of the picture as an hierarchical acyclic structure which is the basis for the interaction [ISO, 1989b]. This structure allows an efficient way of modelling pictures where specific items are reused several times. The user, however, sees a picture which is generated from the structure by traversal which extends the acyclic structure into a tree structure. Multiple instances are visible as individual items. For the user, it is natural to do both, editing a particular item on the display as an individual item (part) or as a multiply used building block. PHIGS only supports the editing of (multiply used) building blocks in a simple way. Individual parts can only be identified via a pick path; manipulations are possible only after a laborious restructuring of the acyclic graph to a tree. However, in this case all information of common origin of parts is totally lost [Wisskirchen, 1989].

GKS on the other hand does not have these problems [Enderle et al., 1987]. The reason does not lie in better concepts but in the restricted functionality which does not support a multi-level picture structure and editing of the graphics structure and, hence, avoids the mentioned pitfalls.

The advantage of existing graphics standards is based on the well defined functionality which meets the needs of significant constituencies. A model is provided for defining and structuring application objects by means of graphics primitives. A set of manipulation functions is provided in terms of this model. Therefore, the overall model gives more benefits than just the sum of the single functions. Graphics primitives cannot be used in an arbitrary way: their use within the given model is restricted, e.g., in PHIGS primitives are used only within a structure where the control of the display, the transformation, and the attribute setting is exercised by the structure mechanism. The model forces the user to obey certain rules when writing a graphics program. This discipline is rewarded by additional services provided by the graphics kernel: device independence, well formed attribute and transformation concept, inquiry facilities, predefined matching of input and output (pick operation). A traditional graphics kernel, therefore, provides more than a mere graphical toolbox.

3.2. Characteristics of Existing Object-Oriented Graphics Kernels

There are several reasons why graphics standardization cannot be based on any of the graphics kernel within existing object-oriented systems, e.g., the Smalltalk-80 graphics kernel [Goldberg and Robson, 1983]. These kernels are language-dependent. They do not provide all the functionality that has proved useful and necessary for traditional graphics kernels and which, therefore, is expected from a graphics standard by the graphics community.

Many of the graphics tools developed in object-oriented systems aim at the support of software development on graphical workstations. These tools include graphical oriented text editors and debuggers, windowing systems for concurrent editing of several documents, dialogue control via pop-up menus, etc. These developments are not assessed negatively, on the contrary, they have played an important role in the progress of computing technology especially for the development of modern workstations. Nevertheless, these efforts have not led to a graphics kernel which could replace current graphics standards like GKS and PHIGS.

Object-oriented graphics kernels typically provide graphics primitives, mechanisms for handling event input, and specialized complex graphics classes, for example, to generate windows, menus, and dialogue boxes. They do not provide a set of kernel functions for device-independent graphics programming which is sufficiently rich, complete and harmonized. They provide no model for the generation, maintenance, and long term storage of graphical object hierarchies or other general purpose *graphics semantics.* There is no pick device which directly relates input to a graphics object structure. In short, they can be characterized as toolboxes or kernels in a narrower sense rather than a consistent complete *system* [Goldberg and Robson, 1983]. The notion of a system is suggested to a certain extent by the model-view-controller concept of Smalltalk-80, which provides for the coordination between often used input/output tools like menu display and menu interaction (view-controller). The coupling of input/output, however, is not directly related to the generation and editing of general graphics data structures [Krasner and Pope, 1988].

Experience has shown that existing object-oriented graphics kernels offer many concepts and methods which can be used with profit as a good starting point for future graphics standards. These concepts include inheritance, flexibility and elegance of input models, and graphical constraints.

4. General Advantages of an Object-Oriented Graphics Standard

Interactive graphics, in an intuitive way, has been object-oriented since its very beginning because the presentation and manipulation of graphical objects on a display was the central objective of interactive computer graphics.

Unfortunately, when graphics standards have been defined, object-oriented languages and object-oriented graphics have not been taken into close consideration. As a consequence, computer graphics has not been influenced significantly by the important and interesting results of object-oriented system design. In our opinion, there is a great gap which has to be closed. The next generation graphics standard should be object-oriented — this is our objective! To motivate this intent, we will outline the advantages and potential of an object-oriented graphics standard.

4.1. Transformation of a Mental Model into Programming Code

We start with a general but, in our view, most significant criterion for the quality of a new standard. To make our point clear, we will first consider the way how an application programmer usually designs an interactive interface.

First, the application programmer has to become familiar with the functionality of the given application: he/she develops a *mental model* of the intended result. This model has to be transformed into the language and functionality of a given standard, it must be *verbalized* in terms of the standard. The main criterion for the quality of an standard should be the capability to verbalize the mental model in a straightforward and natural way. The fewer structure clashes that exist between mental model and graphics capabilities, the less rethinking has to be performed by the programmer. He will be able to generate a better and more consistent program in a shorter time.

Thinking in objects as guided by the object-oriented paradigm is thinking in structured items with attached methods. This basic concept alone is a good starting point for defining the right new standard, since users "have intuitions which correspond closely to the notion of objects within the object-oriented paradigm" [Blake and Wisskirchen, 1989]. It leads to a model

- with direct naming of visual items,
- with attributes directly assigned to visual objects as their own inherent information,

- with concurrently existing and instantiated graphical objects which may be freely selected and edited by the user,
- where different objects with the same behaviour can be seen as instances of one class.

This does not necessarily mean that the right specification is automatically obtained by the use of an object-oriented model. Rather, we are in the appropriate environment and framework for the right generation and definition of the graphics programmer's interface.

In [Wisskirchen, 1990] many examples of the advantages of an object-oriented approach are given. Comparisons with the PHIGS model of traversing an acyclic graph show very clearly the disadvantages of the PHIGS approach which supports a view of an abstract multi-level graph traversing machine rather than the mental model of the application programmer.

4.1.1. Object-Centred View

The object-centred view of the object-oriented paradigm is a decentralized model. All relevant objects of a graphics systems can be described directly: an object is owner of its proprietary data, e.g., attributes and transformations. These data may be assigned and requested by using the object's identifier as receiver for such messages. This avoids artificial mechanisms (sequential lists, temporal sequencing, additional names) used in existing graphics systems for indirect assignment of attributes to single output primitives or groups of them.

4.1.2. Multiple References and Consistent Update

In object-oriented systems, it is common practice and nearly trivial to use multiple references to one single object. This feature is also needed in computer graphics for handling predefined geometrical figures *(building patterns)* which can be used for multiple insertions into a picture.

There are two possible interpretations when editing a building pattern: the changes apply for all visual representations of a building pattern in a consistent way or they apply to one individual item only. Both operations are needed in computer graphics. The *consistent* modification of all instances is very easy to achieve. For *individual* modifications, object-oriented systems provide powerful copy operations, e.g., deep and shallow copying in Smalltalk-80.

4.1.3. Flexible Communication

The well known layer model of traditional graphics systems is a typical subroutine paradigm, where the lower kernel is always called and never calling. There are no components of the kernel, no input device that may directly call the functionality of an application. In object-oriented system, application and kernel objects may call each other, mutually. Through these mechanisms, the reaction to user input can be programmed in a more natural way than in traditional systems. No centralized dialogue controller is necessary for the analysis of input and for branching to the different submodules of the application or the kernel handling specific kinds of reaction.

4.1.4. Inheritance

Inheritance can be used by an object-oriented graphics system in many different situations. Subclasses of the prefabricated graphics kernel classes allow the modification of the given functionality. The traditional way of modifying existing functionality (of a hidden kernel) requires the definition of additional layers on top of the kernel. Such a layer for a modified segment, for example, has to provide all segment functions (attributes, pick-ids, deletions, insertions, transformations). For all these operations new subroutine calls have to be defined, because a modification of the standard interface is not allowed. Inheritance provides a better alternative for modification, it is very natural and easy to implement. By the use of inheritance, additional knowledge (geometric modelling, application specific knowledge) may be integrated into a graphics object, a segment/structure say, without changing the predefined functionality, and with making heavily use of inherited methods. This is real integration, because no naming is required, and the whole application programmer's interface is seen as a real kernel with enhanced functionality.

This principle can be used for new types of primitives (composed primitives, special purpose primitives for cartography, etc.) as long as the internal realization (as a method of a user defined subclass) is done only by means of the given programming language and the functionality of the standardized graphics kernel. It should be noted that the old practice of layer definition on top of a kernel is of course possible and quite similar to the traditional case. This can be done through the definition of additional classes with methods using the functionality of the predefined kernel by message passing.

5. Requirements for an Object-Oriented Graphics Standard

In the following, we will list some requirements we believe are important for a current object-oriented graphics standard. The major points are discussed in more detail in Section 6.

a. The standard should fulfill the general goals of a graphics standard: *application independence, language independence, device independence,* and *information hiding*. Information hiding means that the internal implementation is completely hidden. This requirement will provide portability of application programs. In addition, it will give the implementor of the kernel enough freedom for an efficient implementation. This is an old requirement for graphics standards. The advantages are clear, but in combination with an object-oriented approach some special questions arise which are a matter for further discussions.

b. For object-oriented language binding, *inheritance* should be supported for all methods defined in the standard. Inheritance is meant here in the sense employed in object-oriented systems: inheritance of behaviour. There are many advantages in the field of computer graphics, if all relevant object descriptions in an object-oriented graphics kernel are defined as classes. Many drawbacks which are found in GKS and PHIGS, e.g., the definition of new types of primitives and attributes, integration of geometric modelling in a kernel, can be solved in a very elegant way by inheritance. A new primitive, even if it is constructed by geometric modelling algorithms can be defined (semi-internally) as a subclass of a given kernel class. The external access to such an object will deliver an instance seen as a new graphical object of an extended kernel *(virtual part).* Inheritance can automatically provide methods like attribute assignment, deletion and transformation.

c. The standard should provide a *multi-level part hierarchy* with a well defined semantics. This means that a precise definition for all aspects of building up and editing graphical hierarchies must be worked out for all components of the hierarchy. This requirement reflects the fact that in most applications part hierarchies play a dominant role. The support by a graphics kernel means that the main semantic aspects of a graphical hierarchy are supported by the kernel: inheritance (in the part-of sense) of attributes, deletion and copying of parts and wholes, support of graphical interaction (picking, transformation) for parts and wholes, etc.

d. The standard should support a *dynamic model for part editing.* The number of subparts may change dynamically during run time. This is in accordance to the GKS and PHIGS model. There are no predefined methods (slots) for the insertion or the access of specific subparts, as implemented in frame-oriented systems.

e. In contrast to traditional standards, where communication is only supported by a top-down layer model, more *flexible communications patterns* between kernel and application should be provided (mutual communication between different modules, call back messages for input devices). This allows so-called external control, initiated by the user via an input object. It means, e.g., that any picked part may directly call any other object.

f. *Rule* interpreters and *constraint* solvers become more and more important for supporting new declarative (and less imperative) styles for graphics programming. Therefore, all prerequisites for adding rules and constraints should at least be provided.

g. Besides portability of graphics applications, a *graphical archive* for storage and transfer of pictures 9hould be supported. Different applications may access the contents of the archive. This is a traditional requirement which has to be solved again in this context.

6. Discussion of Some Questions

Our discussion is based on some guidelines which have to be obeyed. They reflect general rules which have proved useful with traditional standards and which should be obeyed as far as possible for new developments. These guidelines include:

- In the functional standard, a set of classes and methods (visible to the outside) should be defined for use of the application programmer in a language independent way (*language independence*). In a set of language dependent documents (worked out for object-oriented languages and language extensions) the same classes and methods should be defined as a concrete application programmer's interface.

- The application programmer will be provided with an implementation which conforms with the standard. Such an implementation consists of a library of classes and methods, in accordance to the standardized language binding. One way of using this implementation is through the creation of instances of the delivered classes and message passing to these instances. This is a certain analogy to the traditional procedural binding of predefined functionality.
- In addition to this, subclassing is allowed for all standardized (visible) classes.
- Changing methods of standardized classes is prohibited. Access to internal methods should be impossible or at least not allowed. This is a strict principle for a secret implementation of a graphics standard. We call it the *principle of privacy* for the kernel.
- Graphical applications should be portable between the same types of environment.
- Graphical presentations should be portable in general via a language independent picture format.
- In addition it should be possible to store and retrieve graphical objects in an archive.

Under these preconditions we will now discuss some problems.

6.1. Language Independence

If we try to describe an object-oriented system the first problem that arises has to do with the great variety of object-oriented models. This has been described in the well known paper of [Stefik and Bobrow, 1985].

Firstly, we have to decide whether the language independent description should be based on the model of classes and inheritance or on prototypes and delegation.

There is one good argument for delegation: "Delegation permits more flexibility, since communication patterns can be determined at message reception time rather than at compile time or object creation time" [Lieberman, 1986].

The good argument for inheritance is that the actual candidates for an object-oriented standard are based on inheritance (Smalltalk-80, C++, CLOS).

There are controversial debates about the pros and cons of the two principles. For others [Stein, 1987] inheritance and delegation are essentially equivalent. But for the pure verbal description of a graphics standard the two models are quite different. Inheritance would suggest a description of the document as a set of stable classes and methods. Delegation would, while defining graphics editing, lead to a description of dynamically changing instances and types *(types on-the-fly)*.

If we use inheritance, i.e., a description of predefined classes and methods, we must think about a convenient functionality for providing all the aspects of flexibility in computer graphics programming. The dynamics of graphics systems are mainly required when graphical object hierarchies have to be edited at runtime. This is obvious when graphics editing has to be realized by use of the application programmer's interface, where new objects are created by copying and editing, and where part hierarchies are continuously changing. For solving this problem however a compromise can be achieved. This means that the graphics hierarchy can be modelled by collection classes. Collection classes may access subparts by using key-value pairs. These classes can dynamically grow and shrink, whereas part access through specific message patterns would require a prototype model.

In [Wisskirchen, 1990] the two different approaches were discussed in connection with some examples, showing that from a purely technical view the delegation model was easier to program. Fortunately, in the case of the experimental system GEO++ considered in that book, it was quite easy to reformulate the class-inheritance specification into an "equivalent" prototype-inheritance specification. Thus we hope that the problems caused by the coexistence of the two alternative models can be solved.

6.2. Inheritance in a Private Kernel

Besides the different models, discussed in Section 6.1, it has to be mentioned that even in the case of class-inheritance a lot of different inheritance mechanisms are offered by different programming environments. If one describes the functionality of a kernel, different organizational principles are possible, depending on the different concepts of inheritance (hierarchical inheritance, different mechanisms of multiple inheritance, up to a more method centred model as supported by CLOS [Bobrow et al., 1988]). This diversity led us ask whether, and to what extent, this has to be taken into consideration as well.

For a decision on what to do, let us ask how crucial inheritance is for the description (not usage) of a kernel with a private internal implementation. Fortunately we came to the conclusion that the organization of the class tree or lattice of the prefabricated kernel is not very important for the application programmer. We will illustrate this with an example.

Suppose that a graphics kernel describes the class Primitive with subclasses PolyLine, Line, Circle. Let attribute: be a method, defined for Primitive. We would like to change attribute: in a way such that the modification is also valid for the subclasses of Primitive. If our kernel were completely transparent we could edit the method for attribute: directly. In this case the modification would have become valid for the subclasses automatically. But this is not allowed in a private kernel. Alternatively if we try to define attribute: for a direct subclass NewPrimitive, this cannot be used for the existing subclasses in an environment with hierarchical inheritance. The only way is to define for each of the subclasses PolyLine, Line, Circle, three new subclasses PolyLineNew, LineNew, CircleNew, and to implement the new method in each of them. It is of course possible to combine this with the given functionality of the superclass (see Figure 1).

To do all this, we do *not* use the information, contained in the specification of the kernel, that Primitive is superclass of the subclasses, and that attribute: is inherited by these

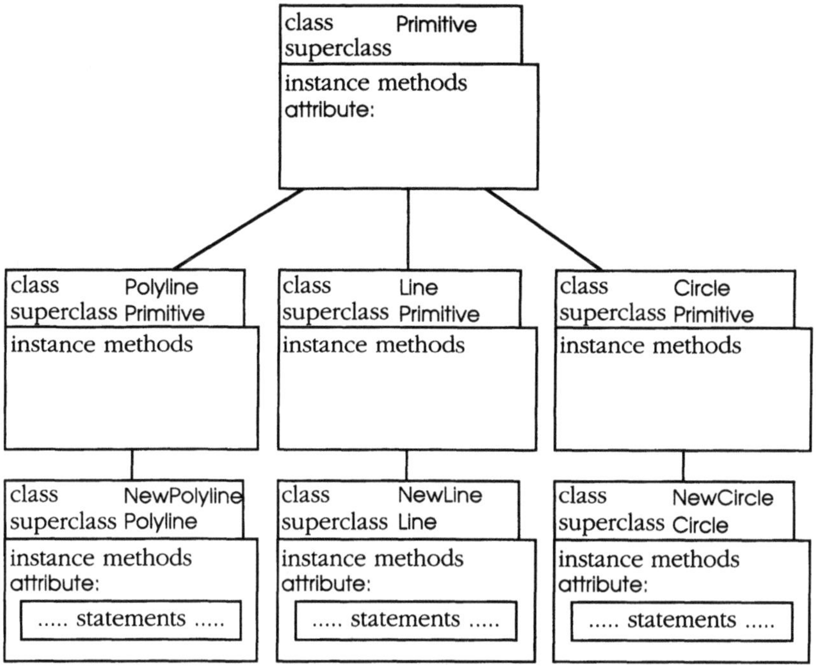

Figure 1: Subclassing in a private kernel (hierarchical inheritance). In the case of hierarchical inheritance, 'attribute:' must be re-implemented three times. The inheritance tree of the private kernel cannot be used.

classes. All this would happen in the same way if each of the methods were defined for each of the subclasses at the very beginning.

In the case of multiple inheritance the subclass PrimitiveNew can be used for PolyLineNew, LineNew, CircleNew. This shows that a given kernel can be used in a more flexible way in this type of environment. But also in this case the fact that the class Primitive is superclass of the other three classes is not really used (see Figure 2).

It should be noted that all of our attempts to loosen the above rule always led to problems. All alternatives would have dismantled the principle of a private kernel, and restricted the freedom for the manufacturer of the kernel. Therefore we propose not to modify the above rules about the privacy of the kernel's internals. This means that we cannot make any technical use of the way how the hierarchy of the kernel is defined. Therefore, for example, the fact that Primitive is superclass of the other four classes need not to be described or even prescribed. This reduces the problem with the different inheritance concepts. At most a hierarchical or poly-hierarchical *description* could be chosen for a more compact verbal description of the document. The key point for the definition of the standard is that a clear description of the messages which can be sent by the application programmer to instances or classes of the kernel must be given. Therefore we come to the conclusion that a language independent description of a kernel can be worked out. Another question is whether and to what extent a language

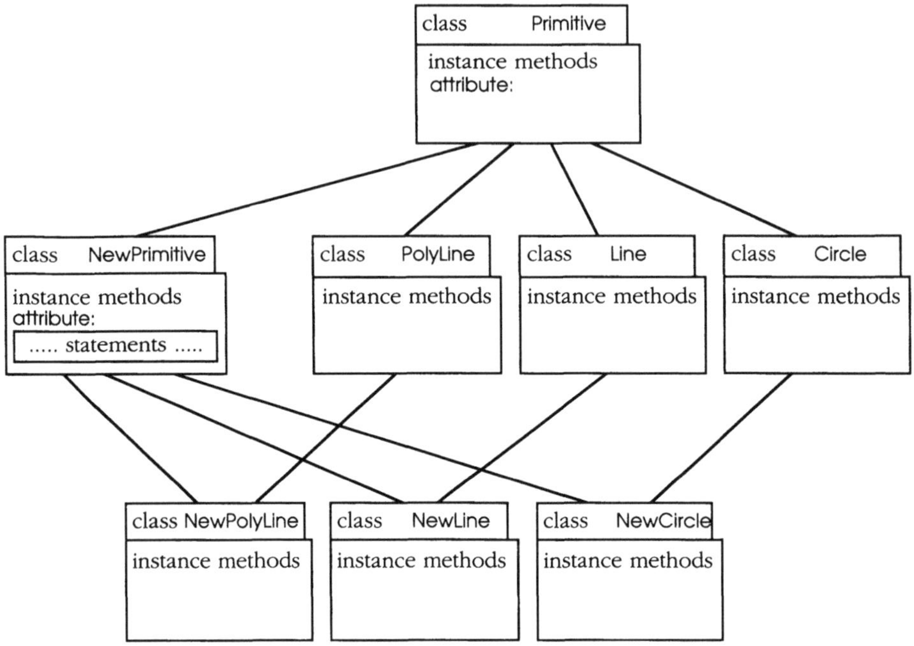

Figure 2: Multiple inheritance. In the case of multiple inheritance the method for 'attribute:' must only be re-implemented once. But also in this case, no use is made of the inheritance graph of the kernel.

binding for non object-oriented environments can be developed. This seems to be more or less possible too, but will not be discussed here.

It is important to note that though the hierarchy of the kernel classes is not an essential topic, environments with different inheritance mechanisms may use the kernel in different ways. This has already be shown by our small example.

6.3. Modelling Part Hierarchies

A graphics system like PHIGS provides a lot of functions for the construction and editing of high level graphics elements called structures which consist of output primitives, attributes and references to other structures, and form an acyclic graph. Object-oriented languages contain several distinct mechanisms to construct object hierarchies. We shall explain it with the graphical object hierarchy shown in Figure 3.

The first possibility is the part hierarchy which provides special methods for the insertion of and the access to subparts. We call this technique *frame-oriented*. In this model, class radio has the preprogrammed methods (*slots*) left: right: which accept parts and left, right for enquiring about parts. The components belong to the class SwitchBoard. For each of the buttons, this class has methods to insert and interrogate a button.

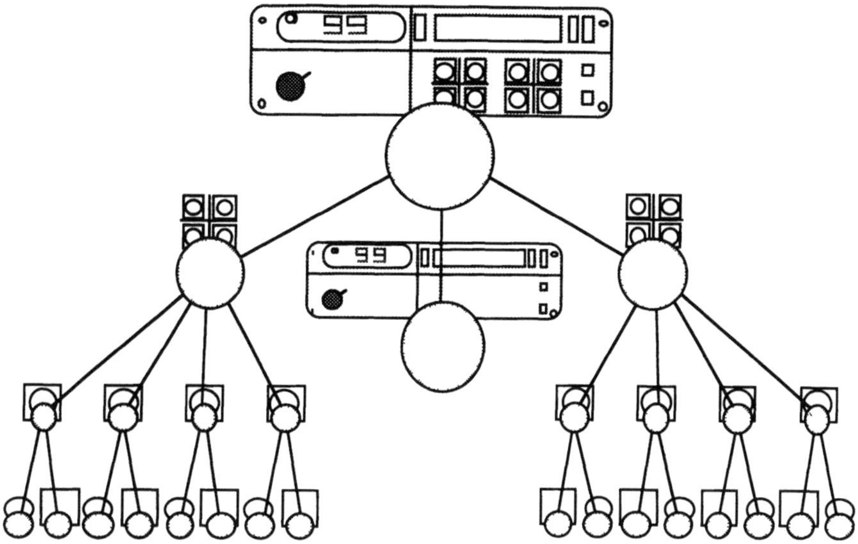

Figure 3: Part Hierarchy

Characteristics of this approach are:

- The number of substructures and the names of methods are established as message-selectors at compile time. This is done via the program editor which informs the frame how many substructures it possesses.
- At run time the predefined methods can be used but cannot be changed.
- For providing a third component middle: besides left: and right: the class definition has to be changed and be recompiled. This limits the usefulness of this possibility.

The given example is a standard motivation for the introduction of *prototypes*. Prototypes are advantageous if new objects are to be generated at run time which are close to existing objects with respect to methods. Prototypes can use delegation to obtain methods from existing objects. If new methods are needed, programming and compilation on-the-fly cannot be avoided.

As we do not want to use delegation for the description of the standard (the reasons have been explained before), we have to look for other techniques to overcome the inflexibility of the frame-concept. One solution is the use of special *collection classes* rather than slots. When inserting into a collection class, a new key-value pair is generated. A dynamic change (addition or deletion of parts) is possible. Parts are accessed via key rather than a specific message pattern. This is more elegant than the technique applied in PHIGS where inserted parts can be addressed via an integer pointers which reflects the parts position within the structure. The address is changed if other parts are inserted previously. Collection classes can be regarded as an evolutionary step from traditional approaches. It has been used in the definition of GEO++ [Blake and

Wisskirchen, 1989]. Similarly to PHIGS, one starts with an empty structure and fills it up via the insert method. Besides a change via insert:, this approach allows the multiplication of code by copying. Furthermore, GEO++ includes a well defined concept for attribute assignment and transformation assignment, a pick input integrated into the multi-level concept and flexible input handling via call-backs. We call systems of the GEO++ type *multi-level collection systems.*

Up to now we have focussed on the disadvantages of frame type structures. On the other hand, frames have the advantage of a stronger typing than alternative approaches. Frames can be ordered into inheritance hierarchies. The structure can be used to define rules or other relationships between slots at frame definition time. For special types of applications, it is therefore desirable to build up frame hierarchies. How can this be done with a graphics standard which uses collection classes as a basic model for describing part hierarchies? [Wisskirchen, 1990] has given a solution for this problem where frames can simply be generated by subclassing of a multi-level collection system. This is a good compromise which models both static and dynamic structuring in computer graphics.

6.4. Part Hierarchies and Constraints

Multi-level graphics systems like PHIGS support part hierarchies, although this terminology is not used in the graphics context. Collecting parts in a whole can be considered in the graphics context as the generation of high level primitives with editing and management facilities. It is evident that a graphics standard has to support part hierarchies for diverse application purposes.

Borning's ThingLab is an object-oriented system which focuses on the definition and satisfaction of graphical constraints [Borning, 1979]. ThingLab does support part hierarchies. However, they do not form a central concept. The semantics related to part hierarchies seems to us to be negligible. The main purpose of part hierarchies in ThingLab is the elegant addressing facility of objects in part hierarchies (in comparison, e.g., with PHIGS structures) which simplifies the formulation of constraints. The internal definition is decentralized, i.e., local to individual parts. ThingLab shows that constraints can put additional semantics on part hierarchies which allows for an "intelligent" graphics system. The background to the development is the fact that there are additional semantics beside that of parts which has to be taken into account. Such semantic aspects are difficult to realize in traditional procedural systems, whereas constraints (or rules) allow for an direct declarative specification.

This discussion leads to the question whether a new graphics standard should provide for a constraint mechanism. We think that this should not be tried at the moment. It seems very difficult to characterize a set of allowed and useful constraints which does not lead to problems during satisfaction. On the other hand, it is essential to define a graphics kernel which allows the formulation of constraints and to which a constraint satisfaction capability can be added. We think that this can be achieved if an easy way exists to address all objects in a part hierarchy, together with their attributes and geometrical data. For the purpose of constraint definition it must be possible to generate graphics objects (primitives, attributes) within part hierarchies which are not (completely) instantiated. This is an important difference with existing graphics system like GKS and PHIGS where primitives have to be completely instantiated before they can be used in the graphics system. For non instantiated objects the addressing mechanism of part hierarchies can be used to formulate predicates. Some variables used in the predicates can be assigned a value and other can be computed via constraint satisfaction. New graphics standards should at least provide the prerequisites for modern declarative programming concepts.

It should be pointed out that the exclusion of constraints is done to avoid inconsistencies in a graphics standard. If it were already possible to define a useful set of constraints which could not lead to unresolvable situations we would be happy to propose its inclusion into a graphics standard.

6.5. How Can Portability Be Achieved?

One of the major objectives of standardization is portability. What should be portable within a computer graphics system?

Portability of application programs can be achieved if all application specific methods which use the graphics kernel, as well as the subclasses which the application has defined to extend the graphics kernel, are transferable. This should not give any major problems.

For storage and transfer of pictures, a metafile standard (Computer Graphics Metafile CGM[ISO, 1987]) has been defined which allows the sequential storage of graphical data structures. This does not cover the storage of a part hierarchy as present in, for example, PHIGS. PHIGS uses a long term storage called an archive for its graphics data structures. This archive can be read in by the same application at a later time or by another application to make the defined structures available.

Object-oriented systems with part hierarchies have two additional problems when storing graphical data:

- The part hierarchy allows the mixture of graphics and application data by subclassing. How can the graphics portions be extracted? Our solution to this problem is that we can use a process similar to the posting of a part hierarchy to determine which data have visual effects and generate a purely graphical part hierarchy. For this purpose, the following method is provided:

```
aGroup myGroup extractGraphics
```

- If constraints are defined for a graphic, these will not be stored if we look only at those elements of the part hierarchy which have an effect on the display. Constraints can only be ported if the whole program is ported which defines the constraints.

7. Résumé

This chapter has discussed the benefits future graphics system could obtain by the use of an object-oriented philosophy and principles. However, there is a gap between the definition of a powerful object-oriented graphics system and an object-oriented graphics standard which has to be bridged.

The authors believe that the definition of an object-oriented graphics standard is currently feasible. To develop this standard the help and active cooperation of experts from the field of object-oriented programming in the respective standards committees within ISO/IEC JTC 1 SC24 is necessary as there are still problems and open questions which must be resolved. The solution should reflect the current state of the art in object-oriented graphics and should cover the requirements spelled out by the graphics community. Cooperation could be achieved by active participation in the formulation of the new standards or by commenting on the developing papers.

There is a double reward to be expected from such an effort:

- The quality and hence the acceptance of the new graphics standard would be enhanced considerably.
- Object-oriented graphics systems could leave the status of research and experimentation and find widespread acceptance.

The present moment is very promising as the graphics committees are just in the initial stages of collecting requirements from the potential constituency of the intended standard and are ready to accept new ideas and suggestions. It is the express objective to develop a "standard of the nineties" which is not necessarily restricted by the existing standards.

References

Blake, E. and Wisskirchen, P. (1989) "Object-oriented graphics," In: W. Purgathofer and J. Schönhut (ed.) *Advances in Computer Graphics V*, Springer-Verlag, Heidelberg.

Bobrow, D.G., DeMichiel, L.G., Gabriel, R.P., Keene, S.E., Kiczales, G., and Moon, D.A. (1988) "Common Lisp Object System Specification," X3J13 Document 88-002R.

Borning, A.H. (1979) "ThingLab: A constraint-oriented simulation laboratory," Xerox Palo Alto Research Center report SSL-79-3. (revised version of Stanford University PhD thesis STAN-CS-79-746)

Brodlie, K., Duce, D., and Hopgood, F.R.A. (1989) "GKS-N Initial Draft," Document ISO/IEC JTC1 SC24 WG1 N79.

Enderle, G., Kansy, K., and Pfaff, G. (1987) *Computer Graphics Programming. GKS — The Graphics Standard (2. Ed.)*, Springer-Verlag, Berlin.

Goldberg, A. and Robson, D. (1983) *Smalltalk-80· the language and its implementation*, Addison-Wesley, Reading, Massachusetts.

ISO (1987) "Metafile for the storage and transfer of picture information," International Standard ISO 8632.

ISO (1989a) "Programmer's Hierarchical Interactive Graphics System (PHIGS)," International Standard ISO/IEC 9592.

ISO (1989b) "Final Report of the Study Group on an Improved Graphics Input Model," Document ISO/IEC JTC1 SC24 N353.

ISO (1989c) "PHIGS PLUS Working Draft," Document ISO/IEC JTC1 SC24 WG2 N37.

Kansy, K. and Wisskirchen, P. (1989) "An object-oriented approach towards a New API for Computer Graphics," Document ISO/IEC JTC1 SC24 WG1 N94

Krasner, G.E. and Pope, S.T. (1988) "A cookbook for using the model-view-controller user interface paradigm in Smalltalk-80," *J. Object-Oriented Programming*, vol. 1, no. 3, 26-48.

Lieberman, H. (1986) "Delegation and inheritance: Two mechanisms for sharing knowledge in object-oriented systems," In: J. Bezivin and P. Cointe (ed) *3ème Journées d'Etudes Languages Orientés Objet*, pp. 79-89.

Stefik, M. and Bobrow, D.G. (1985) "Object-oriented programming: Themes and variations," *The AI Magazine*, vol VI, no. 4, 40-62.

Stein, L.A. (1987) "Delegation is inheritance," *SIGPLAN Notices*, vol. 22, no 12, 138-146.

Wisskirchen, P. (1989) "GEO++ — A system for both modelling and display," In. *Procs. Eurographics '89*, Elsevier Publ., Amsterdam, pp. 403-414. (Hamburg, Sept 1989)

Wisskirchen, P. (1990) *Object-Oriented Graphics*, Springer-Verlag, Berlin.

Authors' Addresses

Edwin Blake, Centre for Mathematics and Computer Science (CWI), Kruislaan 413, 1098 SJ Amsterdam, Netherlands.
Email: edwin@cwi.nl

Patrick Borras, Altaïr, BP 105, 78153 Le Chesnay Cedex, France.
Email: borras@dbblues.altair.fr

Jan van den Bos, Department of Computer Science, University of Leiden, P.O. Box 9512, 2500 RA Leiden, The Netherlands.

Jonathan Burns, Department of Computer Science, LaTrobe University, Bundoora, Victoria, Australia, 3083.
Email: burns@latcs1.oz

Maarten J.G.M. van Emmerik, Delft University of Technology, Faculty of Industrial Design Engineering, Jaffalaan 9, 2628 BX Delft, The Netherlands.
Email: mve@dutio.uucp

Michael Gleicher, School of Computer Science, Carnegie Mellon University, Pittsburgh, PA 15213-3890, USA.
Email: gleicher@cs.cmu.edu

Ralph D. Hill, Bellcore, 445 South Street, 2D 295, Morristown, NJ 07962-1910, USA.
Email: rdh@bellcore.com

Klaus Kansy, German National Research Center for Computer Science (GMD), Postfach 1240, 5205 Sankt Augustin 1, FRG.
Email: kansy@f3.gmd.dbp.de

Michael R. Kaplan, Apple Computer, Inc. Advanced Technology Group, 160 Peck Terrace, Santa Cruz, CA 95062, USA.
Email: mrk@apple.com

Chris Laffra, Department of Computer Science, University of Leiden, P.O. Box 9512, 2500 RA Leiden, The Netherlands.
Email: laffra@cs.leidenuniv.nl.

Didier Lévêque, Altaïr, BP 105, 78153 Le Chesnay Cedex, France.
Email: bishop@dbblues.altair.fr

Jean-Claude Mamou, Altaïr, BP 105, 78153 Le Chesnay Cedex, France.
Email: mamou@dbblues.altair.fr

Peter van Oosterom, TNO Physics and Electronics Laboratory, P.O. Box 96864, 2509 JG The Hague, The Netherlands.
Email: oosterom@fel.tno.nl

Daan Otten, Interactive Systems (IS), Centre for Mathematics and Computer Science (CWI), Kruislaan 413, 1098 SJ Amsterdam, The Netherlands.
Email: daan@cwi.nl

Didier Plateau, Altaïr, BP 105, 78153 Le Chesnay Cedex, France.
Email: didier@dbblues.altair.fr

John R. Rankin, Department of Computer Science, LaTrobe University, Bundoora, Victoria, Australia, 3083.
Email: johnr@latcs1.oz

Jan Rogier, Institute of Applied Computer Science (ITI), Netherlands Organization for Applied Scientific Research (TNO), Schoemakerstraat 97, 2628 VK Delft, The Netherlands.
Email: rogier@cwi.nl

Yen-Ping Shan, IBM Cary, P.O. Box 60000, Cary, NC 27512-9968, USA.
Email: shan@cs.unc.edu

Didier Tallot, Altaïr, BP 105, 78153 Le Chesnay Cedex, France.
Email: tallot@dbblues.altair.fr

Andrew Witkin, School of Computer Science, Carnegie Mellon University, Pittsburgh, PA 15213-3890, USA.

Peter Wisskirchen, German National Research Center for Computer Science (GMD), Postfach 1240, 5205 Sankt Augustin 1, FRG.
Email: wissk@gmdzi.gmd.de

EurographicSeminars

Tutorials and Perspectives in Computer Graphics

Eurographics Tutorials '83. Edited by P. J. W. ten Hagen.
XI, 425 pages, 164 figs., 1984

User Interface Management Systems. Edited by G. E. Pfaff.
XII, 224 pages, 65 figs., 1985

Methodology of Window Management. Edited by F. R. A. Hopgood, D. A. Duce, E. V. C. Fielding, K. Robinson, A. S. Williams.
XV, 250 pages, 41 figs., 1985

Data Structures for Raster Graphics. Edited by L. R. A. Kessener, F. J. Peters, M. L. P. van Lierop. VII, 201 pages, 80 figs., 1986

Advances in Computer Graphics I. Edited by G. Enderle, M. Grave, F. Lillehagen.
XII, 512 pages, 168 figs., 1986

Advances in Computer Graphics II. Edited by F. R. A. Hopgood, R. J. Hubbold, D. A. Duce. X, 186 pages, 96 figs., 1986

Advances in Computer Graphics Hardware I. Edited by W. Straßer.
X, 147 pages, 76 figs., 1987

GKS Theory and Practice. Edited by P. R. Bono, I. Herman.
X, 316 pages, 92 figs., 1987

Intelligent CAD Systems I. Theoretical and Methodological Aspects.
Edited by P. J. W. ten Hagen, T. Tomiyama. XIV, 360 pages, 119 figs., 1987

Advances in Computer Graphics III. Edited by M. M. de Ruiter.
IX, 323 pages, 247 figs., 1988

Advances in Computer Graphics Hardware II. Edited by A. A. M. Kuijk, W. Straßer.
VIII, 258 pages, 99 figs., 1988

CGM in the Real World. Edited by A. M. Mumford, M. W. Skall.
VIII, 288 pages, 23 figs., 1988

Intelligent CAD Systems II. Implementational Issues. Edited by V. Akman, P. J. W. ten Hagen, P. J. Veerkamp. X, 324 pages, 114 figs., 1989

Advances in Computer Graphics IV. Edited by W. T. Hewitt, M. Grave, M. Roch.
XVI, 255 pages, 138 figs., 1991

Advances in Computer Graphics V. Edited by W. Purgathofer, J. Schönhut.
VIII, 223 pages, 101 figs., 1989

User Interface Management and Design. Edited by D. A. Duce, M. R. Gomes, F. R. A. Hopgood, J. R. Lee. VIII, 324 pages, 117 figs., 1991

Advances in Computer Graphics Hardware III. Edited by A. A. M. Kuijk. VIII, 214 pages, 88 figs., 1991

Advances in Object-Oriented Graphics I. Edited by E. H. Blake, P. Wisskirchen. X, 218 pages, 74 figs., 1991

In preparation:

Advances in Computer Graphics VI. Edited by G. Garcia, I. Herman. Approx. 465 pages, 1991

Advances in Computer Graphics Hardware IV. Edited by R. L. Grimsdale, W. Straßer. Approx. 290 pages, 1991

Intelligent CAD Systems III. Practical Experience and Evaluation. Edited by P. J. W. ten Hagen, P. J. Veerkamp. Approx. 280 pages, 1991

MIX
Papier aus verantwortungsvollen Quellen
Paper from responsible sources
FSC® C105338

If you have any concerns about our products,
you can contact us on
ProductSafety@springernature.com

In case Publisher is established outside the EU,
the EU authorized representative is:
Springer Nature Customer Service Center GmbH
Europaplatz 3, 69115 Heidelberg, Germany

Printed by Libri Plureos GmbH
in Hamburg, Germany